THE DIGBY MARY
MAGDALENE PLAY

The Middle English Texts Series are scholarly texts designed for research and classroom use. Its goal is to make available to teachers, scholars, and students texts that occupy an important place in the literary and cultural canon but have not been readily available in print and online editions. The series does not include those authors, such as Chaucer, Langland, or Malory, whose English works are normally in print in good student editions. The focus is, instead, upon Middle English literature adjacent to those authors that are needed for doing research or teaching. The editions maintain the linguistic integrity of the original work but within the parameters of modern reading conventions. The texts are printed in the modern alphabet and follow the practices of modern capitalization, word formation, and punctuation. Manuscript abbreviations are silently expanded, and *u/v* and *j/i* spellings are regularized according to modern orthography. Yogh (ȝ) is transcribed as *g*, *gh*, *y*, or *s*, according to the sound in Modern English spelling to which the medieval pronunciation corresponds; thorn (þ) and eth (ð) are transcribed as *th*. Distinction between the second person pronoun and the definite article is made by spelling the one *thee* and the other *the*, and final *-e* that receives full syllabic value is accented (e.g., *charité*). Hard words, difficult phrases, and unusual idioms are glossed either in the right margin or at the foot of the page. Explanatory and textual notes appear at the end of the text, often along with a glossary. The editions include short introductions on the history of the work, its merits and points of topical interest, and brief working bibliographies.

This series is published in association with the University of Rochester.

Medieval Institute Publications is a program of
The Medieval Institute, College of Arts and Sciences

 WESTERN MICHIGAN UNIVERSITY

THE DIGBY MARY MAGDALENE PLAY

Edited by
Theresa Coletti

TEAMS • Middle English Texts Series • University of Rochester

MEDIEVAL INSTITUTE PUBLICATIONS
Western Michigan University
Kalamazoo

Printed and bound by CPI Group (UK) Ltd, Croydon, CR0 4YY

**Library of Congress Cataloging-in-Publication Data
are available from the Library of Congress.**

ISBN: 978-1-58044-285-5 (paperback)
ISBN: 978-1-58044-301-2 (hardback)

P 5 4 3 2 1

CONTENTS

 ## ACKNOWLEDGMENTS

I'm happy for the opportunity, at long last, to express my gratitude to the institutions and individuals who have encouraged and underwritten my work. At the beginning of this endeavor, a research grant from the University of Maryland's College of Arts and Humanities enabled me to consult Bodleian Library MS Digby 133 in Oxford. I am grateful to the staff at the Bodleian who assisted me in my consultation of Digby 133. At this project's conclusion, and like many METS editors before me, I am pleased to recognize the National Endowment for the Humanities for its long support of this series.

This project has benefitted from the work of my smart and capable student research assistants at the University of Maryland: Carissa Baker, Christine Maffuccio, Maggie Ray, and Jeffrey Griswold. Gail McMurray Gibson provided astute commentary on portions of the introduction and remains my trusted fellow traveler in all things East Anglian. Emily Steiner's seminar in medieval performance at the University of Pennsylvania test-drove an early version of the edited text; Genelle Gertz's students at Washington and Lee University read a later version and welcomed me to talk about it.

METS staff at the University of Rochester have made major contributions to this project. I'm delighted to thank the cohort of graduate student editors who worked on producing the text of Mary Magdalene for this edition. For their ever meticulous and insightful reading of (too) many versions of this project, assistant METS editors Martha Johnson-Olin and Pamela Yee deserve my deepest thanks, as well as staff editors Leah Haught, Alison Harper, and Ashley Conklin. And it's my great pleasure to have a new occasion to express my life-long gratitude to METS General Editor and my teacher, mentor, and friend, the incomparable Russell Peck.

🌿 INTRODUCTION

The Digby *Mary Magdalene* — as the play is called after the Oxford University Bodleian Library manuscript (Digby 133) that preserves its unique copy — hails from East Anglia, the region of England comprising the counties of Norfolk and Suffolk and, to the south and west, parts of Essex and Cambridgeshire; in the north and east, East Anglia reaches to the North Sea.[1] Excepting cycles of biblical plays performed or compiled in Chester, Coventry, York, and other northern towns, virtually the entire extant corpus of medieval English drama made its home in East Anglia.[2] This region was distinguished in the late Middle Ages by its internationally linked urban centers in Norwich and Bishop's (now King's) Lynn, its densely populated and prosperous rural landscape, and the vibrant religious culture that permeated both, weaving together city, village, and countryside. Drama is the most social and communal of literary forms, firmly embedded in the cultural locales that produce it. Late medieval East Anglian material, textual, and visual traditions offer resources both broad and deep for exploring, to echo Gail McMurray Gibson's phrase, its "theaters of devotion."[3]

The Digby *Magdalene* play and its eponymous subject intersect repeatedly with these medieval East Anglian traditions. Mary Magdalene appears regularly in major devotional, hagiographic, and other dramatic texts of East Anglian auspices. She numbers among the female saints most often represented on the painted rood screens that still embellish fifteenth-century East Anglian parish churches; she was a familiar dedicatee of those churches, the guilds that they supported, and other religious foundations in the region. This proliferation of Magdalenes attests to the congruence of the saint's medieval identities and the commitments of East Anglian religious culture.[4]

Despite the wealth of evidence tying the Digby play's saintly subject to East Anglia, the play itself remains geographically unmoored, its medieval locale unmarked by any sign that it was home to one of the most eclectic and ambitious projects of the late medieval English

---

[1] This introduction draws occasionally from my two contributions to *The Oxford Encyclopedia of British Literature*, "The Digby Plays," and "The Digby *Mary Magdalene*." Where noted, it also draws from my monograph, *Mary Magdalene and the Drama of Saints*.

[2] For a useful discussion distinguishing the northern biblical plays known as "cycles" and East Anglian dramatic forms and traditions, including the N-Town Plays, see Sugano, "Introduction," *N-Town Plays*. The foundational study of late medieval East Anglian religious drama and culture is Gibson, *Theater of Devotion*.

[3] Gibson, *Theater of Devotion*. For a stellar illustration of the radical cultural and historical particularities of medieval performance practices, see Carol Symes' *A Common Stage*, a work on the theater of medieval Arras.

[4] See Coletti, *Mary Magdalene and the Drama of Saints*, pp. 22–99 and pp. 240–60.

1

stage. Although records of medieval performative activities in the region document local habits of staging and theatrical organization, such as theaters in the round and multi-community productions, none of these records can be linked to extant East Anglian dramatic texts.[5] Paradoxically, the richest regional tradition of late medieval English theater — as represented by the corpus of extant texts — has left the fewest documentary traces of its existence beyond the manuscript page. Fortunately, in the case of the Digby *Magdalene*, the manuscript page offers up important information pointing to the play's now widely accepted East Anglian attribution, information that relies on linguistic evidence and traces of ownership inscribed in Bodleian Library MS Digby 133 (see discussion of the "Manuscript" below). This lack of a documentary record of performance has not impeded medieval drama scholars from advancing informed hypotheses about the Digby play's precise locale, auspices, and occasion. Attempting to account for the play's panoramic scope and ambitious theatricality, one hypothesis asserts that the play must have been produced by a city "of major size and considerable dramatic experience." Another imagines a "prosperous market town" capable of attracting the mixed audience to which the Digby *Magdalene* seems to appeal.[6] Chelmsford, Norwich, King's Lynn, Ipswich, and Lincoln have all been proposed as possible homes for the Digby play.[7] Pending a future discovery of lost dramatic records, readers of the Digby *Magdalene* in search of its origins will keep coming back to both the intricacies of its manuscript text and opportunities for interpretation offered up by late medieval East Anglian culture and society.

The Digby saint play is one of many important Middle English lives of Mary Magdalene, and these other native vitae furnish crucial intertexts for her dramatic biography.[8] But these insular lives also participate in broader hagiographic traditions that both understood, and so produced, Mary Magdalene as one of the most important saints — male or female — of Western Europe. Like medieval Latin clerical culture itself, medieval hagiography is an international phenomenon; its legends and images travel back and forth, accruing new meanings as they encounter and inhabit new cultural locations. The Mary Magdalene who figures so prominently in late medieval East Anglia — especially the Magdalene of the Digby play — was tied to and shaped by continental traditions that represented her across textual and visual media. East Anglian cultural and commercial exchanges with the European continent provided important conduits for such trading of hagiographical motifs

---

[5] Here I adapt several paragraphs from Coletti, "Social Contexts," pp. 287–89. On East Anglian dramatic traditions, see Beadle, "Medieval Drama of East Anglia," and "Plays and Playing at Thetford"; Wright, "Community Theatre in Late Medieval East Anglia"; and Galloway and Watson, *Records of Plays and Players in Norfolk and Suffolk*. For a succinct overview of the manuscript and documentary records of East Anglian dramatic traditions, see Sugano, "Introduction," *N-Town Plays*.

[6] See, respectively, Ritchie, "Suggested Location," p. 52; and A. Johnston, "*Wisdom* and the Records," p. 94.

[7] Coldewey, "Chelmsford Records"; Davidson, "Middle English Saint Play," pp. 74–75; Bennett, "*Mary Magdalene* of Bishop's Lynn"; Wickham, "Staging of Saint Plays," pp. 113–15; and Ritchie, "Suggested Location."

[8] For a sample of Middle English lives of Mary Magdalene, see *Middle English Legends of Women Saints*, ed. Reames, pp. 51–110. Other important vitae include those of East Anglian hagiographer Osbern Bokenham (see *Legendys of Hooly Wummen*, pp. 136–72) and John Mirk (see *Festial*, pp. 203–08). For a discussion of the English narrative vitae in relation to the Digby play, see Carter, "The Digby *Mary Magdalen*."

and images.[9] The peregrinations of Margery Kempe, medieval East Anglia's most important Magdalene devotee and rival, underscore the easy converse of the region's devotional and mercantile activities with interests that cross seas and traverse continents.

Beyond the late medieval East Anglian sphere, then, continental resources have much to offer a reading of the Digby *Magdalene*, providing insight into imaginative genealogies of representation that furnish a far-flung back story for the late medieval dramatic saint. Attending to such resources can also shed light on the East Anglian Magdalene's departures from preoccupations of continental texts, images, and performances dedicated to her. Recent scholarship, for instance, has established the major contribution of mendicant preaching, especially by French and Italian Franciscans and Dominicans, to the saint's multi-faceted medieval identity. Although there is no established record of medieval English fraternal investment in this cause, issues raised in continental mendicant preaching occasionally surface in the Digby *Magdalene*. Across northern Europe and extending to the Mediterranean region, well-documented lay and clerical patronage produced — in words, images, and sounds — creative collaborations between the beliefs and aspirations of medieval people and the sheer potential of Mary Magdalene's labile biography to inspire unique devotional expressions.[10] In visual cultures especially, the Digby saint play resonates far more with the rich continental lexicon of Magdalene imagery than it does with late medieval English visual evocations of Mary Magdalene's spiritual biography.[11] Hence, understanding the achievement of the Digby *Magdalene* as dramatic vita, visual spectacle, and devotional endeavor requires understanding the play's creative negotiation of the East Anglian locales and traditions that inform it and the capacious, international archive that accrued to Mary Magdalene as a premier saint of medieval Western Christendom.[12]

Such negotiation of local priorities and perspectives imported from the wider world is typified in the Digby play's certain resemblance to, and likely dependence upon, the vita of the saint made available in Jacobus de Voragine's international bestseller, *Legenda Aurea* or *Golden Legend* (1270s). Jacobus' achievement was to weave together in a single expansive narrative several distinct biographical strands of the saint's life. One involved the Mary Magdalene created by Gregory the Great's influential conflation of the woman who witnesses

---

[9] See Gibson and Coletti, "Lynn, Walsingham, Norwich"; and Hill, *Women and Religion*, pp. 1–16.

[10] Here I can only gesture toward the vast, recent bibliography exploring medieval Mary Magdalene in continental Europe, with some consideration of resources covering expanses of geography and genre. See Haskins, *Mary Magdalen*; Jansen, *Making of the Magdalen*; Taylor, "Apostle to the Apostles"; Loewen, "Conversion of Mary Magdalene" and "Mary Magdalene Preaches through Song." See also the various visual, verbal, and musical archives explored in essays collected by Loewen and Waugh, *Mary Magdalene in Medieval Culture*.

[11] Medieval England does not lack testimony to Mary Magdalene's important presence in visual culture, particularly that which still survives in parish churches; see Coletti, *Mary Magdalene and the Drama of Saints*, pp. 50–72. But compared to that of Western Europe, the medieval English record is thin, a finding that can be explained by complex factors, including, of course, the destruction of religious art during the English Reformation. For recent studies of continental visual traditions of representing the saint, see Erhardt, "Introduction"; Morris, "German Iconography"; and other essays collected in Erhardt and Morris, *Mary Magdalene: Iconographic Studies*.

[12] The approach suggested here affirms Gibson's characterization of late medieval East Anglia's simultaneous cultivation of "regional consciousness and character" and a determined embrace of economic and religious resources continental in origin; *Theater of Devotion*, p. 22.

Christ's resurrection in all the gospels; the sinner who anoints Jesus in the home of Simon the Pharisee (Luke 7); and Mary, sister of Martha and Lazarus (Luke 10).[13] The other strand advanced legendary accounts of Mary Magdalene's evangelical and ascetic activities that had attained prominence as her cult developed in the eleventh through thirteenth centuries.[14] Although Jacobus' vita cannot be conclusively established as a direct source for the Digby *Magdalene*, we might keep in mind that William Caxton's translation of the *Golden Legend* first appeared in print in 1483 and was followed by nine subsequent editions up through 1527 — the very decades that span what scholars believe to be the composition of the Digby play and its eventual copying into its single extant manuscript.[15] Evidence from testamentary bequests points to late medieval East Anglian familiarity with Jacobus' *Legenda*.[16] Whatever the exact relationship between the Digby *Magdalene* and Jacobus' influential work, the play clearly exploits the eclecticism of his social and spiritual narrative, highlighting the paradoxical identities that it promoted — identities that became central to the saint's broad medieval appeal.[17] Thus, the play presents Mary Magdalene as the daughter of a prosperous, genteel family who ends her life as a desert contemplative. It provides for a biblical sinner, famous for sexual profligacy, to recuperate her purity and join the company of heavenly virgins. Although she occupies none of the standard socio-sexual categories available to medieval women (virgin, wife, and widow), the Digby play's Magdalene emerges as a patron of marital procreation, childbirth, and dynastic continuity whom her devotees address in language that would seem better suited to the virgin mother of Jesus: "Heyll be thou, Mary, ower Lord is wyth thee!" (line 1939).

This complex adaptation of hagiographic narrative traditions occurs in the medium of dramatic performance, a fact that one can sometimes lose sight of when investigating the Digby play's relationship to the dense medieval archive of Magdalene phenomena. Recognition of medieval performance practices, English and continental, will — and should — always put pressure on analytical approaches that privilege the written record. At the same time, that record furnishes our sole access to the slippery dramatic genre of the English saint play, of which *Mary Magdalene* and *The Conversion of Saint Paul*, one of the Magdalene play's textual companions in Bodleian Library MS Digby 133, provide the only surviving Middle English witnesses.[18] Consequently, the Digby saint plays have often been invoked as representative instances of a dramatic genre whose very characteristics have been hypothesized based on their own idiosyncratic example. Significant, if scattered, dramatic records in English sources refer to the mounting of *ludi*, *miracula*, plays, games, and

---

[13] Gregory the Great, "Homily 33."

[14] For discussion of the many legends and texts that contribute to the making of the late medieval Magdalene, see *Critical Edition of the Legend*, ed. Mycoff, pp. 4–24.

[15] *Late Medieval Religious Plays*, ed. Baker, Murphy, and Hall, p. xl. The EETS editors Baker, Murphy, and Hall note the distance between the approximate date of the play's language (late fifteenth century) and the likely date of its manuscript (c. 1520–30).

[16] For this point and observations about the play's relationship to its sources, see Coletti, *Mary Magdalene and the Drama of Saints*, pp. 22–23.

[17] Mycoff's examination of the textual traditions informing Jacobus' life of the saint leads him to note the play's many creative departures from the *Legend*. See *Critical Edition of the Legend*, pp. 40–41.

[18] This paragraph adapts material from Coletti, *Mary Magdalene and the Drama of Saints*, pp. 24–27.

pageants on the feast days of saints and other holy days and seasonal commemorations; such records have been taken as evidence that the saint or miracle play was the most ubiquitous and long-lived of medieval English dramatic genres.[19] Lawrence Clopper has challenged this finding, arguing that claims for the widespread popularity of the saint play are, in fact, based on crucial misreadings of the terminology comprising the documentary record; he reads the term "saint play" as signifying only scripted drama.[20] But alternative approaches to ritual and ceremony and to the performative nature of public life in medieval societies have recently revised our conception of what constitutes drama, theater, plays — and play — in these environments.[21] We now understand that medieval performative behaviors, including those considered dramatic and theatrical, occupy a broad continuum of public actions. These insights enable us, for example, to situate John Lydgate's mummings and entertainments in new performative as well as literary contexts; and they inform Claire Sponsler's claim that these unusual and understudied texts of Lydgate may represent "the most important body of dramatic work by a known author in English before the sixteenth century."[22] A more capacious understanding of medieval performance practices as modes of theater also enables us to notice dramas of saints occurring in unexpected guises and in a variety of forms. As Catherine Sanok has shown, even lacking clear evidence of scripted drama, the historical record documenting public performance of female saints, in pageants and tableaux, is sufficient to suggest how such encounters may have been mobilized for social and political ends.[23]

Whether addressing East Anglian regional priorities or continental saints' cults, textual sources or generic forms, these medieval critical contexts provide important analytic tools for grappling with the exuberant and unruly entity that is the Digby *Magdalene*. At the same time, any effort to frame the Digby play and its saintly subject must also acknowledge Mary Magdalene's diachronic existence as a prominent focus of two millennia of scriptural commentary and, over the same period, her ubiquitous presence in verbal and visual artifacts of both learned and popular cultures, all bearing witness to the enduring appeal and provocation of her multi-faceted story.[24] In medieval western Christendom, Mary Magdalene was the female saint whose popularity was second only to that of the Virgin Mary; in the modern and contemporary worlds, she at times seems on the verge of vying with the mother of Jesus for that number one spot. Some of this attention stems from the saint's recent high profile role in sensationalized continuations of biblical story featured in

---

[19] On the medieval English saint play, see Jeffrey, "English Saints' Plays"; Grantley, "Saints' Plays"; Davidson, "Middle English Saint Play"; and Wickham, "Staging of Saint Plays."

[20] Clopper, "*Communitas*." Davidson takes on Clopper's reading of the records in "British Saint Play Records."

[21] See Symes, "Medieval Archive and the History of Theatre"; Holsinger, "Cultures of Performance"; and Chaganti, "The *Platea*: Pre- and Postmodern."

[22] Sponsler, *The Queen's Dumbshows*, p. 7. See also Sponsler's edition of these works: John Lydgate, *Mummings and Entertainments*.

[23] Sanok, *Her Life Historical*, pp. 145–73, 216–24. See also DiSalvo, "Unexpected Saints."

[24] For an overview, see Haskins, *Mary Magdalen*.

films, novels, and dubious histories.[25] More important, though, feminist biblical scholars —
motivated in part by some of the same issues driving fascination with Mary Magdalene in
popular culture — over the past few decades have turned to canonical scriptures and
apocrypha such as *The Gospel of Mary* to recuperate Mary Magdalene's biblical roles as
Christ's witness and first apostle. This work aims to acknowledge the Magdalene specifically
and women more generally as important participants in the birth of the Christian
movement.[26]

Although the remainder of this edition's introduction and all of its explanatory notes
focus primarily on the play as a phenomenon of late medieval dramatic and cultural history,
I gesture here toward this larger panorama of Mary Magdalene studies, in cult and culture,
because of the invitation to link past and present that it offers. As a prominent saint of the
medieval Christian church and a modern icon of gender and religious identities, Mary
Magdalene continues to command attention and to spark inquiry. The Middle English play
that casts her in its starring role imaginatively engages issues and controversies that remain
relevant to these current conversations.

THE MANUSCRIPT

The unique text of *Mary Magdalene* was likely copied in the first quarter of the sixteenth
century (c. 1515–30).[27] It survives in Bodleian Library MS Digby 133, a manuscript that
gathers together an eclectic group of texts: Latin alchemical, magical, and astrological works
appear alongside the sole surviving copies of the other extant Middle English saint play, *The
Conversion of Saint Paul*, and the biblical play known as *Candlemas Day and the Killing of the
Children of Israel*.[28] Also appearing in Digby 133 is a substantial fragment (752 of 1163 lines)
of the morality play *Wisdom*, preserved in its entirety in what we now call the Macro
manuscript (Folger Library MS V.a.354), which includes the unique texts of the East Anglian
plays *Mankind* and *Castle of Perseverance*.[29] The Macro manuscript and Digby 133 are
commonly recognized as two of the three major compilations of East Anglian drama (the
other is British Library MS Cotton Vespasian D Viii, or the N-Town Plays). It is tempting
to use the term "anthology" to characterize the material witnesses represented by the Digby
and Macro manuscripts. But recent research indicates that these two clusters of East Anglian
dramatic texts in manuscript compilations associated, respectively, with Kenelm Digby and
Cox Macro, the early modern antiquarians who lent their names to these endeavors, may

---

[25] In particular, I am thinking of Brown, *The Da Vinci Code*; and Baigent, Leigh, and Lincoln, *Holy
Blood, Holy Grail*. See also Coletti, "Afterword," pp. 276–78.

[26] See K. King, *Gospel of Mary*; Brock, *Mary Magdalene, The First Apostle*; and Ricci, *Mary Magdalene
and Many Others*. Thimmes ("Memory and Re-Vision") provides an important overview of and
bibliography on this development. For a collection that effectively mediates popular and scholarly
perspectives, see Burstein and De Keijzer, *Secrets of Mary Magdalene*.

[27] This discussion adapts material from Coletti, *Mary Magdalene and the Drama of Saints*, pp.
36–37.

[28] Bodleian Library "MS Digby 133" is accessible online through Digital Bodleian:
http://image.ox.ac.uk/show?collection=bodleian&manuscript=msdigby133.

[29] For a detailed discussion of the Digby manuscript, see *Late Medieval Religious Plays*, ed. Baker,
Murphy, and Hall, pp. ix–xv. See also *Macro Plays*, ed. Eccles.

not represent a discernible intention to gather together textual witnesses of medieval drama with the aim of creating, after the fact, an explicit tradition of early English dramatic performance.[30] At the same time, it is intriguing to note that in the case of both Digby 133 and the Macro plays in their original manuscript context, Middle English dramatic works are preserved amongst alchemical, medical (Macro MS), and scientific (Digby 133) treatises.[31] What this similarity might suggest about the motivations — if any — for bringing together dramatic texts and works of alchemical and technical knowledge must remain a matter for future investigations, as do the codicological and antiquarian implications of the fact that texts of the play *Wisdom* are extant in both of these early modern miscellanies.[32]

Despite the apparent lack of organizational purpose or theme in the current configuration of Bodleian Library MS Digby 133 and the likelihood that its dramatic works came to be assembled therein at different times and under different circumstances, the play texts themselves nonetheless exhibit relationships to one another that raise provocative questions about possible connections between their late medieval composition and production.[33] For example, a passage in *Mary Magdalene* (lines 217–24) finds a close echo in *The Killing of the Children* (lines 97–104).[34] *Wisdom*, as I have claimed elsewhere, reads and plays like an allegorical dress rehearsal for the Digby *Magdalene*'s biblical and hagiographical treatment of the same themes.[35] Both plays present a feminine figure whose symbolic mediation of corporeal desires, spiritual longings, and relationship to Christ are informed by exegesis of the Song of Songs. Seduced by evil disguised as a gallant, both heroines are restored through contrition. The morality and the saint play also are similarly preoccupied with knowledge of self, suspicion of learning, and the mediation of active and contemplative lives, similarities that are reinforced by occasional verbal echoes between the two works.[36] EETS editors Donald Baker, John Murphy, and Louis Hall posit other connections among the dramatic works of Digby 133, for example, maintaining that the scribe who copied *The Killing of the Children* is also responsible for the manuscript's substantial fragment of *Wisdom*.[37] Such internal connections of theme and verbal texture

---

[30] Beadle has completely reconstructed the manuscript belonging to Cox Macro's library, from a portion of which nineteenth-century bibliophile Hudson Gurney extracted and bound together what we now call the Macro Plays: *Mankind*, *Wisdom*, and *Castle of Perseverance*; see Beadle, "Macro MS 5." Gibson's study of the antiquarian legacy of the N-Town Plays also sheds light on contexts in which Digby 133 took shape in the seventeenth century; "Manuscript as Sacred Object," pp. 520, 528–29n87. Her forthcoming study of the antiquarian afterlives of medieval English drama manuscripts investigates Digby 133 in greater detail.

[31] Beadle, "Macro MS 5"; *Late Medieval Religious Plays*, ed. Baker, Murphy, and Hall, p. ix.

[32] The relationship between the Digby and Macro versions of *Wisdom* has been studied most extensively in *Play of "Wisdom,"* ed. Riggio, pp. 1–19.

[33] On the sequence in which items collected in Digby 133 entered the current manuscript volume, see *Late Medieval Religious Plays*, ed. Baker, Murphy, and Hall, p. xii.

[34] For the *Killing of the Children*, see *Late Medieval Religious Plays*, ed. Baker, Murphy, and Hall, pp. 96–115.

[35] Here I draw upon Coletti, *Mary Magdalene and the Drama of Saints*, p. 98.

[36] For other similarities between the two plays, see Coletti, "'*Paupertas est donum Dei*,'" pp. 373–75.

[37] *Late Medieval Religious Plays*, p. x. Riggio, however, states that evidence for a common hand is not conclusive; *Play of "Wisdom,"* p. 75.

between plays whose authorship and performance are entirely undocumented also occur among the East Anglian plays assembled in the miscellany that Richard Beadle calls Macro MS 5, after the catalog number of the item when the manuscript was sold in 1820.[38]

I have considered these internal features of Digby 133 in some detail because, in this particular case, relationships between dramatic manuscripts of East Anglian provenance as well as between individual works within and across these rare, regional manuscripts furnish key resources for investigating *Mary Magdalene*. As far as contextualizing the play is concerned, though, other facets of the work's single manuscript text are easier to pin down. That text, as I noted above, is assigned an East Anglian provenance because of linguistic features; it exhibits the identifying characteristics of the East Anglian dialect, including many inflections specific to Norfolk.[39] Beadle's map of scribal locations for Norfolk play manuscripts places the *Magdalene* scribe in the southeastern quadrant of the county.[40] East Anglian physician and alchemist Myles Blomefylde (1525–1603), who was born in Bury St. Edmunds, Suffolk, but long resided in Chelmsford, Essex, reinforced this regional linguistic attribution when he wrote his name or his initials on three of the plays in Digby 133: *The Conversion of St. Paul*, *Wisdom*, and *Mary Magdalene*.[41] No one knows how Blomefylde acquired the manuscript texts destined to become a signature of East Anglian drama generally and the medieval English saint play particularly. But he was an avid book collector who seems especially to have been drawn to dramatic works: his library also included the unique copy of Henry Medwall's *Fulgens and Lucrece* (c. 1497), a play that some scholars consider the first to be assigned to a known dramatic author.

These opportunities to contextualize the *Magdalene* text's medieval linguistic and cultural locations must also reckon with the challenges posed by the material artifact of the play manuscript itself. The copy of *Mary Magdalene* in Digby 133 is the product of a single scribe whose efforts leave much to be desired. Baker, Murphy, and Hall give a full account of these difficulties as well as a complete description of the manuscript.[42] Although the scribe's handwriting varies in size and neatness, it is generally clear. That said, the sole extant copy of *Mary Magdalene* may be missing as many as thirty lines. The scribe has made many mistakes — for example, omitting lines, confusing speeches and speakers, copying

---

[38] "Macro MS 5," p. 36. The primary connections among the Macro plays are those linking *Mankind* and *Wisdom*. Beadle (p. 44) states that both plays were copied by the hand which he identifies as that of Monk Thomas Hyngham of Bury St. Edmunds, who also inscribed his ownership of the works on both play texts. Both the Macro miscellany as reconstructed by Beadle and MS Digby 133 in its current form include one play that does not exhibit features shared by its dramatic companions in their respective collections: *Castle of Perseverance* among the Macro plays and *The Conversion of St. Paul* among those of Digby. These two plays exhibit few or none of the codicological and internal textual features that connect the other plays in their respective manuscripts, although *St. Paul* does bear the autograph of its one-time owner Myles Blomefylde.

[39] *Late Medieval Religious Plays*, ed. Baker, Murphy, and Hall, pp. xxxvi–xl. On those dialectal features, see also Beadle, "Literary Geography," pp. 91–94. A more recent study of the play's language, though, identifies a mixture of dialects, especially — and unusually — present for the sake of rhyme and meter. See Maci, "Language of *Mary Magdalene*."

[40] Beadle, "Literary Geography," p. 101.

[41] For discussion of Blomefylde, see *Late Medieval Religious Plays*, ed. Baker, Murphy, and Hall, pp. xii–xv; and Coletti, *Mary Magdalene and the Drama of Saints*, p. 37 and the sources cited there.

[42] See *Late Medieval Religious Plays*, ed. Baker, Murphy, and Hall, pp. xxx–xxxiii.

lines out of order and stage directions in the wrong place, as well as skipping words and letters. These features suggest that the text was copied from another manuscript in hurried circumstances or other compromised conditions or was derived from a bad exemplar; at one point the scribe may even have glossed his effort with a desperate "Jhesu mercy" (fol. 129r).

The final lines of the *Magdalene* play's manuscript call attention to the complicated cultural status of the textual artifact itself. After Mary Magdalene dies and her soul is joyfully welcomed into heaven, the priest who has ministered to her utters his final speech within the world of the play (lines 2123–30). Then, stepping out of that world, he addresses the "sufferens" (or sovereigns) before whom the "sentens" has been played in "syth" (sight). He once more invokes a present audience when he asks for God's blessing upon "tho that byn here" and extends that extra-dramatic world with his call for "clerkys" to sing "wyth voycys cler" (lines 2131–39). The text then announces its own conclusion — "Explicit oreginale de Sancta Maria Magdalena" (Here ends the original of Saint Mary Magdalena) — employing a word ("oreginale") that elsewhere in medieval dramatic records signifies something along the lines of an official copy (see explanatory note to line 2139 s.d.). But the text gives the playwright, or more likely the scribe, the last word: "Yff ony thing amysse be, / Blame connyng, and nat me. / I desyer the redars to be my frynd, / Yff ther be ony amysse, that to amend" (lines 2140–43). Whereas the priest appeals to "sovereigns" who witness in "sight" the actions of players, thereby calling up present and contingent conditions of a performance that is "here," the scribe expresses concern for the afterlife of his work and the contingencies of writing and reading in a future time, in which "ony thing" can go "amysse." Standing between these phenomena is the manuscript text itself, the "oreginale" that in this instance is itself only a copy. Such are the complex mediations — of playing, writing, and reading in and across times — that medieval dramatic manuscripts themselves perform.[43]

LANGUAGE, WRITING, AND LITERARY FORM

In the Digby *Magdalene*, matters of language have to do with much more than the play's East Anglian dialect. Rather, the play displays a deep awareness of language as both poetic and dramatic medium and as vehicle of communication in its diegetic world. Although best known for its dramatic spectacle, the play unfolds an exuberant linguistic variety, ranging from the doggerel Latin of its pagan priest, to the convoluted diction of its evil spirits, to the saint's plain-spoken articulations of scripture. At the same time, significant moments in the play's dramatic world often address the materiality of as well as opportunities and constraints afforded by verbal communication. This parallel attention to poetic linguistic forms and language in use would seem to belie the haste and lack of care evidenced by the manuscript itself as material witness.

The text of the Digby *Magdalene*, and by that I mean words on the manuscript page, offers many delights but also many frustrations; the very act of producing the text for this edition has underscored for me the complexities — and obfuscations — of its language. This edition aims to comprehend — syntactically and lexically — and to gloss every difficult word and turn of phrase. To unpack the Digby *Magdalene*'s linguistic challenges, I have relied heavily on the invaluable resources of the *Middle English Dictionary*. But even these are taxed

---

[43] On the relationship of East Anglian drama manuscripts to private reading, see Granger, *Drama and Liturgy*, pp. 172–92.

by speeches such as Cyrus' introduction of his daughters Mary Magdalene and Martha early in the play: "Here is a coleccyon of cyrcumstance: / To my cognysshon nevyr swych anothyr, / As be demonstracyon knett in contynens, / Save alonly my lady that was ther mother" ("Here is a group of qualities / Knit together in modest behavior, as is openly shown; / To my knowledge there was never such another, / Except for my wife, who was their mother" [lines 75–78]). The EETS editors Baker, Murphy, and Hall, whose gloss I adapt here, note the difficulties of syntax and lexical meaning in these lines.[44] At later moments in the play, Mary Magdalene's exchange with her wooer and tempter Curiosity as well as the comedic banter that the pagan priest and shipmaster pursue with their respective boys differently illustrate the play's verbal complexities. These conversations are rich in sexual and homoerotic innuendo, lending a compelling undercurrent of masculine verbal aggression to a play devoted to the biblical woman best known for sexual profligacy. What exactly does the shipmaster's boy mean when he laments that all his "corage is now cast" (line 1421)?[45]

The Digby playwright also manipulates linguistic and poetic idioms to good dramatic effect to distinguish, for example, demonic from divine diction as well as the pre- from the post-conversion speech of the king and queen of Marseilles; they introduce themselves in obscure, aureate language whose marked alliteration nearly stumbles over itself. The king is a "sofereyn semely" who "fare[s] fresly [eagerly] and fers [fiercely] to the feld" and commands "brawling breellys [rascals] and blabyr-lyppyd bycchys [thick-lipped scoundrels], / Obedyenly to obbey . . . [him] wythowt offense" (lines 929, 931, and 927–28). His queen lauds his "dilectabyll dedys [that] devydytt . . . [her] from dyversyté" ("Your admirable deeds separate [protect] me from adversity" [line 955]). Once they are received and baptized by Saint Peter in the Holy Land, though, their speech is both stripped of its ornament and, syntactically, rendered more straightforward: "Syr, the soth I shall yow seyn, / And tell yow myn intentt wythin a whyle. / Ther is a woman hyth Mary Maudleyn, / That hether [hither] hath laberyd [brought] me owt of Marcyll," says the king to Peter (lines 1819–22). At the same time, the play's shifting verbal idioms do not line up along an axis that differentiates the complex and sometimes convoluted diction of ethically challenged characters from the simpler speech of the avowed Christians. Restored from death to life, the queen of Marseilles recovers her verbal flourishes too, lauding Mary Magdalene as "sowlys confortacyon" and "bodyys sustynauns" that "hast wrappyd us in wele from all varyawns" ("You have wrapped [surrounded] us in well-being, protected from all change" [lines 1901–03]). Through the course of the play, the dramatic Magdalene herself speaks in a range of idioms. When she becomes an apostle to the people of Marseilles, her sermon (lines 1481–1525) offers a kind of verbal fresh air, cutting through the aureation and obscure innuendo of the dramatic language preceding her major homiletic moment with simple English vocabulary and phrases that relocate the creation narrative from the Book of Genesis to the late medieval work week: "On the Weddysday, ower lord of mythe / Made more at hys plesyng, / Fysche in flod, and fowle in flyth, / And all this was for ower hellpyng" (lines 1504–07). Yet, when dramatic circumstances call for a different kind of rhetorical self-awareness, the Digby saint rises to the occasion. For example, elevated from her wilderness retreat and led by angels to receive heavenly food "wyth reverent song" (line 2030, s.d.), Mary Magdalene responds with alliterative language far more decorative than

---

[44] *Late Medieval Religious Plays*, ed. Baker, Murphy, and Hall, p. 198.

[45] See the explanatory note for this line.

her homiletic idiom: "But [unless] I shuld serve my Lord, I were to blame, / Wych [who] fullfyllyt me wyth so gret feliceté, / [Who] Wyth melody of angyllys shewit me gle and game, / And have fed me wyth fode of most delycyté!" (lines 2035–38).

Joanne Findon's study of the Digby *Magdalene* raises the stakes on considerations of the play's language by showing how it intersects with verbal idioms of other late medieval literary genres. Imagery from secular, especially courtly, love poetry and religious lyric, for instance, frequently echoes in the dramatic text, providing a "multivalent language" that aptly articulates the fluid, boundary-crossing identities that the dramatic saint represents.[46] Findon's capacious notion of the play's intertexts usefully frames other important moments of verbal ingenuity, such as the often-remarked Latin liturgical parody (lines 1186–97) that signals the false faith of the people of Marseilles whom Mary Magdalene has been ordered to convert.[47] Findon identifies the play's dense verbal texture — shifting languages (Latin and vernacular), vocabularies, and levels of style — as key to the essential multivalency of the work itself. This insight helps to situate the Digby *Magdalene* in larger discursive fields and raises questions about the relationship of such linguistic plenitude to conditions of late medieval authorship and literary culture.[48]

The formal and poetic play *with* language in *Mary Magdalene* accompanies a dramatic preoccupation with the capacities *of* language as the medium of written and spoken communication. Tiberius Caesar, Herod, and Pilate, the boastful secular rulers who dominate the play's early scenes, rely on both modes, but the messenger who flies from one to another is most importantly a bearer of letters (lines 133, 216 s.d., 225–26, 252, 1261–1330). Tiberius Caesar urges his followers to "[t]ake hed [heed]" that his commandments "wretyn be" (line 120), and his messenger directs Pilate to "take avysement" of the writing that he presents to him (line 254). These characters understand — and the play's assumed audience implicitly does too — that official writing is a matter of "grett aprise [worth or value]" (line 1298). As Hyunyang Kim Lim has argued, dramatic representations of the circulation and significance of public, political writing locates the Digby play's narrative within the larger realm of late medieval documentary culture, a culture marked by an increased use of propaganda and thus also by "anxiety about written documents and textual authority."[49]

The play's characters invest written documents with various forms of power. Whereas Pilate may assert for himself that Jesus "is resyn agayn, as before he tawth (taught)" (line 1259), his sergeants advise him that such news, as far as Herod and Tiberius Caesar are concerned, must be "taken care of [concealed] by cunning" in a "pystyll of specyallté" (lines 1262 and 1267). Hence Caesar receives a "special letter" reporting that Jesus' dead body was stolen and carried off by his disciples (lines 1322–24), a story whose "[c]rafty . . . connyng" he is more than happy to perpetuate: "I wyll have cronekyllyd the yere and the reynne, / That nevyr shall be forgott" (lines 1327, 1329–30). But this glimpse of the instability of documentary culture, its potential for use as a "tool of oppression and

---

[46] Findon, *Lady, Hero, Saint*, p. 55.

[47] See Scherb, "Blasphemy and the Grotesque."

[48] In a more technical vein, a recent study of dialectal variants in the *Magdalene* text suggests that the author or perhaps the scribe frequently employs loan words from other dialects for the sake of sustaining meter or rhyme; Maci, "Language of *Mary Magdalene*," p. 135.

[49] Lim, "Pilate's Special Letter," p. 2. See also "'Take Writing.'"

bureaucratic corruption," finds a dramatic foil in the sacred writing to which Herod's philosophers appeal.[50] Their lord is not happy to hear that "skreptour gevytt informacyon, / And doth rehersse . . . verely [truly report]" the birth of a child who shall reign and be glorified by the entire world (lines 171–74). Unfortunately for the play's Herod, Holy Scripture resists manipulation, firm in its capacity to "verify" the truth (lines 178–79).

Through her own verbal testimony, Mary Magdalene later invokes the "pleyn" (line 1521) declaration of scripture when she preaches in Marseilles a sermon derived from Genesis 1 (lines 1481–1525). Like writing, the spoken word is invested with power. The king mocks the saint's great "resonnys [her remarks or words]" and threatens to cut out her tongue (lines 1526 and 1528–29). Yet it is precisely Mary Magdalene's capacity to speak her prayer to God that bests the pagan idols, whom the king repeatedly implores to "[s]peke . . . speke." But to no avail; they are apparently rendered mute "whyle Chriseten here is" (lines 1540–46). The saint's very audible prayer accomplishes the miracle that puts the king on the path to conversion. Even so, the Digby play also suggests that, as a mode of verbal communication, speech too has its limitations. Although divine prayers and petitions can create on stage the spectacular destruction of Marseilles' pagan temple along with that of its priest and his boy (line 1561, s.d.), Mary Magdalene admits human speech's inefficacy in communicating the heavenly joys she experiences in her desert retreat, where she talks only to angels (lines 2053–60). Paradoxically, the distance between human and divine that can be bridged by devout prayer does not apply to human endeavors to mingle more fluidly with and report back about experiences of the sacred. Within the world of the play, even Jesus, who would seem to transcend all communicative limits, concludes his densely metaphoric and paratactic encomium to his mother (lines 1349–63) by declaring the insufficiency of spoken and written expression in the face of perfection: "The goodnesse of my mothere no tong can expresse, / Nere no clerke of hyre, hyre joyys can wryth" (lines 1364–65).

REGIONAL CONTEXTS

As we have seen, the Mary Magdalene who commands the starring role in one of Middle English drama's most ambitious theatrical projects represents the intersection of a long-lived, ubiquitous universal cult and the preoccupations and investments of a local culture. Furthermore, the Digby play takes full interpretive advantage of the sprawling biblical and legendary vita popularized by Jacobus' *Legenda aurea*, finding therein a story about institutions, spiritual identities, and religious practices. The late medieval contexts that might be brought to bear upon the Digby *Magdalene* are as eclectic as the play itself. Prominent among them, though, are the play's ties to a Magdalene-saturated regional culture and its conversation with contemporary spiritual and religious discourses.

The Digby saint play culminates a long tradition of medieval English Magdalene devotion extending back to the Anglo-Saxon period, when early veneration of the saint was firmly established through works such as the ninth-century *Old English Martyrology* and Æthelwold of Winchester's late tenth-century *Benedictional*. Through its iconography and liturgy, Æthelwold's service book associates Mary Magdalene with the Virgin Mary and, probably more important, with East Anglian Æthelthryth, the Anglo-Saxon virgin saint and

---

[50] Lim, "Pilate's Special Letter," p. 3.

founder of Ely. Running counter to the sinful biblical woman promoted by Gregory the Great's influential life, Mary Magdalene's assumption of virginal attributes in Æthelwold's work would become a distinguishing feature of her early English cult.[51] This East Anglian re-inscription of Mary Magdalene's biography under the aegis of the virginal, authoritative Æthelthryth also occurs in a late thirteenth-century Anglo-Norman legendary produced at or for the Augustinian priory of nuns at Campsey Ash, Suffolk. British Library MS Additional 70513 brings together lives of Anglo-Saxon virgin princesses and royal abbesses (including Æthelthryth, or Audrey in Anglo-Norman), virgins, ascetics, English male ecclesiastics — and Mary Magdalene, the single biblical saint and one of only three non-British saints appearing in the collection. Within and for this wealthy monastic community, the inclusion of the Magdalene's vita in the Campsey Ash legendary underscores her association with the spiritual values espoused by the collection's other exemplary female saints, virgins, and ascetics.[52] Mary Magdalene keeps company with Audrey/Æthelthryth in the Campsey Ash manuscript and appears alongside Æthelthryth on decorated East Anglian rood screens because both holy women participate in a tradition of female sanctity that emphasized virginity and the spiritual authority of feminine purity. These central emphases of their early English cults contributed to East Anglian religious culture an image of feminine holiness that appealed to a broad demographic of monastic and lay patrons and audiences, enduring for centuries after Æthelwold's *Benedictional* first included Mary Magdalene in its choir of virgins.[53]

Mary Magdalene's cultic centers may have been located physically in Burgundy and Provence, but later medieval East Anglia emerges as a virtual hub of devotion to the saint.[54] Before she ever appeared in the eponymous Digby saint play, Mary Magdalene had figured crucially in unique East Anglian devotional, hagiographical, and dramatic texts that represent some of the most significant examples of imaginative religious writing in late medieval England.[55] These works feature Mary Magdalene in her many roles — witness to the Resurrection, intimate of Jesus, penitent sinner, model contemplative, apostle to the apostles as well as to Marseilles. Both the Short and Long Texts of Julian of Norwich's

---

[51] Ortenberg, "Le Culte de Sainte Marie Madeleine," pp. 25–31. See also Coletti, *Mary Magdalene and the Drama of Saints*, pp. 54–57.

[52] The Campsey Ash legendary contains the only copy of *La Vie seinte Audrée*, an Anglo-Norman life of Æthelthryth. On the manuscript see Wogan-Browne, *Saints' Lives and Women's Literary Culture*, and Coletti, *Mary Magdalene and the Drams of Saints*, pp. 57–58.

[53] See Ortenberg, "Le Culte de Sainte Marie Madeleine," and Wogan-Browne, *Saints' Lives and Women's Literary Culture*.

[54] The late medieval East Anglian counties of Norfolk and Suffolk were particularly attentive to feminine religious values and ideals. East Anglia was the cultic center of devotion to the Virgin Mary in England. Across the medieval centuries, English and international pilgrims flocked to the Marian shrine at Walsingham in northwest Norfolk. East Anglia was also home to a lively cult of the Virgin Mary's mother, Saint Anne. Feminine sacred symbols proliferated in East Anglia's celebrated parish churches, especially through painted images on rood screens and carvings on bench ends. See Gibson and Coletti, "Lynn, Walsingham, Norwich," pp. 311–12; Gibson, "Saint Anne and the Religion of Childbed"; Coletti, "Genealogy, Sexuality, and Sacred Power"; and Duffy, "Holy Maydens, Holy Wyfes."

[55] This paragraph draws from Coletti, *Mary Magdalene and the Drama of Saints*, p. 229. For more on regional contexts for the play, see pp. 50–99 of that work.

Revelation invoke Mary Magdalene's scripturally authentic witness to the Crucifixion as a touchstone for the affective yearnings that lead to Julian's daring theological explorations.[56] Margery Kempe makes the saint her alter ego, appropriating for herself the Magdalene's closeness to Jesus, sinful past, renounced sexual nature, and reconstituted virginity.[57] Osbern Bokenham accords the saint's vita the central position in his all-woman hagiography, exploiting her symbolic complexity to argue for a female apostolate and feminine genealogy of secular rule in fifteenth-century England.[58] When Bokenham's East Anglian patron Isabel Bourchier, countess of Eu, commissioned the Augustinian friar to write a life of Mary Magdalene, she acted as did other East Anglian noble women, who variously professed their devotion to the saint.[59] In the Macro and Digby morality play *Wisdom*, the corporeal experience of Mary Magdalene shadows that of the fallen Anima, whose spiritual state is imaged in a bodily expulsion of demons that mirrors the saint's own purgation.[60] The compiler-reviser of the *N-Town Play* places Mary Magdalene at the Last Supper, establishing her apostolic authority along with that of the other disciples.[61] Implicitly capitalizing on textual and visual traditions attesting to late medieval East Anglia's romance with Mary Magdalene, the Digby play, on the eve of the Reformation, also marks their culmination.

STAGING AND PERFORMANCE

This introduction has focused thus far on the Digby play's ties to an expansive English and continental archive documenting Mary Magdalene's ubiquitous and influential across the medieval centuries. I have pursued this approach because the East Anglian dramatic text invites — and deserves — such scrutiny. Extensive explanatory notes to this edition establish in greater detail the rationale for this scrutiny by identifying, to borrow Findon's term, the Digby *Magdalene*'s many intertexts. At the same time and even as a written text, the play constantly communicates to the reader awareness of the medium of its own performance. As a specimen of theatrical performance, the play's requirements for its staging are every bit as ambitious as are the challenges and varieties of its verbal idioms.

---

[56] *Writings of Julian of Norwich*, ed. Watson and Jenkins, pp. 63, 125.

[57] *Book of Margery Kempe*, ed. Meech and Allen, pp. 49, 191–97, 210.

[58] So argues Delaney, *Impolitic Bodies*; on Bokenham's life of the saint, see Delaney, *Impolitic Bodies*, pp. 53–57, 89–94.

[59] Bokenham, "Prolocutorye into Marye Mawdelyns lyf," in *Legendys of Hooly Wummen*, p. 137, lines 5065–75. Other East Anglian noblewomen who realized their devotion to the saint in works of art include Anne Harling, Lady Scrope, who commissioned an image of Mary Magdalene for her church at East Harling, Norfolk (Sugano, "Apologies for the Magdalene," pp. 172–74), and Alice Chaucer, Duchess of Suffolk and wife of William de la Pole, whose cadaver tomb in her chapel at Ewelme includes an image of the saint on its roof (Goodall, *God's House at Ewelme*, pp. 175–91). Isabel Bourchier's niece, Margaret of York, had herself represented as Mary Magdalene in a Flemish Deposition painting c. 1500; see Pearson, "Gendered Subject, Gendered Spectator."

[60] *Wisdom*, in *Macro Plays*, ed. Eccles, p. 144, line 912, s.d.

[61] *N-Town Play*, 1:264–73, lines 141–204, s.d. Here I adopt the singular "Play" of Spector's edition, though the N-Town manuscript's status as compilation is now generally accepted. See *N-Town Plays*, ed. Sugano, pp. 1–2.

Copious stage directions, primarily in English but occasionally in Latin, open a welcome window on possibilities for the play's medieval performances. These "astonishing and informative" instructions for stage business orchestrate the characters' traversing of a playing space whose geography is simultaneously domestic (Magdalene's castle), global (Rome and Jerusalem) and sacred (heaven and hell).[62] These directions also give notice that characters do not simply move across the expansive theatrical space; they also rise above and fall below it. The play is remarkably spectacular. It provides for frequent journeying of human and divine messengers, sudden appearances and disappearances of Jesus on earth and in heaven, a cloud that descends from on high to set a pagan temple on fire, and seven devils that "devoyde" (line 691, s.d.) from Mary during the feast at the home of Simon the Pharisee. A floating ship crosses the playing space with saintly and regal cargo; Jesus orders visionary appearances of Mary and attendant angels; the saint is elevated into the clouds for daily feedings with heavenly manna.[63] The sheer material demands of the play — e.g., for a ship sufficiently large to bear sailors as well as a king and queen, or for a hoisting device enabling transport between heaven and earth — point to great mechanical and technical virtuosity.[64] And all of these objects, spaces, and special effects are mobilized to create the multiple dramatic worlds occupied and transformed by the play's heroine.

I stated above (pp. 1–2) that the authorship, locale, and auspices of the Digby *Magdalene* remain a mystery to the many scholars who nonetheless continue to investigate the mechanics as well as the theatrical potential of its staging.[65] One piece of this mystery is the very fact that "no one seemed even to want to record what must have been considerable expenditures in relation to" the play's performance. As Godfrey notes, the mechanical feats and specialized locales that the play calls for "would generate, one might think, both curiosity and provoke response sufficiently to leave evidence of itself behind."[66] Despite the archive's muteness on this point, we can confidently observe, however, that the Digby play employs *platea* and *loca*, or place and scaffold staging. In general terms, this method requires an open area, called the *platea* or place, and a group of scaffolds or *loca* arranged around and/or within it. Whereas the *platea* as playing space is available for multiple and shifting significations, the *loca* constitute specific architectural or other designated structures; in the case of the Digby *Magdalene*, the tyrants' scaffolds, Magdalene's castle and her bower, the Jerusalem tavern, and Lazarus' tomb constitute some of these *loca*. Dramatic actions on or at the *loca* are knit together by activities occurring on the *platea*, which furnishes the basic ground for the play's staging.[67] Evidence indicates that *platea* and *loca* staging, including theaters in the round, was a regular feature of late medieval East Anglian performances. In his comprehensive analysis of dramatic staging in the region, Victor Scherb

---

[62] Quotation from Godfrey, "*Mary Magdalen* in Performance," p. 109.

[63] Here I draw from Coletti, *Mary Magdalene and the Drama of Saints*, p. 25.

[64] For detailed discussion of requirements of and possibilities for the ship in performance, see Godfrey, "Machinery of Spectacle," pp. 155–56n6.

[65] In addition to sources cited in footnotes 5–7 above, see also Godfrey, "Machinery of Spectacle," and "*Mary Magdalen* in Performance."

[66] Godfrey, "Machinery of Spectacle," pp. 146–47.

[67] This description is adapted from Scherb, *Staging Faith*, p. 55. Bush ("Resources of *Locus* and *Platea* Staging") provides a good overview of such staging in relation to the Digby play.

connects the Digby saint play with *The Castle of Perseverance* and the two Passion sequences in the *N-Town Play*, as examples of the "large-scale play."[68] Recent studies of the scope of the Digby *Magdalene* indicate exactly how large that scale might have been. Matthew Evan Davis identifies the play's requirement for over fifty characters and thirty-seven different locations.[69] An analysis of the play's dramatic action posits that at least thirty-one of the fifty-two action sequences comprising it occur on the *platea*, its primary space where audience members may have been invited or expected not simply to follow but to join, promenade fashion, a dramatic action kinetically dedicated to horizontal and vertical traveling.[70]

Who was occupying this proliferation of dramatic roles and enacting all of this movement? As for medieval English drama as a whole, it is generally assumed that the Digby *Magdalene* in performance — though the issue has largely eluded scholarly debate — would be the work of an all-male cast, accustomed to conventions of theatrical crossdressing that prevailed in the period.[71] From Cyrus' extolling his daughter Mary's femininity (line 71) and Jesus' praising that of his mother (line 1356), to the scabrous sexual innuendo that punctuates masculine rivalry in the play's comedic master-servant scenes, to the gender-norming exemplified by the king and queen of Marseilles, the Digby *Magdalene* is not shy about exploring — and exploiting — gender roles for theatrical meaning and dramatic effect.[72] Crossdressing on its medieval stage could lead to provocative manipulation of the gender categories and behaviors that are so often at issue in the play. For example, men playing the female roles might interject homoerotic valences into scenes of heterosexual wooing (like that occurring between Mary Magdalene and Curiosity, or the king and queen of Marseilles). Theatrical gestures highlighting the instability of gender categories seem especially apt in light of Mary Magdalene's own association with sexual transgression.[73] Still we should not entirely rule out the possibility of women performing on the Digby *Magdalene*'s stage. New evidence from Suffolk discovered by James Stokes, for instance, provides a portrait of women, across the social spectrum, who were involved in a range of performative activities in what he calls "pre-evangelical" England, that is, the England of the provinces where traditional cultural festivities, games, and plays endured up to the late sixteenth century.[74]

But if particulars of performing the Digby *Magdalene* on its late medieval stage must elude us, the play itself invites, indeed almost requires, that we think about how and why it may have worked in theatrical terms. Weaving together hagiographical narrative, courtly discourse, mercantile and anticlerical satire, scriptural texts, and contemplative and mystical idioms, the play unfolds on a stage in which dramatic action vacillates between naturalistic

---

[68] Scherb, *Staging Faith*, pp. 146–90; for his discussion of *Mary Magdalene*, see pp. 172–89.

[69] Davis, "As Above, So Below," pp. 74, 76. Of the thirty-seven, nineteen are mentioned in the stage directions; five are mentioned in characters' speeches; ten are mentioned in character speeches but "do not appear to exist in the physical play space" (p. 76); and three are inferred.

[70] Godfrey, "*Mary Magdalen* in Performance," pp. 112, 116–17.

[71] Normington, *Gender and Medieval Drama*, pp. 55–70.

[72] On these explorations, see Coletti, *Mary Magdalene and the Drama of Saints*, pp. 151–89.

[73] On such possibilities in performance, see Evans, "Signs of the Body." For comment on the potential impact of crossdressing on the performance of female saint plays, see Sanok, "Performing Feminine Sanctity," pp. 286–87.

[74] Stokes, "Women and Performance," p. 40.

representation, allegory, ritual, parody, and dreamscapes. Its stage comprehends all the world and the supernatural realms too. As a recent study observes, in its dramatic tale of travel the play must "grapple with the challenge of how to present a geographically and temporally sprawling story in a limited performance space."[75] One way to address this challenge may have involved the re-use or resignification of *loca* or scaffolds. Scherb notes clusters of associations that attend various *loca*, allowing for memorial recapitulation of earlier scenes and actions under entirely new meanings: thus the tavern in which Mary Magdalene falls for Curiosity may give way to the bower in which she awaits her lovers; that in its turn is refigured in the *hortulanus* scene in which Mary encounters the risen Christ as a gardener. In this model, the resignification of dramatic *loca* also heralds changes in spiritual commitments associated with those spaces.[76] Findon's study of the play's staging further attends to its "spatial semantics," the conceptual kinds of spaces in and through which dramatic action unfolds. Thus, in addition to their sheer number and potential for doubling, the spaces of dramatic *loca* may be domestic or public, closed or open, fortified or vulnerable.[77]

Our contemporary awareness of these signifying possibilities of location and movement inscribed within the Digby text invites larger questions about how medieval performance practice, in this instance, is not simply an action done to and with the dramatic text but is instead the necessary condition for realizing the play's complex spiritual and aesthetic vision.[78] From this perspective, then, to inquire about the staging of *Mary Magdalene* is also to ask how a play that depicts its own spectacle as a medium of conversion can also present a Jesus who enjoins his followers to pursue a faith without corporeal signs; or it is to consider how a play so committed dramatically to interrogating sources and forms of knowledge of the sacred might also offer its own embodied project as part of that effort.[79] To inquire about the staging of the Digby saint play, then, is to encounter a metatheatricality that recognizes, even celebrates, the extraordinarily good fit between the inescapable materiality of dramatic performance and the demands and opportunities of Mary Magdalene's rich late medieval biography.

EDITORIAL STATEMENT

This text has been edited from the single extant copy of *Mary Magdalene* in Bodleian Library MS Digby 133 (fols. 95r–145r). Although I have not attempted a complete collation

---

[75] Rochester, "Space and Staging," p. 44.

[76] Scherb, *Staging Faith*, pp. 176–79. On reuse of the play's many locations in staging, see also Davis, who provides a detailed model of what this layering might look like; "As Above, So Below."

[77] Findon, "Enclosure, Liberation, and Spatial Semantics."

[78] For a fuller discussion of performance, embodiment, and the spiritual interests of the play, see Coletti, *Mary Magdalene and the Drama of Saints*, pp. 190–217.

[79] Reflecting on his experience acting in and directing the Digby *Magdalene* for Poculi Ludique Societas in 2003, Peter Cockett ("The Actor's Carnal Eye") speaks of the actor's somatic and affective experience as a vehicle for spiritual knowledge. Lim's study of the play's relationship to late medieval documentary culture ("Pilate's Special Letter") argues that the play offers the experiential truth of performance as a counterweight to the instability of writing. Ehrstine analyzes the potential of mansion staging in continental performances to serve as visual, spiritual mnemonic; see "Framing the Passion."

with prior editions, I have recorded all substantive departures from Baker, Murphy, and Hall's Early English Text Society (EETS) edition of the play, *The Late Medieval Religious Plays of Bodleian MSS Digby 133 and e Museo 160* (1982), which collates all previous editions. I have also consulted the text of *Mary Magdalene* in David Bevington's *Medieval Drama* (1975), probably the version of the play best known to readers in recent decades. Bevington's text renders a collation difficult because his edition fully normalizes spelling. I have recorded significant departures from Bevington, however, and also noted my agreement with his readings when these seem preferable to those of the EETS edition. Bevington's text is closest to F. J. Furnivall's first edition of the play for EETS, *The Digby Plays* (1896). The edition of *Mary Magdalene* in John Coldewey's *Early English Drama: An Anthology* (1993) is largely derived from Baker, Murphy, and Hall.

This edition renders the manuscript's Middle English text according to guidelines consistent with editorial practices of the METS series:

- Thorn (*þ*) is modernized as *th*; yogh (*ȝ*) as *y*, *g*, *gh*, and occasionally as *z* and *s*.
- *i/j* and *u/v* are regularized.
- East Anglian *x* (*xall*) for the digraph [ʃ] is normalized as *sh*; *qw* (*qwat*) is normalized as *wh*. First occurrences of these practices are recorded in the textual notes.
- Scribal *w* for *v* is regularized (*volunté*).
- An *e* has been added to *the* (*þe*) used as a pronoun (*thee*).
- Single final *e* with full syllabic value is accented (*degré, nessesyté*).
- All Latin and English abbreviations are silently expanded.
- Modern punctuation has been added.
- Latin words and stage directions are printed in italics.
- Speech markers and setting changes are printed in boldface.

Several of the scribe's practices deserve special mention. The scribe uses thorn and yogh interchangeably, especially in combination with the letter *e*, thereby creating confusion between the article *þe* (*the*) and forms of the second person pronoun *þe* (*thee*) and *ȝe* (*ye*).[80] For example, see line 168, where the scribe has written the identical word to signify *ye* (*ȝe*) and the article *the* (*þe*): "Þe [ye] be þe [the] rewlar of this regyon"; or compare lines 101, "O þe [ye] good fathyr," and 105, "Ȝe [ye] shew us poyntys . . ." In such instances, my transcriptions reflect the best modern usage as determined by context.

As the EETS editors observe, the "scribe seems not to have had a very firm grip on the significance of some of the traditional abbreviation symbols."[81] Thus the scribe may write *yr* for *ys*, or *us* for *ys*. Discernible patterns of irregularity are recorded in the textual notes. Because of these scribal inconsistencies, my expansion of abbreviations occasionally differs from those of Baker, Murphy, and Hall. I have not recorded these minor differences and have sought to expand all abbreviations as consistently as possible.

In this edition, divisions in the text correspond to changes in speaker only, not stanzaic form, as in the case of the EETS edition, the only one that attempts to reconstruct the play's

---

[80] Benski's study of orthographic confusion and exchange in paleographic contexts sheds light on this manuscript quirk; "The Letters <þ> and <y> in Later Middle English."

[81] *Late Medieval Religious Plays*, ed. Baker, Murphy, and Hall, p. xxxi.

chaotic verse form and stanzaic structure.[82] The EETS editors posit that the confusing verse forms of the Digby text are probably a function of the play's copying and recopying over time, compounded by scribal lapses. Whereas the scribe has bracketed stanzaic patterns only intermittently, he has otherwise attempted to assert order on the text by drawing lines between the speeches of individual speakers. This edition, then, follows the scribe's lead in attending to organization along these lines.

The manuscript's speech markers generally appear in the right margin, though the scribe has occasionally placed them at the left or at the top of the page, especially when a page break occurs in the middle of a speech (e.g., fol. 99v). The Digby *Magdalene* scribe appears to have been incapable of designating the play's characters consistently by the same names, and of spelling or abbreviating a name in the same way twice consecutively. Speech markers in the text, therefore, are wildly inconsistent. To cite the most egregious example, Mary Magdalene is designated by speech markers as *Mary Mau*, *Mary Magleyn*, *Maria*, *Marya*, *Mary*, *Mari Maugleyn*, *Mary M*, *M Magdleyn*, *Magdleyn*, *Mauleyn*, etc. I have regularized all of these to *Mary Maudleyn*, the name the saint gives when asked by the King of Marseilles to identify herself (line 1675). I have regularized other names in speech markers to the form or spelling most frequently used by the scribe (e.g., *Herodys* rather than *Herowdys*). Where no one form appears with obvious frequency, I have selected the first or best spelling based on clarity. When the same character is identified by two or even three different names, I have retained all names and provided glosses where clarification is needed; for example, the shipmaster is called *Nauta* and *Mastyr* as well as *Shepmaster*; the character *Satan* is also identified as *Primus* and *Rex Diabolus*. Like other abbreviations in the text, all abbreviated speech markers have been silently expanded. When the scribe has omitted a speech marker, as occurs when a speaker is identified by a stage direction, I have supplied the speaker's name in brackets. Because I have regularized the speech markers in this manner, I have not recorded variations with Baker, Murphy, and Hall's EETS text, which treats the speech markers inconsistently, sometimes silently expanding and sometimes designating expansions with brackets. The list of Dramatis Personae normalizes these differences to facilitate entry to and reading of the text.

---

[82] *Late Medieval Religious Plays*, ed. Baker, Murphy, and Hall, pp. xxxiii–xxxvi.

THE DIGBY MARY MAGDALENE PLAY

DRAMATIS PERSONAE

(in order of appearance)

IMPERATOR, Tiberius Caesar
  SERABYL, his scribe
  PROVOST
SYRUS, lord of Magdalene castle
  his children:
    LAZARUS
    MARY MAGDALENE
    MARTHA
NUNCIUS, messenger to Caesar
HEROD, lord of Jerusalem
  PRIMUS PHILOSOPHER
  SECUNDUS PHILOSOPHER
  PRIMUS MILES (soldier)
  SECUNDUS MILES (soldier)
PILATE, judge in Jerusalem
  PRIMUS SERGEANT
  SECUNDUS SERGEANT
WORLD
  PRIDE
  COVETISE
FLESH
  LECHERY (LUXURIA)
  GLUTTONY
  SLOTH
DEVIL (SATAN; DIABOLUS)
  WRATH
  ENVY

SENSUALITY, messenger to WORLD
BAD ANGEL (SPIRITUS MALIGNI)
TAVERNER
CURIOSITY, a gallant
SYMOND LEPER
GOOD ANGEL
JESUS
TWO DEVILS, Belfagour and Belzabub
TWO SOLDIERS, attendant upon Lazarus
DISCIPLES
A JEW
KING (REX) OF MARSEILLES
QUEEN (REGINA) OF MARSEILLES
MARY JACOBE
MARY SALOME
TWO ANGELS, at Christ's tomb
PETER, the disciple
JOHN, the disciple
PRESBYTER, a heathen priest
  CLERICUS, his BOY
NUNCIUS, PILATE's messenger
MARY'S DISCIPLE
ANGEL, called Raphael
SHIPMAN, or NAUTA and MASTER
  GROBBE, his BOY
TWO ANGELS, attendant upon MARY MAGDALENE
and JESUS
PRIEST, a hermit

fol. 95r **[Rome]**

INPERATOR I command sylyns, in the peyn of forfetur,   *Emperor; silence; under penalty of loss*
        To all myn audyens present general!   *audience*
        Of my most hyest and mytyest volunté,   *volition*
        I woll it be knowyn to all the world unyversal
5   That of heven and hell chyff rewlar am I,   *chief ruler*
        To wos magnyfycens non stondyt egall.   *whose; equal*
        For I am soveren of al soverens subjugal   *subjugated*
        On to myn empere, beyng incomparable   *empire*
        Tyberyus Sesar, wos power is potencyal.   *whose; mighty*
10   I am the blod ryall, most of soverenté,   *royal highest in*
        Of all emperowers and kynges my byrth is best,
        And all regeons obey my myty volunté.   *will*
        Lyfe and lem and goodys all be at my request,   *limb*
        So, of all soverens, my magnyfycens most mytyest
15   May nat be agaynsayd of frend nor of foo;   *opposed by; by foe*
        But all abydyn jugment and rewle of my lyst.   *endure; pleasure*
        All grace upon erth from my goodnys commyt fro,   *kindness comes*
        And that bryngis all pepell in blysse so.
19   For the most worthyest, woll I rest in my sete.   *As; will; seat*

SERYBYL Syr, from your person growyt moch grace!   *much grace emanates*

INPERATOR Now, for thin answer, Belyall blysse thi face!   *your; Belial*
        Mykyl presporyté I gyn to porchase;   *Great; begin to acquire*
        I am wonddyn in welth from all woo.   *wrapped; woe*
fol. 95v Herke thou, provost, I gyff thee in commandment   *command you*
25   All your pepull preserve in pesabyl possessyon.   *peaceful*
        Yff any ther be to my goddys disobedyent,   *gods*
        Dyssever tho harlottys and make to me declaracyon.   *Isolate those scoundrels*
        And I shall make all swych to dye,   *such*
        Thos precharsse of Crystys incarnacyon!   *preachers*

PROVOST Lord of all lorddys, I shall gyff yow informacyon.

INPERATOR Lo, how all the world obeyit my domynacyon!
32   That person is nat born that dare me dysseobey!
        Syrybbe, I warne yow, se that my lawys
        In all your partyys have dew obeysauns.   *regions; due*
35   Inquere and aske, eche day that daunnes,   *dawns*
        Yf in my pepul be found ony weryons
        Contrary to me in ony chansse,
        Or with my goldyn goddys grocth or grone

	I woll marre swych harlottys with mordor and myschanse!¹	
40	Yff ony swyche remayn, put hem in repreffe,	*such; reprove them*
	And I shall you releff.	*reward*

SERYBYL Yt shall be don, lord, withowtyn ony lett or withowt doth.   *delay; doubt*

INPERATOR Lord and lad to my law doth lowte.   *bow*
Is it nat so? Sey yow all with on showte!   *one shout*

Here answerryt all the pepul at onys: "Ya, my lord, ya."   *once*

INPERATOR So, ye froward folkes, now am I plesyd!   *disobedient*
46   Sett wyn and spycys to my consell full cler.
fol. 96r   Now have I told yow my hart, I am wyll plesyd.
Now lett us sett don alle and make good chyr.   *cheer*

[Castle of Magdalene]

Her entyr Syrus, the fader of Mary Maudleyn.

SYRUS	Emperor and kyngges and conquerors kene,	*brave*
50	Erlys and borons and knytes that byn bold,	*barons; knights; are*
	Berdys in my bower so semely to senne,	*Young women; house; attractive; see*
	I commaund yow at onys my hestes to hold.	*at once; orders to obey*
	Behold my person, glysteryng in gold,	*glittering*
	Semely besyn of all other men.	*Deemed comely among*
55	Cyrus is my name, be cleffys so cold,	*cliffs*
	I command yow all obedyent to beyn.	*be*
	Woso woll nat, in bale I hem bryng,	*Whoso; suffering; them*
	And knett swyche caytyfys in knottys of care.	*bind such wretches*
	Thys castell of Maudleyn is at my wylddyng,	*command*
60	With all the contré, bothe lesse and more,	*surrounding lands*
	And Lord of Jherusalem. Who agens me don dare?	*Who dares act against me?*
	Alle Beteny at my beddyng be.	*Bethany is at my bidding*
	I am sett in solas from al syyng sore,	
	And so shall all my posteryté,	
65	Thus for to leven in rest and ryalté.²	
	I have her a sone that is to me ful trew,	*very*
	No comlyar creatur of Goddys creacyon;	*more attractive*
	To amyabyll douctors full brygth of ble	*Two; daughters; very; countenance*

---

¹ Lines 36–39: *If there be found among my people any inconstancy / [That is] Against me in any circumstance, / [Or anyone who] grouches or complains about my golden gods, / I will harm such scoundrels with murder and misfortune*

² Lines 63–65: *I am in solace protected from all sorrowful sighs, / And so shall all my posterity / live thus royally in tranquility*

Ful gloryos to my syth an ful of delectacyon.   *sight and; delight*

fol. 96v Lazarus, my son in my resspeccyon,   *regard (sight)*

71   Here is Mary, ful fayur and ful of femynyté,   *very fair*

And Martha, ful of beuté and of delycyté,   *completely beautiful and delightful*

Ful of womanly merrorys and of benygnyté.   *virtues; kindness*

They have fulfyllyd my hart with consolacyon.

75   Here is a coleccyon of cyrcumstance:

To my cognysshon nevyr swych anothyr,

As be demonstracyon knett in contynens,

Save alonly my lady that was ther mother.[1]

Now Lazarus, my sonne, whech art ther brothyr,   *who*

80   The lordshep of Jherusalem I gyff thee aftyr my dysses;   *death*

And Mary, thys castell alonly an non othyr;   *only; and*

And Martha shall have Beteny, I say exprese.   *expressly*

Thes gyftes I graunt yow withowtyn les   *lie*

Whyll that I am in good mynd.   *While*

LAZARUS   Most reverent father, I thank yow hartely

86   Of yower grett kyndnes shuyd onto me.   *For; shown*

Ye have grauntyd swych a lyfelod worthy   *livelihood*

Me to restreyn from all nessesyté.   *keep; hardship*

Now, good Lord, and hys wyll it be,   *may it be*

90   Graunt me grace to lyve to thy plesowns,

And agens hem so to rewle me,

Thatt we may have joye wythowtyn veryans.[2]

MARY MAUDLEYN   Thatt God of pes and pryncypall counsell,   *[fol. 97r]; peace*

More swetter is thi name than hony be kynd.   *sweeter; by nature*

95   We thank yow, fathyr, for your gyftes ryall,   *royal*

Owt of peynes of poverté us to onbynd.[3]

Thys is a preservatyff from streytnes we fynd,   *impoverishment*

From worldly labors to my coumfortyng,

For thys lyfflod is abyll for the dowttyr of a kyng,

100   Thys place of plesauns, the soth to saye.[4]

---

[1] Lines 75–78: *Here is a group of qualities / knit together in modest behavior, as is openly shown; / To my knowledge there was never such another, / Except for my wife, who was their mother*

[2] Lines 90–92: *Grant me grace to live according to your desires / And so to govern myself with respect to them / That we may have lasting joy*

[3] *For releasing us from poverty's pains*

[4] Lines 97–100: *This [gift], we find, will preserve us from penury, / [And] from worldly labors, thus comforting me, / For this livelihood (Magdalene Castle) is fitting for a king's daughter, / This pleasant place, truth be told*

MARTHA   O, ye good fathyr of grete degré,   *father of great social stature you are good*
Thus to departe with your ryches,   *Thus to part with*
Consederyng ower lowlynes and humylyte,   *lowly estate*
Us to save from worldly dessetres.   *To spare us worldly distress*
105   Ye shew us poyntes of grete jentylnes,   *examples; great*
So mekly to mayntyn us to your grace.   *benevolently; keep us*
Hey in heven avansyd mot yow be high;   *High; may you be advanced*
In blysse, to se that Lordys face
Whan ye shal hens passe.   *pass from here (die)*

SYRUS   Now I rejoyse wyth all my mygthtys.   *to the fullness of my abilities*
111   To enhanse my chyldryn, it was my delyte.   *to elevate to prosperity*
Now, wyn and spycys, ye jentyll knyttes,
Onto thes ladys of jentylnes.

Here shal they be servyd wyth wyn and spycys.

[Rome]

INPERATOR   Syr provost and skrybe, juggys of my rem,   *scribe; judges; realm*
115   My massengyr I woll send into ferre cuntré   *distant region*
Onto my sete of Jherusalem,   *city*
Onto Herowdys, that regent ther ondyr me,
fol. 97v   And onto Pylat, jugges of the countré.
Myn entent I woll hem teche.   *them*
120   Take hed, thou provost, my precept wretyn be,   *heed that my orders be in writing*
And sey I cummaund hem, as they woll be owit wrech,   *that harm will come to them*
Yf ther be ony in the cuntré ageyn my law doth prech,   *anyone*
Or ageyn my goddys ony trobyll tellys,   *against; gods; speaks ill*
That thus agens my lawys rebellys,   *Who*
125   As he is regent and in that reme dwellys,   *realm*
And holdyth his croun of me be ryth,   *crown; right*
Yff ther be ony harlettys that agens me make replycacyon,[1]
Or ony moteryng agens me make with malynacyon.   *muttering; evil intent*

PROVOST   Syr, of all this they shall have informacyon,
130   So to uphold yower renoun and ryte.   *prerogative*

[INPERATOR]   Now, massengyr, withowtyn taryyng,
Have here gold onto thi fe.   *as your payment*
So bere thes lettyrs to Herowdys the kyng,
And byd hem make inquyrans in every cuntré,   *inquiries*
135   As he is jugge in that cuntré beyng.   *Since*

---

[1] *If there are any scoundrels who argue against me*

NUNCYUS   Soveren, your arend it shall be done ful redy,   *errand; readily*
    In all the hast that I may;   *haste*
    For to fullfyll your byddyng,
    I woll nat spare nother be nyth nor be day.   *neither; night*

        Here goth the masengyr toward Herowdys.

[Herod's Palace]

HERODYS   In the wyld, wanyng world, pes all at onys!   *[fol. 98r]; Curse on you, silence at once*
141   No noyse, I warne yow, for greveyng of me.   *angering me*
    Yff yow do, I shal hourle off yower hedys, be Mahondys bonys,   *hurl off; heads*
    As I am trew kyng to Mahond so fre.   *noble*
    Help, help, that I had a swerd!   *sword*
145   Fall don, ye faytours, flatt to the ground.   *down; scoundrels*
    Heve off your hodes and hattys, I cummaund yow alle;   *Take off; hoods*
    Stand bare hed, ye beggars! Wo made yow so bold?   *bare headed; Who*
    I shal make yow know your kyng ryall.
    Thus woll I be obeyyd thorow al the world,
150   And who so wol nat, he shal be had in hold,   *restrained*
    And so to be cast in carys cold,   *into a miserable condition*
    That werkyn ony wondyr agens my magnyfycens.   *Who; devises*
    Behold these ryche rubyys, red as ony fyr,   *any*
    With the goodly grene perle ful sett abowgth.   *about*
155   What kyng is worthy or egall to my power?   *equal*
    Or in this world, who is more had in dowt   *feared*
    Than is the hey name of Herowdys, kyng of Jherusalem,   *high*
    Lord of Alapye, Assye, and Tyr,
    Of Abyron, Beryaby, and Bedlem?
160   All thes byn ondyr my governons.   *are; control*
    Lo, all thes I hold withowtyn reprobacyon.   *reproof*
    No man is to me egall, save alonly the emperower,   *equal; except for*
    Tyberyus, as I have in provostycacyon.   *whom I serve as provost*
fol. 98v How sey the phylyssoverys be my ryche reyne?   *philosophers about; reign*
165   Am nat I the grettest governowur?
    Lett me ondyrstond; whatt can ye seyn?   *say*

PHYLYSOFYR   Soveren, and it plece yow, I woll expresse: *please*
    Ye be the rewlar of this regyon,   *ruler*
    And most worthy sovereyn of nobylnes
170   That evyr in Jude barre domynacyon.   *Judea held*
    Bott, syr, skreptour gevytt informacyon,   *scripture; gives*
    And doth rehersse it verely,   *truly report*
    That chyld shal remayn of grete renoun,   *continue in*
    And all the world of hem shold magnyfy: *shall glorify him*

175   *Et ambulabunt gentes in lumine tuo et reges*
      In splendore ortus tui.[1]

HERODYS   And whatt seyst thow?

SECUNDUS PHYLYSOFYR   The same weryfyyt my bok; as how,   *verifies*
      As the skryptour doth me tell,
180   Of a myty duke shal rese and reyn,   *mighty duke [who] shall rise*
      Whych shal reyn and rewle all Israell.   *Who*
      No kyng agens hys worthynes shall opteyn,   *prevail*
      The whech in profesy hath grett eloquence:
      Non auferetur sceptrum de Juda et dux de
185   *Femore eius, donec veniet qui mitendus est.*[2]

HERODYS   A, owt, owt! Now am I grevyd all wyth the worst!   *[fol. 99r]; completely grieved*
      Ye dastardys! Ye doggys! The dylfe mote yow draw![3]
      With fleyyng flappys I byd yow to a fest.   *flaying whips; command; feast*
      A swerd, a swerd! Thes lordeynnes wer slaw!
190   Ye langbaynnes! Loselles! Forsake ye that word![4]
      That caytyff shall be cawth, and suer I shall hem flaw;   *caught; surely; him; flay*
      For hym many mo shal be marryd with mordor.[5]

PRIMUS MILES   My sovereyn lord, dyssemay yow ryth nowt.   **First Soldier**; *dismay; not at all*
      They ar but folys, ther eloquens wantyng;   *fools; lacking*
195   For in sorow and care sone they shall be cawt.   *soon; caught*
      Agens us they can mak no dysstonddyng.   *They cannot withstand us*

SECUNDUS MILES   My lord, all swych shall be browte before your audyens,[6]
      And levyn ondyr your domynacyon,
      Or elles dammyd to deth wyth mortal sentense,
200   Yf we hem gett ondyr ower gubernacyon.

HERODYS   Now thys is to me a gracyows exsortacyon,   *exhortation*
      And grettly rejoysyth to my sprytes indede.   *spirits indeed*

---

[1]   Lines 175–76: *And the Gentiles shall walk in thy light, and kings / in the brightness of thy rising* (Isaias 60:3)

[2]   Lines 183–85: *Of which the prophecy eloquently speaks: / The scepter shall not be taken from Judea, nor a ruler from / his thigh, until he comes that is to be sent* (Genesis 49:10)

[3]   *You dastards! You scoundrels! May the devil tear you apart*

[4]   Lines 189–90: *A sword! A sword! Would that these rascals were slain! / You longbones! Scoundrels! Retract that word (i.e., the prophecy of the coming of Christ)*

[5]   *Because of him many more shall be ruined by murder*

[6]   Lines 197–200: **Second Soldier**: *My lord, all such shall be brought before your presence, / And [they shall] live under your domination, / Or else [they shall be] condemned to death by mortal sentence, / If we get them under our control*

	Thow these sottes agens me make replycacyon,	*Although; fools oppose me*
	I woll suffer non to spryng of that kenred,	*allow no one; from that lineage*
205	Some voys in my lond schall sprede,	
	Prevely or pertely in my lond abowth.	
fol. 99v	Whyle I have swych men, I nede not to drede	
	But that he shal be browt ondyr, withowtyn doth.[1]	

Her commyt the emperowers masengyr, thus sayyng to Herodys:

MESENGYR	Heyll, prynse of bountyowsnesse!	*generous prince*
210	Heyll, myty lord of to magnyfy!	*worthy to extol*
	Heyll, most of worchep of to expresse!	
	Heyll, reytyus rewlar in thi regensy!	*righteous ruler; kingdom*
	My sofereyn, Tyberyus, chyff of chyfalry,	*chief of chivalry*
	Hys soveren sond hath sent to yow here:	*message*
215	He desyrth yow and preyyt on eche party	*desires; beseeches; in every way*
	To fulfyll hys commaundment and desyre.	

Here he shall take the lettyrs onto the kyng.

HERODYS	Be he sekyr, I woll natt spare	*He may be sure; hesitate*
	Forto complyshe his cummaunddment,	*to fulfill*
	Wyth sharp swerddes to perce them bare	*pierce bare flesh*
220	In all countres wythin this regent	*kingdom*
	For his love to fulfyll his intentt.	
	Non swych shall from ower handys stertt,	*escape*
	For we woll fulfyll his ryall juggement	
	Wyth swerd and spere to perce thorow the hartt!	
225	But, masengyr, reseyve thys lettyr wyth,	*in haste*
	And ber ytt onto Pylattys syth.	*bear; sight*

| **MESENGYR** | My lord, it shall be done ful wygth. | *[fol. 100r]; quickly* |
| | In hast I woll me spede! | *hurry* |

[Jerusalem — Pilate's Palace]

PYLATT	Now ryally I reyne in robys of rychesse,	*reign; robes*
230	Kyd and knowyn both ny and ferre	*Recognized; near*
	For juge of Jherusalem, the trewth to expresse,	*As judge*
	Ondyr the Emperower Tyberius Cesar.	
	Therfor I rede yow all, bewarre	*advise*
	Ye do no pregedyse agen the law.	*do no damage to existing law*

---

[1] Lines 205–08: *[Should] some rumor [of him] spread in my lands, / privately or publically, around my jurisdiction / While I have such men, I need not fear / That he (Christ) shall be anything except under our control, without a doubt*

235	For and ye do, I wyll yow natt spare,	*if you do*
	Tyl ye have judgment to be hangyd and draw.	*torn to pieces*
	For I am Pylat, prommyssary and presedent.	*procurator and ruler*
	All renogat robber inperrowpent,	
	To put hem to peyn, I spare for no peté.[1]	
240	My serjauntes semle, what seye ye?	*attractive; say you*
	Of this rehersyd I wyll natt spare.[2]	
	Plesauntly, syrrys, aunswer to me,	*sirs*
	For in my herte I shall have the lesse care.	*So that; concern*

PRIMUS SERJUNT	As ye have seyd, I hold it for the best,	**First Sergeant**
245	Yf ony swych among us, may we know.	*If [there be] any such*

SECUNDUS SERJUNT	For to gyff hem jugment, I holdd yt best,	**Second Sergeant**; *give them*
	And so shall ye be dred of hye and low.	*feared by high and low*

PYLATT	A, now I am restoryd to felycyté!	

fol. 100v   *Her comyt the emprorys masengyr to Pylat.*

MESENGYR	Heyll, ryall in rem in robis of rychesse!	*realm*
250	Heyl, present thou prynsys pere!	*present one; peer of princes*
	Heyl, jugge of Jherusalem, the trewth to expresse!	
	Tyberyus, the emprower, sendyt wrytyng herre,	*emperor; writing here*
	And prayyt yow, as yow be his lover dere,	*beseeches; since you are his loyal subject*
	Of this wrytyng to take avysement	*notice*
255	In strenthyng of his lawys cleyr,	*strengthening; plain*
	As he hath set yow in the state of jugment.	*Since; seat*

Her Pylat takyt the lettyrs with grete reverens.

PYLATT	Now, be Martes so mythy, I shal sett many a snare	*Mars so mighty*
	His lawys to strenth in al that I may.	*strengthen; can do*
	I rejoyse of his renown and of his wylfare,	*I am happy for; well-being*
260	And for thi tydyngges, I geyff thee this gold today.	*give*

MESENGYR	A, largeys, ye lord, I crye this day!	*largesse (generosity)*
	For this is a geft of grete degré.	*gift; quality*

PYLATT	Masengyr, onto my sovereyn thou sey	
	On the most specyall wyse recummend me.	

Her avoydyt the masengyr, and Syrus takyt his deth.   *exits; dies*

---

[1] Lines 238–39: *Rebuking all renegade robbers, / For no pity do I spare to put them to pain*

[2] *I will not back down from what I have just rehearsed (said)*

[Castle of Magdalene]

SYRUS	A, help, help! I stond in drede!	
266	Syknes is sett ondyr my syde.	
	A, help! Deth wyll aquyte me my mede!	*grant me my reward*
fol. 101r	A gret God, thou be my gyde!	*guide*
	How I am trobyllyd both bak and syde.	*troubled (pained in)*
270	Now, wythly help me to my bede.	*quickly*
	A, thys rendyt my rybbys! I shall nevyr goo nor ryde.	*tears my ribs*
	The dent of deth is hevyar than led.	*stroke; heavier*
	A, lord, lord, what shal I do this tyde?	*at this time*
	A gracyows God, have ruth on me,	*mercy*
275	In this world no lengar to abyde.	*I shall not remain long in this world*
	I blys yow, my chyldyrn. God mot with us be!	*bless; May God be*

> *Her avoydyt Syrus sodenly, and than sayyng Lazarus:*   *exits*

[LAZARUS]	Alas, I am sett in grete hevynesse!	
	Ther is no tong my sorow may tell,	
	So sore I am browth in dystresse.	*sorrowfully; put in distress*
280	In feyntnes I faltyr for this fray fell;	*weakness; deadly attack*
	This dewresse wyl lett me no longar dwelle,	
	But God of grace sone me redresse.[1]	
	A, how my peynys don me repelle.	*do attack me*
	Lord, withstond this duresse!	*[may I] withstand*

MARY MAUDLEYN	The inwyttissymus God that evyr shal reyne,	*most wise*
286	Be his help an sowlys sokor.	*[May] he be your soul's succor*
	To whom it is most nedfull to cumplayn,	*necessary to appeal*
	He to bryng us owt of ower dolor.	*That he may bring us out of our sadness*
	He is most mytyest governowre,	
290	From soroyng us to restryne.	*restrain (keep)*

MARTHA	A, how I am sett in sorowys sad,	**[fol. 101v]**
	That long my lyf I may nat indeure.	*no longer; endure*
	Thes grawous peynes make me ner mad.	*grievous pains; nearly*
	Undyr clowyr is now my fathyris cure,	
295	That sumtyme was here ful mery and glad.[2]	
	Ower Lordes mercy be his mesure,	*desert (reward)*
	And defeynd hym from peynes sad.	*protect; sorrowful*

---

[1] Lines 281–82: *This duress will permit me to live no longer, / Unless God in his grace restores me soon*

[2] Lines 294–95: *Under clover now lie buried the cares of my father, / Who was once here, very merry and happy*

LAZARUS   Now, systyrs, ower fatherys wyll we woll exprese;   *fulfill*
             Thys castell is owerys with all the fee.   *ours; income*

MARTHA   As hed and governower, as reson is,
301   And on this wyse abydyn with yow wyll wee.
             We wyll natt desevyr, whattso befalle.[1]

MARY MAUDLEYN   Now, brothyr and systyr, welcum ye be,
             And therof specyally I pray yow all.[2]

> Her shal entyr the Kyng of the World, the Flesch, and the Dylfe
> with the Seven Dedly Synnys, a Bad Angyll, an an Good Angyl,   *and a*
> thus seyyng the World:

[Stage of the World]

[WORLD]   I am the World, worthyest that evyr God wrowth,   *wrought (made)*
306   And also I am the prymatt portature   *principal supporter*
              Next heveyn, yf the trewth be sowth,   *Next to heaven; sought*
              And that I jugge me to skryptur.   *For that I call scripture as my witness*
              And I am he that longest shal induere   *endure*
310   And also most of domynacyon.   *greatest in*
fol. 102r Yf I be hys foo, woo is abyll to recure?   *someone's foe; who; thrive*
              For the whele of fortune wyth me hath sett his senture.   *center*
              In me restyt the ordor of the metellys sevyn,   *is fixed; metals*
              The whych to the seven planyttys ar knett ful sure: *planets; securely knit*
315   Gold perteynyng to the sonne, as astronemere nevyn;   *sun; says*
              Sylvyr to the mone, whyte and pure;   *moon*
              Iryn onto the Maris that long may endure;   *Iron; Mars*
              The fegetyff mercury onto Mercuryus;   *fugitive (unstable)*
              Copyr onto Venus, red in hys merrour;   *Copper; mirror (image)*
320   The frangabyll tyn to Jubyter, yf ye can dyscus;   *breakable tin; Jupiter*
              On this planyt Saturne, ful of rancure,   *And to; rancor*
              This soft metell led, nat of so gret puernesse.   *lead; purity*
              Lo, alle this rych tresor wyth the World doth indure.   *treasure; endure*
              The seven prynsys of hell of gret bowntosnesse,   *princes; bounty (generosity)*
325   Now who may presume to come to my honour?   *approximate my*

PRYDE   Ye, worthy World, ye be gronddar of gladnesse   *founder*
            To them that dwellyn ondyr yower domynacyon.

---

[1] Lines 300–02: *By reason [you, Lazarus,] are our leader and governor; / Therefore we will remain with you. / We will never separate [from you], whatever should happen*

[2] *And especially [because we are brother and sister], I entreat you [to enter the Castle]*

COVETYSE And who so wol nat, he is sone set asyde,
　　　　　Wher as I, Covetyse, take mynystracyon.[1]

MUNDUS Of that, I pray yow, make no declareracyon.   *World*
331　　　Make swych to know my soverreynte,
　　　　　And than they shal be fayn to make supplycacyon,
　　　　　If that they stond in ony nesessyté.[2]

fol. 102v　　　*Her shal entyr the Kyng of Flesch wyth Slowth, Gloteny, Lechery.*

[Stage of the King of Flesh]

FLESCH I, Kyng of Flesch, florychyd in my flowers,   *adorned*
335　　　Of deyntys delycyows I have grett domynacyon.   *By means of delicious luxuries*
　　　　　So ryal a kyng was nevyr borne in bowrys,   *royal; bowers*
　　　　　Nor hath more delyth ne more delectacyon.   *Nor has [one]; delight; pleasure*
　　　　　For I have comfortatywys to my comfortacyon:
　　　　　Dya galonga, ambra, and also margaretton —-
340　　　Alle this is at my lyst, agens all vexacyon.
　　　　　Alle wykkyt thyngys I woll sett asyde.
　　　　　Clary, pepur long, wyth granorum paradysy,
　　　　　Zenzybyr and synamom at every tyde —[3]
　　　　　Lo, alle swych deyntyys delycys use I.   *dainties*
345　　　Wyth swyche deyntyys I have my blysse.
　　　　　Who woll covett more game and gle   *could wish for greater mirth and sport*
　　　　　My fayere spowse Lechery to halse and kysse?[4]
　　　　　Here is my knyth Gloteny, as good reson is,   *knight; as reason would have it*
　　　　　Wyth this plesaunt lady to rest be my syde.   *remain*
350　　　Here is Slowth, anothyr goodly of to expresse;   *another good one to speak of*
　　　　　A more plesaunt compeny doth nowhere abyde.   *cannot be found anywhere*

LUXURIA O ye prynse, how I am ful of ardent lowe,   ***Lechery**; prince; love*
　　　　　With sparkylles ful of amerowsnesse!   *amorousness*
　　　　　With yow to rest fayn wold I aprowe,   *remain; gladly would I agree*
355　　　To shew plesauns to your jentylnesse.   *show; gentility*

---

[1] Lines 328–29: *And whoever will not [dwell under World's domination] will soon be passed over [for advancement] / Wherever I, Covetousness, am in charge*

[2] Lines 330–33: *I ask you please to make no mention of that (the prospect of refusal mentioned by Covetyse). / [Instead] make such as these to know my sovereignty, / And then they will be pleased to make supplication [to me], / If they find themselves in any need*

[3] Lines 338–43: *For I have comforting cordials to restore me / compounds of galingale, amber, and pearls — / All this is for my pleasure, to combat all vexations. / All noxious things I shall set aside (remove from me). / Clary (a medicinal plant), long pepper, with grains of paradise / Ginger and cinnamon [I shall have] all the time*

[4] *[Than] to embrace and kiss my fair spouse Lechery*

THE FLESCH   O ye bewtews byrd, I must yow kysse!   *beauteous young woman*
    I am ful of lost to halse yow this tyde.   *lust (desire) to embrace you right now*

fol. 103r   *Here shal entyr the prynse of dyllys in a stage and*   *devils*
       helle ondyrneth that stage, thus seyyng the Dylfe: *Devil*

[The Devils' Stage]

[**DYLFE**]   Now I, prynse pyrles, prykkyd in pryde,   ***Devil**; peerless; dressed up*
    Satan, yower sovereyn, set wyth every cyrcumstanse,[1]
360   For I am atyred in my towyr to tempt yow this tyde.   *fitted out; time*
    As a kyng ryall I sette at my plesauns,   *sit; pleasure*
    Wyth Wrath and Invy at my ryall retynawns.   *in my royal retinue*
    The bolddest in bowyr I bryng to abaye,[2]
    Mannis sowle to besegyn and bryng to obeysauns.   *besiege; obedience*
365   Ya, wyth tyde and tyme I do that I may,   *time; what I can*
    For at hem I have dysspyte that he shold have the joye
    That Lycyfer wyth many a legyown lost for ther pryde.[3]
    The snarys that I shal set wher nevyr set at Troye.   *snares (traps); were never*
    So I thynk to besegyn hem be every waye wyde.   *plan to besiege them by every means*
370   I shal getyn hem from grace whersoevyr he abyde,[4]
    That body and sowle shal com to my hold,   *So that; control*
    Hym for to take.   *[And thus] I will capture him*
    Now, my knythtys so stowth   *stout (strong)*
    Wyth me ye shall ron in rowte,   *run together*
375   My consell to take for a skowte,
    Whytly that we were went for my sake.[5]

WRATH   Wyth wrath or wyhyllys we shal hyrre wynne.   *wiles; win her over*

ENVY   Or wyth sum sotyllté sett hur in synne.   *subtlety cause her to sin*

DYLFE   Com of, than, let us begynne
380   To werkyn hure sum wrake!   *cause her some harm*

fol. 103v   *Her shal the Deyvl go to the World wyth hys compeny.*

---

[1] *[I am] Satan, your sovereign, endowed with every circumstance (advantage)*

[2] *The boldest in bower (dwelling) are put at my mercy*

[3] Lines 366–67: *For I despise them (mankind) for having the joy / That Lucifer with his legions lost because of pride*

[4] *I will remove him (mankind) from grace wherever he lives*

[5] Lines 375–76: *And you shall accept my counsel as a guide, / Oh, that we were quickly gone for my sake*

[Stage of the World]

SATAN   Heyle, World, worthyest of abowndans!   *abundantly worthy*
         In hast we must a conseyll take: *take counsel*
         Ye must aply yow wyth all your afyauns,
         A woman of whorshep ower servant to make.[1]

MUNDUS   Satan, wyth my consell I wyll thee avansse.   *advance (promote) you*
386   I pray thee, cum up onto my tent.
         Were the Kyng of Flesch her with hys asemlanus![2]
         Masengyr! Anon that thou werre went   *were on your way*
         Thys tyde.   *At this time*
390   Sey, the Kyng of Flesch wyth grete renown,
         Wyth hys consell that to hym be bown,   *bound*
         In alle the hast that evyr they mown,   *may*
         Com as fast as he may ryde.

MESENGYR   My Lord, I am your servant, Sensualyté.
395   Your masege to don, I am of glad chyr.   *deliver; cheer (disposition)*
         Ryth sone in presens ye shal hym se,   *Very soon; before you*
         Your wyl for to fulfylle her.   *here*

         Her he goth to the Flesch, thus seyyng:

[Stage of the King of Flesh]

         Heyl, lord in lond, led wyth lykyng!   *by pleasure*
         Heyl, Flesch in lust, fayyrest to behold!   *fairest*
400   Heyl, lord and ledar of emprore and kyng!   *leader*
         The worthy World, be wey and wold,   *by highway and forest*
         Hath sent for yow and your consell.
         Satan is sembled wyth hys howshold,   *assembled*
         Your counseyl to have most for aweyle.   *for the greatest profit*

FLESCH   Hens in hast that we ther where!   *[fol. 104r]; were there*
406   Lett us make no lengar delay.

SENSWALITÉ   Gret myrth to ther hertys shold yow arere,[3]   **Sensuality**
         By my trowth I dare safly saye.   *safely*

         Her commyt the Kyng of Flesch to the World, thus seyyng:

---

[1] Lines 383–84: *You must dedicate yourself, and all those pledged to you / To make this worshipful woman (Mary Magdalene) our servant*

[2] *Would that the King of Flesh were here with his assembly*

[3] *You shall bring great mirth to their hearts [by appearing before them]*

[Stage of the World]

[FLESCH] Heyl be yow, soverens lefe and dere!	*beloved*
410 Why so hastely do ye for me send?	

MUNDUS A, we are ryth glad we have yow here,	*very pleased [that]*
Ower counsell togethyr to comprehend.	*to plan*
Now, Satan, sey your devyse.	*tell your device (plan)*

SATAN Serys, now ye be set, I shal yow say:	*that you are seated*
415 Syrus dyyd this odyr day.	*died*
Now Mary, hys dowctor, that may,	*daughter; maiden*
Of that castel beryt the pryse.	*bears the prize*

MUNDUS Sertenly, serys, I yow tell,	*Certainly*
Yf she in vertu stylle may dwelle,	*remains virtuous*
420 She shal byn abyll to dystroye helle,	*be able*
But yf your counseyll may othyrwyse devyse.	*Unless*

FLESCH Now ye, Lady Lechery, yow must don your attendans,	*attend upon her*
For yow be flowyr fayrest of femynyté.	*femininity*
Yow shal go desyyr servyse and byn at hure atendauns,	
425 For ye shal sonest entyr, ye beral of bewte.[1]	

LECHERY Serys, I abey your counsell in eche degré.	*obey; in every way*
Stryttwaye thethyr woll I passe.	*Straightaway there; go*

SATAN Spiritus malyngny shal com to thee,	*An evil spirit*
Hyre to tempt in every plase.	*Her; everywhere*
430 Now all the six that here be,	
fol. 104v Wysely to werke, hyr favor to wynne,	
To entyr hyr person be the labor of Lechery,	
That she at the last may com to helle.[2]	
How, how, *spiritus malyng*, thou wottyst what I mene?	*do you know*
435 Cum owt, I sey! Heryst nat what I seye?	*Do you not hear*

BAD ANGYL Syrrys, I obey your counsell in eche degree.	
Stryttwaye thethyr woll I passe.	
Speke soft, speke soft, I trotte hyr to tene.	*hurry in order to torment her*
I prey thee pertly, make no more noyse.	*ask you openly*

---

[1] Lines 424–25: *You shall ask to be in her service and attend upon her, / For you [rather than others] shall soonest enter [the Castle], you beautiful beryl*

[2] Lines 430–33: *Now all of the six (remaining deadly sins) who are here, / To win her (Mary Magdalene's) good will, work in this manner / To enter her person through Lady Lechery's effort, / So that she (Mary Magdalene) may at last be condemned to hell*

Her shal alle the Seven Dedly Synnys besege the castell tyll Mary   besiege
agre to go to Jherusalem. Lechery shall entyr the castell wyth   agrees
the Bad Angyl, thus seyyng Lechery:

[The Castle of Magdalene]

[LUXURIA]   Heyl, lady, most laudabyll of alyauuns!   kindred
441   Heyl, oryent as the sonne in hys reflexité!   brilliant
         Myche pepul be comfortyd be your benyng afyauns.
         Bryter than the bornyd is your bemys of bewté,
         Most debonarius wyth your aungelly delycyté.[1]

MARY MAUDLEYN   What personne be ye that thus me comendyd?[2]

LUXURIA   Your servant to be, I wold comprehende.   intend

MARY MAUDLEYN   Your debonarius obedyans ravyssyt me to trankquelyté.[3]
448   Now, syth ye desyre, in eche degree,   since; desire [it]; every way
         To receyve yow I have grett delectacyon.   pleasure
450   Ye be hartely welcum onto me!   sincerely
         Your tong is so amyabyll, devydyd wyth reson.[4]

LUXURIA   Now, good lady, wyll ye me expresse   [fol. 105r]; say to me
         Why may ther no gladdnes to yow resort?[5]

MARY MAUDLEYN   For my father I have had grett hevynesse;
455   Whan I remembyr, my mynd waxit mort.   becomes deadened

LUXURIA   Ya, lady, for all that, be of good comfort,
         For swych obusyons may brede myche dysese.   abuses; breed; unease
         Swych desepcyons potyt peynys to exsport;
         Prynt yow in sportys whych best doth yow plese.[6]

MARY MAUDLEYN   Forsothe, ye be welcum to myn hawdyens!   Truly; presence
461   Ye be my hartys leche.   healer of my heart
         Brother Lazarus, and it be yower plesauns,   if; pleasure

---

[1] Lines 440–44: *Hail, lady, most praiseworthy of family connection! / Hail, [oh one] brilliant as the shining sun! / Many people are comforted by your kind trust. / Brighter than burnished are your beams of beauty, / Most gracious [one] with your angelic delights*

[2] *Who are you that have thus commended me?*

[3] *Your gracious obedience transports me to tranquility*

[4] *Your tongue (speech) is so amiable and rationally arranged*

[5] *Why no happiness resorts to (remains with) you*

[6] Lines 458–59: *Take pains to put aside such disappointments / Commit yourself to the pastimes that best please you*

And ye, systyr Martha, also in substawns,   *truly*
This place I commend onto your governons,   *entrust*
465   And onto God I yow betake.   *commend*

LAZARUS   Now, systyr, we shal do your intente,
In this place to be resydent
Whyle that ye be absent,
To kepe this place from wreche.   *harm*

Here takyt Mary hur wey to Jherusalem wyth Luxsurya, and
they shal resort to a tavernere, thus seyyng the tavernere:

[A Tavern in Jerusalem]

[TAVERNERE]   I am a taverner, wytty and wyse,
471   That wynys have to sell, gret plenté.   *wines; in great abundance*
Of all the taverners, I bere the pryse,   *take the prize*
That be dwellyng wythinne the ceté.   *Who are; city*
fol. 105v Of wynys I have grete plenté,
475   Both whyte wynne and red that is so cleyre.   *white; clear*
Here is wynne of Mawt and malmeseyn,
Clary wynne, and claret, and other moo,
Wyn of Gyldyr and of Galles, that made at the Grome,
Wyn of Wyan and Vernage, I seye also,
480   Ther be no bettyr as ferre as ye can goo.[1]

LUXURIA   Lo, lady, thee comfort and thee sokower.   *help yourself*
Go we ner and take a tast;   *Let's go closer; taste*
Thys shal bryng your sprytys to favor.   *comfort your spirits*
Tavernere, bryng us of the fynnest thou hast.   *finest*

TAVERNERE   Here, lady, is wyn, a repast   *refreshment*
486   To man and woman, a good restoratyff.   *cordial*
Ye shall nat thynk your mony spent in wast;   *is spent wastefully*
From stodyys and hevynes it woll yow relyff.   *cares and burdens; relieve*

MARY MAUDLEYN   Iwys, ye seye soth, ye grom of blysse.   *Certainly; the truth; man*
490   To me ye be courtes and kynde.   *courteous*

Her shal entyr a galaunt, thus seyyng: *young man of fashion*

---

[1] Lines 476–80: *Here is wine from Malta and malmsey (a strong sweet wine), / Clary wine (sweet drink of wine, honey, and spice), claret, and many more, / (Dutch) Wine from Guelder and (Spanish wine) from Galicia, and [wine] made at Groine (Spain), / Wine from Guienne (France) and vernage (Italy), I say too, / There are no better, however far you travel*

GALAUNT Hof, hof, hof! A frysch new galaunt!   *lively*
       Ware of thryst; ley that adoune![1]
       What? Wene ye, syrrys, that I were a marchant   *Do you suppose; sirs*
       Because that I am new com to town?   *newly arrived in*
fol. 106r Wyth sum praty tasppysstere wold I fayne rownd![2]
496   I have a shert of reynnys wyth slevys peneawnt,[3]
       A lase of sylke for my lady constant.   *silken sash; faithful*
       A, how she is bewtefull and ressplendant!
       Whan I am from hyre presens, lord, how I syhe!   *away from her; sigh*
500   I wol awye sovereyns and soiettys I dysdeyne.[4]
       In wyntyr a stomachyr, in somyr non att al;   *[I wear] a waistcoat; summer*
       My dobelet and my hossys evyr together abyde.[5]
       I woll, or even, be shavyn for to seme yyng.   *before evening; look young*
       With here agen the her I love mych pleyyng —[6]
505   That makyt me ilegant and lusty in lykyng.   *elegant; amorous in my desires*
       Thus I lefe in this world; I do it for no pryde.   *live*

LUXURIA Lady, this man is for yow, as I se can,
       To sett yow in sporttys and talkyng this tyde.   *pleasures; at this time*

MARY MAUDLEYN Cal him in, tavernere, as ye my love will han,   *if; have*
510   And we shall make ful mery yf he wolle abyde.   *stay (remain)*

TAVERNERE How, how, my mastyre, Coryossyté!   *Curiosity (the gallant)*

CORYOSTÉ What is your wyll, syr? What wyl ye wyth me?

TAVERNERE Here ar jentyll women dysyore your presens to se,   *are; [who] desire*
       And for to drynk with yow this tyde.

CORYOSTÉ A, dere dewchesse, my daysyys iee!   *duchess; daisy*
516   Splendaunt of colour, most of femynyté!   *Bright; complexion*
       Your sofreyn colourrys, set wyth synseryté!   *sovereign disposition; sincerity*
fol. 106v Consedere my love into yower alye,[7]
       Or ellys I am smet wyth peynnes of perplexité.   *else; smitten (struck); pains*

MARY MAUDLEYN Why, syr, wene ye that I were a kelle?   *think; loose woman*

---

[1] *Beware of thirst; set down that [drink]*

[2] *With some pretty barmaid I would gladly speak privately*

[3] *I have a shirt of Rennes linen with wide, loose sleeves*

[4] *I will advise sovereigns and disdain subjects*

[5] *My doublet (jacket) and my hose always match perfectly*

[6] *With hair against hair I love to play very much*

[7] *Accept my love into your alliance (may I be among those closest to you)*

CORYOSTÉ Nay, prensses, parde, ye be my hertys hele.
522   So wold to God ye wold my love fele![1]

MARY MAUDLEYN What cause that ye love me so sodenly?   *Why do you; suddenly*

CORYOSTÉ O, nedys I must, myn own lady.   *necessarily*
525   Your person, itt is so womanly,
    I can nat refreyn me, swete lelly.   *restrain myself; lily*

MARY MAUDLEYN Syr, curtesy doth it yow lere.[2]

CORYOSTÉ Now, gracyus gost wythowtyn pere,   *spirit; peer*
    Mych nortur is that ye conne.[3]
530   But wol yow dawns, my own dere?   *dance*

MARY MAUDLEYN Syr, I asent in good manyr.
    Go ye before, I sue yow nere,   *I will follow close behind you*
    For a man at alle tymys beryt reverens.   *times possesses*

CORIOSTÉ Now, be my trowth, ye be with other ten.   *you are grieved by other things*
535   Felle a pese; tavernere, let us sen   *Fill a cup; let's see (we'll have)*
    Soppes in wynne. How, love ye?   *Sops*

MARY MAUDLEYN As ye don, so doth me.
    I am ryth glad that met be we;
    My love in yow gynnyt to close.   *begins*

CORYOSTÉ Now, derlyng dere, wol yow do be my rede?   *[fol. 107r]; counsel (advice)*
541   We have dronkyn and ete lytyl brede.
    Wyll we walk to another stede?   *place*

MARY MAUDLEYN Evyn at your wyl, my dere derlyng,   *Even*
    Thowe ye wyl go to the worldys eynd   *Though; end*
545   I wol nevyr from yow wynd,   *wend (go)*
    To dye for your sake.

    Here shal Mary and the galant avoyd, and the Bad Angyll goth to   *depart*
    the World, the Flych and the Dylfe, thus sayyng the Bad Angyl:

---

[1] *No, princess, by God, you are my heart's healer / I wish to God you would feel my love*

[2] *Courtesy teaches you [to restrain yourself]*

[3] *You know a lot about nurture (good breeding)*

[The Stage of the World]

[BAD ANGYL] A lorges, a lorges, lorddys alle at onys![1]	
Ye have a servant fayur and afyabylle,	*affable*
For she is fallyn in ower grogly gromys.	*grisly snares*
550 Ya, Pryde, callyd Coriosté, to hure is ful laudabyll,	*laudable*
And to hure he is most preysseabyll,	*worthy of praise*
For she hath graunttyd hym al hys bonys.	*boons (requests)*
She thynkyt hys person so amyabyll,	*thinks*
To here syte, he is semelyare than ony kyng in tronys.[2]	

DIABOLUS A, how I tremyl and trott for these tydyngys!	*tremble; news*
556 She is a soveryn servant that hath hure fet in synne.	*feet*
Go thow agayn and ewer be hur gyde.	*ever; guide*
The laudabyll lyfe of lecherry let hur nevyr lynne,	*cease*
559 For of hure al helle shall make rejoysseyng.	*Because of*

Her goth the Bad Angyl to Mari agayn.

REX DIABOLUS Farewell, farewell, ye to nobyl kyngys this tyde,	***King of Devils**; two*
For hom in hast I wol me dresse.	*home; go*

MUNDUS Farewell, Satan, prynsse of pryde!	***[fol. 107v]***

FLESCH Farewell, semlyest, alle sorowys to sesse.[3]	

Her shal Satan go hom to hys stage, and Mari shal entyr into
the place alone, save the Bad Angyl, and all the Seven Dedly Synnys
shal be conveyyed into the howse of Symont Leprous. They shal be
arayyd lyke seven dylf, thus kept closse. Mari shal be in an erbyr,   *garden (arbor)*
thus sayyng:

MARY MAUDLEYN A, God be wyth my valentynys,	
565 My byrd swetyng, my lovys so dere!	*lover dear*
For they be bote for a blossum of blysse,[4]	
Me mervellyt sore they be nat here!	*marvel greatly*
But I woll restyn in this erbyre,	
Amons thes bamys precyus of prysse,	*Among; balms of price*
570 Tyll som lover wol apere	*Until*
That me is wont to halse and kysse.	*accustomed to embrace*

---

[1] *A, largess, largess (the gift of Mary's fall) to all you lords at once*

[2] *To her sight he is more attractive than any enthroned king*

[3] *Farewell, [Satan, who is] best suited to bring all [our] sorrows to an end*

[4] *For they are beneficial to a blossom of [amorous] bliss (i.e. herself)*

Her shal Mary lye doun and slepe in the erbyre.

[House of Simon Leper]

SYMONT LEPRUS This day holly I pot in rememberowns		*completely I intend to keep*

	To solas my gestys to my power.[1]	
	I have ordeynnyd a dynere of substawns,	*prepared a sumptuous dinner*
575	My chyff freyndys therwyth to chyre.	*best friends; cheer*
	Into the seté I woll apere,	*city; appear (go)*
	For my gestys to make porvyawns,	*guests; preparations*
fol. 108r	For tyme drayt ny to go to dynyr,	*draws near*
	And my offycyrs be redy with this ordynowns.[2]	
580	So wold to God I myte have aqueyntowns	*make the acquaintance*
	Of the profyth of trew perfytnesse,	*prophet (Christ); perfection*
	To com to my place and porvyowns.	*purveyance (the dinner)*
	It wold rejoyse my hert in gret gladnesse,	
	For the report of hys hye nobyllnesse	*high*
585	Rennyt in contreys fer and nere.	*Runs (circulates)*
	Hys precheyng is of gret perfythnes,	
	Of rythwysnesse, and mercy cleyre.	*righteousness; pure*

*Her entyr Symont into the place, the Good Angyll thus
seyyng to Mary:*

	[GOOD ANGYL] Woman, woman, why art thou so onstabyll?	
	Ful byttyrly thys blysse it wol be bowth.	*bitterly; bought*
590	Why are thou agens God so veryabyll?	*inconstant (variable)*
	Wy thynkys thou nat God made thee of nowth?[3]	
	In syn and sorow thou art browth,	*brought*
	Fleschly lust is to thee full delectabyll,	*very pleasurable*
	Salve for thi sowle must be sowth,	*Salve (salvation); sought*
595	And leve thi werkys vayn and veryabyll.	*abandon; actions*
	Remembyr, woman, for thi pore pryde,	*because of*
	How thi sowle shal lyyn in helle fyre.	*lie; fire*
	A, remembyr how sorowful itt is to abyde	
	Wythowtyn eynd in angure and ir!	*end in anger and ire*
600	Remembyr thee on mercy, make thi sowle clyre.	*pure*
	I am the gost of goodnesse that so wold thee gydde.	*spirit; guide*

---

[1] *To entertain my guests to the best of my ability*

[2] *And my household servants are ready with the arrangements*

[3] *Why do you not consider that God created you from nothing*

MARY MAUDLEYN   A, how the speryt of goodnesse hat promtyt me this tyde.   *[fol. 108v]*
      And temtyd me wyth tytyll of trew perfythnesse!¹
      Alas, how bettyrnesse in my hert doth abyde!   *bitterness*
605   I am wonddyd with werkys of gret dystresse.   *grieved by works*
      A, how pynsynesse potyt me to oppresse,
      That I have synnyd on every syde!²
      O, Lord, wo shall put me from this peynfulnesse?   *who; remove*
      A, woo shal to mercy be my gostly gyde?   *who; spiritual guide*
610   I shal porsue the prophett, wherso he be,   *pursue; wherever*
      For he is the well of perfyth charyté.   *perfect*
      Be the oyle of mercy he shal me relyss.   *By; oil; relieve*
      With swete bawmys, I wyl sekyn hym this syth,   *seek; time*
      And sadly folow hys lordshep in eche degré.   *earnestly*

        Here shal entyr the prophet with hys desyplys, thus seyyng   *disciples*
        Symont Leprus:

SYMOND LEPRUS   Now ye be welcom, mastyr most of magnyfycens.
616   I beseche yow benyngly ye wol be so gracyows,   *kindly; gracious*
      If that it be lekyng onto yower hye presens   *If it be to your high presence's liking*
      Thys daye to com dyne at my hows.

JHESUS   Godamercy, Symont, that thou wylt me knowe,³
620   I woll entyr thi hows with pes and unyté.   *peace; unity*
      I am glad for to rest ther grace gynnyt grow,   *where; begins to grow*
      For wythinne thi hows shal rest charyté,   *charity shall remain*
      And the bemys of grace shal byn illumynows.   *beams; enlightening*
fol. 109r But syth thou wytystsaff a dynere on me,⁴
625   With pes and grace I entry thi hows.

SYMOND   I thank yow, mastyr most benyng and gracyus,   *kind*
      That yow wol, of your hye soverenté.
      To me itt ys a joye most speceows,   *most pleasing*
      Wythinne my hows that I may yow se.
630   Now syt to the bord, mastyrs alle!   *come to the table*

        Her shal Mary folow alonge wyth this lamentacyon:

---

¹ Lines 602–03: *Ah, how the spirit of goodness (good spirit) has prompted me this time / And tempted me with the title (name) of true perfection*

² Lines 606–07: *Ah, how pensiveness (anxiety) overwhelms me / Because I have sinned everywhere*

³ *God reward you, Simon, that you wish to know me*

⁴ *But since you graciously offer (vouchsafe) me a dinner*

MARY MAUDLEYN   O I, cursyd cayftyff that myche wo hath wrowth

   Agens my makar, of mytys most![1]

   I have offendyd hym with dede and thowth,   *thought*

   But in hys grace is all my trost,   *trust*

635 Or ellys I know well I am but lost,   *else*

   Body and sowle damdpnyd perpetuall!   *eternally damned*

   Yet, good Lord of Lorddys, my hope is perhenuall

   Wyth thee to stand in grace and favour to se.[2]

   Thow knowyst my hart and thowt in especyal;   *especially*

640 Therfor, good Lord, aftyr my hart reward me. *according to the wishes of*

    Her shal Mary wasche the fett of the prophet wyth the terrys
    of hur yys, whypyng hem wyth hur herre, and than anoynt hym
    wyth a precyus noyttment. Jhesus dicit:[3]

[JHESUS]   Symond, I thank thee speceally   *especially*

   For this grett repast that here hath be.   *repast (meal)*

fol. 109v But, Symond, I tell thee fectually,   *earnestly*

   I have thyngys to seyn to thee.   *say*

SYMOND LEPRUS   Mastyr, what your wyll be,   *whatever*

646 And it plese yow, I well yow here;   *If; will hear you*

   Seyth your lykyng onto me,   *Speak what you like*

   And al the plesawnt of your mynd and desyyr.   *pleasure*

JHESUS   Symond, ther was a man in this present lyf,

650 The wyche had to dectours well suere,   *Who; two debtors; surely*

   The whych wher pore and myth make no restoratyf.[4]

   But stylle in ther dett ded induour.   *ever; debt; endure*

   The on owt hym an hondyrd pense ful suere,[5]

   And the other fefty, so befell the chanse; *fifty; as it happened*

655 And becawse he cowd nat hys mony recure, *could not; recover*

   They askyd hym for foryevnesse, and he foryaf in substans.[6]

   But, Symont, I pray thee, answer me to this sentens: *address this problem*

   Whych of thes to personnys was most beholddyn to that man? *two; indebted*

---

[1] Lines 631–32: *Oh I, cursed wretch who has wrought great sorrow / Against my creator, greatest in might*

[2] Lines 637–38: *Yet good Lord of Lords, my enduring (perennial) hope [is] / To stand with you in grace and see [your] favor*

[3] *Here Mary shall wash the feet of the prophet (Jesus) with the tears of her eyes, wiping them with her hair, and then anoint them with a precious ointment. Jesus says*

[4] *Who were poor and could make no restitution*

[5] *One owed him a hundred pence for sure*

[6] *They asked him for forgiveness, and he essentially forgave them*

SYMOND LEPRUS   Mastyr, and it plese your hey presens,   *may it please*
660   He that most owt hym, as my reson yef can.[1]

JHESUS   *Recte judicasti.* Thou art a wyse man,   *You have judged rightly*
            And this quesson hast dempte trewly.   *question; have judged (deemed)*
            Yff thou in thi concyens remembyr can,   *conscience*
            Ye to be the dectours that I of specefy.   *two; debtors of whom I speak*
fol. 110r But, Symond, behold this woman in al wyse,   *in every way*
666   How she wyth terys of hyr bettyr wepyng,   *tears; bitter*
            She wassheth my fete and dothe me servyse,   *serves me*
            And anoytyt hem wyth onymentys, lowly knelyng,   *them; ointments, humbly*
            And with hur her, fayur and brygth shynnyng,   *her hair; bright*
670   She wypeth hem agayn wyth good entent.
            But, Symont, syth that I entyrd thi hows,   *since; entered*
            To washe my fete thou dedyst nat aplye,   *did not offer*
            Nor to wype my fete thou were nat so favorus;   *obliging*
            Wherfor, in thi conscyens, thou owttyst nat to replye.   *ought not*
675   But, woman, I sey to the verely,   *truly*
            I forgeyffe thee thi wrecchednesse,   *forgive*
            And hol in sowle be thou made therby![2]

MARY MAUDLEYN   O, blessyd be thou, lord of evyrlastyng lyfe,
            And blyssyd be thi berth of that puer vergynne!   *birth; pure virgin*
680   Blyssyd be thou, repast contemplatyf,
            Agens my seknes, helth and medsyn.[3]
            And for that I have synnyd in the synne of pryde,   *because*
            I wol enabyte me wyth humelyté.   *clothe myself; humility*
            Agens wrath and envy, I wyl devyde   *oppose*
685   Thes fayur vertuys, pacyens and charyté.   *patience*

JHESUS   Woman, in contrysson thou art expert,   *[fol. 110v]; contrition*
            And in thi sowle hast inward mythe,   *strength (might)*
            That sumtyme were in desert,
            And from therknesse hast porchasyd lyth.[4]
690   Thy feyth hath savyt thee and made thee bryth.   *faith; saved; bright*
            Wherfor I say to thee, "*Vade in pace.*"   *Go in peace*

            Wyth this word sevyn dyllys shall devoyde from the woman,   *depart*
            and the Bad Angyll entyr into hell with thondyr.

---

[1] *He who owed him the most, by my reasoning*

[2] *And may you thereby be made whole (healthy) in your soul*

[3] Lines 680–81: *Blessed are you, contemplative repast (spiritual nourishment) / [May you be my] health and physician for my sickness*

[4] Lines 688–89: *[You] who once were in the desert (spiritual wasteland), / And from the darkness have purchased (gained) the light*

[MARY MAUDLEYN]	O thou, gloryus Lord, this rehersyd for my sped,	
	Sowle helth attys tyme for to recure.[1]	
	Lord, for that I was in whanhope, now stond I in dred,	*because; despair*
695	But that thi gret mercy wyth me may endure.	*Unless*
	My thowth thou knewyst wythowtyn ony dowth.	*thoughts; doubt*
	Now may I trost the techeyng of Isaye in scryptur,	*trust; Isaiah*
	Wos report of thi nobyllnesse rennyt fere abowt.	*Whose; circulates widely*
JHESUS	Blyssyd be they at alle tyme	*those who; times*
700	That sen me nat and have me in credens.	*see; on faith*
	With contrysson thou hast mad a recumpens,	*made recompense*
	Thi sowle to save from all dystresse.	
	Beware and kepe thee from alle neclygens,	*negligence*
	And aftyr thou shal be partenyr of my blysse.	*afterwards; partner*

fol. 111r   *Here devodyt Jhesus wyth hys desipyllys, the Good Angyll*
                 rejoysyng of Mawdleyn:

BONUS ANGELUS	Holy God, hyest of omnipotency,	***Good Angel***
706	The astat of good governons to thee I recummend,[2]	
	Humbylly besecheyng thyn inperall glorye	*imperial*
	In thi devyn vertu us to comprehend.	*divine; include*
	And, delectabyll Jhesu, soverreyn sapyens,	*sapience (wisdom)*
710	Ower feyth we recummend onto your pur peté,	*pure pity (mercy)*
	Most mekely prayyng to your holy aparens,	*spiritual manifestation*
	Illumyn ower ygnorans with your devynyté.	*ignorance; divinity*
	Ye be clepyd redempcyon, of sowlys defens,	
	Whyche shal ben obscuryd be thi blessyd mortalyté.[3]	
715	O *Lux Vera*, graunt us yower lucense,	*True Light; brilliance*
	That wyth the spryte of errour I nat seduet be.	*spirit; seduced (led astray)*
	And, *Sperytus Alme*, to yow most benyne,	*Bounteous Spirit; kind*
	Thre persons in trenyté and on God eterne,	*trinity; one; eternal*
	Most lowly ower feyth we consyngne,	
720	That we may com to your blysse gloryfyed from malyngne,	
	And wyth your gostely bred to fede us, we desyern.[4]	

---

[1] Lines 692–93: *Oh thou, glorious Lord, [who] related this for my advantage / To recover my soul's health at this time*

[2] *I entrust to you those in the state of good [self-]governance*

[3] Lines 713–14: *You are called redemption, the defender of souls / [The spiritual state of which] shall be obscured by your blessed mortality (your humanity)*

[4] Lines 719–21: *Most humbly we attest our faith, / That we, safe from evil, may come glorified to your bliss, / And we desire to be fed by your spiritual food*

[Hell]

REX DIABOLUS   A, owt, owt and harrow! I am hampord wyth hate!¹

      In hast wyl I set our jugment to se!   *haste*

fol. 111v Wyth thes betyll-browyd bycheys I am at debate.²

725   How, Belfagour and Belzabub, com up here to me!

        Here aperytt to dyvllys before the mastyr.   *appear two devils*

SECUNDUS DIABOLUS   Here, Lord, here! What wol ye?   ***Second Devil**; What do you want?*

TERCIUS DIABOLUS   The jugment of harlottys here to se,   ***Third Devil***

      Settyng in judycyal-lyke astate.   *As I sit in my judicial position*

      How, thow Bad Angyll! Apere before my grace.   *Appear*

SPIRITUS MALIGNI   As flat as fox, I falle before your face.   ***Evil Spirit***

PRIMUS DIABOLUS   Thow theffe! Wy hast thou don alle this trespas,   ***First Devil***

732   To lett yen woman thi bondys breke?   *allow that; bonds*

MALINUS SPIRITUS   The speryt of grace sore ded hyr smyth,   *struck her heavily*

      And temptyd so sore that ipocryte.   *greatly; hypocrite*

PRIMUS DIABOLUS   Ya, thys hard balys on thi bottokkys shall byte!³

736   In hast, on thee I wol be wreke.   *avenged*

      Cum up, ye horsons, and skore awey the yche,⁴

      And wyth thys panne, ye do hym pycche!   *pan; darken him with pitch*

      Cum off, ye harlottys, that yt wer don!   *were done*

        Here shall they serve all the sevyn as they do the frest.   *first*

PRIMUS DIABOLUS   Now have I a part of my desyere!   *desire*

741   Goo in to this howsse, ye lordeynnys here,

      And loke ye set yt on afeyere —   *on fire*

      And that shall hem awake!

fol. 112r   *Here shall the tother deyllys sett the howse on afyere*

        and make a sowth, and Mari shall go to Lazar and to Martha.⁵

---

¹ **King of Devils** *(Satan): Ah, out, out and harrow! I am made mad by hate*

² *With these beetle-browed (shaggy-browed) bitches (scoundrels), I am ready to contend*

³ *Ya, these hard scourges on your buttocks will bite*

⁴ *Come up [from hell], you bastards, and whip the itch away*

⁵ *Here shall the other devils set the house on fire and make soot (smoke), and Mary shall go to Lazarus and Martha*

PRIMUS DIABOLUS   So, now have we well afrayyd these felons fals!   *frightened*
745   They be blasyd, both body and hals!   *burned; neck*
         Now to hell lett us synkyn als   *also*
         To ower felaws blake!   *fellows (companions)*

[The Castle of Magdalene]

MARY MAUDLEYN   O brother, my hartys consolacyown!
         O blessyd in lyffe and solytary!
750   The blyssyd prophet, my confortacyown,[1]
         He hathe made me clene and delectary,   *pure; delectable*
         The wyche was to synne a subjectary.   *Who had been a slave to sin*
         Thys kyng, Cryste, consedyryd hys creacyown;   *considered (remembered)*
         I was drynchyn in synne deversarye,   *drowning in many sins*
755   Tyll that Lord relevyd me be hys domynacyon.   *relieved; power*
         Grace to me he wold nevyr denye,
         Thow I were nevyr so synful, he seyd, "*Revertere*."   *Though; extremely; "Turn back"*
         O, I, synful creature, to grace I woll aplye;   *dedicate myself*
         The oyle of mercy hath helyd myn infyrmyté.   *healed; infirmity (sickness)*

MARTHA   Now worchepyd be that hey name Jhesu,
761   The wyche in Latyn is callyd *Savyower*!   *Savior*
         Fulfyllyng that word evyn of dewe,   *just as deserved*
         To alle synfull and seke, he is sokour.   *sick; remedy*

LAZARUS   Systyr, ye be welcum onto yower towere.   *[fol. 112v]*
765   Glad in hart of yower obessyawnse,   *[I am] glad; for; respect*
         Wheyl that I leffe, I wyl serve hym wyth honour,   *While; live*
         That ye have forsakyn synne and varyawns.   *For (Because); instability*

MARY MAUDLEYN   Cryst, that is the lyth and the cler daye,   *light; clear*
         He hath oncuryd the therknesse of the clowdy nyth,   *uncovered; darkness*
770   Of lyth the lucens and lyth veray,[2]
         Wos prechyng to us is a gracyows lyth,   *Whose*
         Lord, we beseche thee as thou art most of myth,   *because*
         Owt of the ded slep of therknesse defend us aye.   *darkness protect us always*
         Gyff us grace evyr to rest in lyth,   *Give*
775   In quyet and in pes to serve thee nyth and day.   *quiet*

          Her shall Lazar take hys deth, thus seyyng:

---

[1] Lines 748–50: *Oh brother (Lazarus), my heart's consolation / The blessed prophet [Jesus who is] singular in his blessedness / And brings me comfort*

[2] *[He is] the brilliance of light and the true light*

[LAZARUS]   A, help, help, systyrs, for charyté!

Alas, deth is sett at my hart!

A, ley on handys! Wher are ye?   *lay your hands on me*

A, I faltyr and falle! I wax alle onquarte.   *become totally uneasy*

780   A, I bome above! I wax alle swertt.[1]

A, good Jhesu, thow be my gyde.

A, no lengar now I reverte!   *I can no more revive myself*

I yeld up the gost. I may natt abyde.   *give up; spirit*

MARY MAUDLEYN   O good brother, take coumforth and myth,   *[fol. 113r]; be strong*

785   And lett non hevynes in yower hart abyde.   *allow*

Lett away alle this feyntnesse and fretth,   *Let pass; fretting*

And we shal gete yow leches yower peynys to devyde.   *doctors; destroy*

MARTHA   A, I syth and sorow and sey, "Alas!"   *sigh*

Thys sorow is apoynt to be my confusyon.   *appointed; ruin*

790   Jentyl systyr, hye we from this place,   *let us go quickly*

For the prophet to hym hatt grett delectacyon.   *takes great pleasure in him*

Good brothere, take somme confortacyon,   *consolation*

For we woll go to seke yower cure.

Here goth Mary and Martha, and mett with Jhesus, thus seyyng: *meet*

[MARY MAUDLEYN AND MARTHA]   O, Lord Jhesu, ower melleflueus swettness,[2]

795   Thowe art grettest lord in glorie!

Lover to thee, Lord, in all lowlynesse,

Comfort thi creatur that to thee crye![3]

Behold yower lover, good Lord, specyally,

How Lazare lyth seke in grett dystresse.   *lies*

800   He is thi lover, Lord, suerly.   *surely*

Onbynd hym, good Lord, of hys hevynesse!   *Release him; from*

JHESUS   Of all infyrmyté, ther is non to deth.

For of all peynnys that is impossyble

To undyrestond be reson; to know the werke,[4]

805   The joye that is in Jherusallem hevenly,

fol. 113v   Can nevyr be compylyd be counnyng of clerke:

To se the joyys of the Fathyr in glory,

The joyys of the Sonne whych owth to be magnyfyed,   *ought*

---

[1] *My head is buzzing! Everything is becoming dark for me*

[2] *Oh, Lord Jesus, Our soothing sweetness*

[3] Lines 796–97: *Lord, [may you] comfort your humble lover (Lazarus), / Your creature who cries out to you*

[4] Lines 802–06: *Of all infirmities, there is none to compare with death; / For of all afflictions, it is impossible / To understand rationally. To comprehend God's creative work / [and] The joy in [his] heavenly Jerusalem / Can never be brought together [and articulated] by clerical knowledge* (John 11:4)

	And of the therd person the Holy Gost truly,	*third*
810	And alle three but on in heven gloryfyed!	*one*
	Now, women that arn in my presens here,	*who are*
	Of my wordys take avysement.	*heed*
	Go hom agen to yower brothyr Lazere —	
	My grace to hym shall be sent.	

MARY MAUDLEYN   O, thow gloryus Lord here present,

816	We yeld to thee salutacyon!	*give; greetings*
	In ower weyys we be expedyent.	*In our woes we have great need*
	Now, Lord, us defend from trybulacyon.	*protect; tribulation*

Here goth Mary and Martha homward, and Jhesus devodyt.   *exits*

[Castle of Magdalene]

LAZARUS   A, in woo I waltyr as wavys in the wynd!   *am tossed like waves*

820	Awey is went all my sokour.	*Gone; help*
	A, deth, deth, thou art onkynd!	
	A, A, now brystyt myn hartt! This is a sharp showyr!	*breaks; pain*
	Farewell, my systyrs, my bodely helth.	*[and] my bodily*

Mortuus est.   *He dies*

MARY MAUDLEYN   Jhesu, my Lord, be yower sokowre,

| 825 | And he mott be yower gostys welth.[1] | |

PRIMUS MILES   Goddys grace mott be hys governour.   *may*

In joy evyrlastyng fore to be.

SECUNDUS MILES   Amonge alle good sowlys, send hym favour,   *[fol. 114r]*

As thi powere ys most of dygnyté.[2]

MARTHA   Now, syn the chans is fallyn soo,   *because; circumstance has thus fallen*

831	That deth hath drewyn hym don this day,	*drawn him down*
	We must nedys ower devyrs doo:	*do our duty*
	To the erth to bryng hym wythowt delay.	*him (his body)*

MARY MAUDLEYN   As the use is now, and hath byn aye,   *custom; always*

835	Wyth wepars to the erth yow hym bryng.	*weepers (mourners)*
	Alle this must be donne as I you saye,	*as I tell you*
	Clad in blake, wythowtyn lesyng.	*black; truly*

---

[1] Lines 824–25: *May Jesus, my Lord, be your help / And may he be your spirit's well-being*

[2] *Since your (God's) power is most honorable*

[Grave of Lazarus]

PRIMUS MILES Gracyows ladyys of gret honour,
    This pepull is com here in yower syth,   *sight*
840 Wepyng and weylyng with gret dolour,   *wailing; sadness*
    Because of my lordys dethe.

    Here the on knyght make redy the ston, and
    other bryng in the wepars, arayyd in blak.[1]

PRIMUS MILES Now, good fryndys that here be,   *friends*
    Take up thys body wyth good wyll,
    And ley it in hys sepoltur, semely to se.   *sepulchre; reverently*
845 Good Lord, hym save from alle manyr ille! *every kind of harm*

    Lay him in. Here al the pepyll resort to the castell, *return*
    thus seyyng Jhesus:

[JHESUS] Tyme is comyn of very cognysson.[2]
    My dyssyplys, goth wyth me   *go*
    For to fulfyll possybyll peticion.[3]
    Go we together into Jude.   *Judea*
fol. 114v There Lazar, my frynd, is he.
851 Gow we together as chyldyurn of lyth,   *children; light*
    And from grevos slepe, sawen heym wyll we.   *save*

DISSIPULUS Lord, it plese yower myty volunté, *Disciple; [if] it please; powerful intent*
    Thow he slepe, he may be savyd be skyll.[4]

JHESUS That is trew, and be possybilyté;   *it is possible*
856 Therfor of my deth shew yow I wyll.
    My fathyr, of nemyows charyté,   *boundless*
    Sent me, hys son, to make redemcyon,
    Wyche was conseyvyd be puer verginyté, *Who; conceived; by pure*
860 And so in my mother had cler incarnacyon.[5]
    And therfore must I suffyre grevos passyon   *pain*
    Ondyre Pounse Pylat, wyth grett perplexité, *Under Pontius Pilate; distress*
    Betyn, bobbyd, skoernyd, crownnyd with thorne — *mocked; scorned*
    Alle this shall be the soferens of my deité. *suffering; divinity*

---

[1] *Here the one knight makes the [grave]stone ready, and another brings in the weepers, arrayed in black*

[2] *The time of true knowledge (recognition) has come*

[3] *To fulfill a petition that is within my power [to grant]*

[4] *If he [only] sleeps, he may be saved by [your] knowledge*

[5] *And so in my mother I was incarnated in purity*

865   I, therfor, hastely folow me now,
        For Lazar is ded, verely to preve;
        Wherfor I am joyfull, I sey onto yow,
        That I knowlege yow therwyth, that ye may it beleve.[1]

                Here shal Jhesus com with hys dissipulys, and on Jew tellyt Martha: *one*

[JEW]   A, Martha, Martha, be full of gladnesse!
870   For the prophett ys comyng, I sey trewly,
        With hys dyssypyllys in grett lowlynesse.   *humility*
fol. 115r He shall yow comfortt wyth hys mercy.

                Here Martha shall ronne agen Jhesus, thus seyyng: *run toward*

[MARTHA]   A, Lord, me, sympyl creatur, nat denye,   *do not deny me*
        Thow I be wrappyd in wrecchydnesse.   *Although*
875   Lord, and thou haddyst byn here, verely,   *if you had been*
        My brother had natt a byn ded, I know well thysse.   *this*

                Jhesus dicit   *Jesus says*

[JHESUS]   Martha, docctor, onto thee I sey,   *daughter*
        Thy brother shall reyse agayn.   *rise*

MARTHA   Yee, Lord, at the last day,
880   That I beleve ful pleyn.   *I clearly believe that*

JHESUS   I am the resurreccyon of lyfe, that evyr shall reynne,   *reign*
        And whoso belevyt verely in me   *whoever believes*
        Shall have lyfe evyrlastyng, the soth to seyn.
        Martha, belevyst thow this?

MARTHA   Ye, forsoth, the Prynsse of blysch!   *bliss*
886   I beleve in Cryst, the son of sapyens,   *sapience (wisdom)*
        Whyche wythowt eynd ryngne shall he,   *Who shall reign without end*
        To redemyn us freell from ower iniquité.   *frail ones; our*

                Here Mary shall falle to Jhesus, thus seyyng Mary: *before*

MARY MAUDLEYN   O, thou rythewys regent, reynyng in equité,[2]   ***[fol. 115v]***
890   Thou gracyows Lord, thou swete Jhesus!

---

[1] Lines 865–68: *Therefore, quickly follow me now, / To demonstrate truly that Lazarus is dead; / Wherefore I am joyful, I tell you, / That I may acquaint you [with this circumstance], so that you may believe it*

[2] *O, you righteous regent, reigning in justice*

And thou haddyst byn here, my brothyr alyfe had be.   *If; would be alive*
Good Lord, myn hertt doth this dyscus.   *ponder*

JHESUS   Wher have ye put hym? Sey me thys.

MARY MAUDLEYN   In hys monument, Lord, is he.

JHESUS   To that place ye me wys.   *direct me*
896   Thatt grave I desyre to se.
    Take off the ston of this monument.   *from*
    The agrement of grace here shewyn I wyll.   *covenant; will I show*

MARTHA   A, Lord, yower preseptt fulfyllyd shall be.   *your order*
900   Thys ston I remeve wyth glad chyr.   *remove*
    Gracyows Lord, I aske thee mercy.
    Thy wyll mott be fullfyllyd here!   *May thy will*

Here shall Martha put off the grave ston.

JHESUS   Now, Father, I beseche thyn hey paternyté,   *your high*
    That my prayour be resowndable to thi Fathyrod in glory,   *may resound; Fatherhood*
905   To opyn theyn erys to thi Son in humanyté,   *your ears*
    Nat only for me, but for thi pepyll verely,
    That they may beleve and betake to thi mercy.   *commend themselves*
    Fathyr, fore them I make supplycacyon.
909   Gracyows Father, graunt me my bone!   *boon (request)*
fol. 116r Lazer, Lazer! Com hethyr to me!   *hither*

Here shall Lazar aryse, trossyd wyth towellys, in a shete.[1]

LAZARUS   A, my makar, my savyowr, blyssyd mott thu be!   *may you be*
    Here men may know thi werkys of wondyre.   *wondrous works*
    Lord, nothyng is onpossybyll to thee.   *impossible*
    For my body and my sowle was departyd asondyr.   *separated*
915   I shuld a rottytt, as doth the tondyre,
    Fleysch from the bonys a-consumyd away.
    Now is aloft that late was ondyr![2]
    The goodnesse of God hath don for me here,   *enacted this*
    For he is bote of all balys to onbynd,   *remedy; suffering*
920   That blyssyd Lord that here ded apere.   *did appear*

---

[1] *Here shall Lazarus arise, bound with linen clothes [and covered], in a sheet*

[2] Lines 915–17: *I should have rotted, like the tinder (i.e. wood) / Flesh [should have been] eaten away from the bones. / Now is above ground that which (Lazarus's body) lately was under [it]*

> *Here all the pepull and the Jewys, Mari, and Martha, wyth*
> *on voys sey thes wordys: "We beleve in you, Savyowr, Jhesus,*   *one*
> *Jhesus, Jhesus!"*

[JHESUS] Of yower good hertys I have advertacyounys,   *evidence*
    Wherethorow in sowle, holl made ye be.[1]
    Betwyx yow and me be nevyr varyacyounys,   *Between; divergence*
    Wherfor I sey, "*Vade in pace.*"   *Go in peace*

> *Here devoydyt Jhesus wyth hys desypyllys. Mary and Martha*
> *and Lazare gon hom to the castell, and here begynnyt*
> *[Rex Marcylle] hys bost:*

[Marseilles]

[REX MARCYLLE] Avantt! Avant thee, onworthy wrecchesse![2]   *[fol. 116v]; **King of Marseilles***
926   Why lowtt ye nat low to my lawdabyll presens,   *bow; praiseworthy*
    Ye brawlyng breellys and blabyr-lyppyd bycchys,   *rascals; thick-lipped scoundrels*
    Obedyenly to obbey me wythowt offense?   *[Thus] obediently*
    I am a sofereyn semely that ye se butt seyld,   *seldom see*
930   Non swyche ondyr sonne, the sothe for to say!   *sun*
    Whanne I fare fresly and fers to the feld,[3]
    My fomen fle for fer of my fray!   *foes; fear; attack*
    Even as an enperower I am onored ay,   *ever honored*
    Wanne baner gyn to blasse and bemmys gyn to blow.
935   Hed am I heyest of all hethennesse holld![4]
    Both kynggys and cayserys I woll they shall me know,   *emperors*
    Or ellys they bey the bargayn that evyr they were so bold!   *pay the price*
    I am Kyng of Marcylle, talys to be told,
    Thus I wold it were knowyn ferre and nere.
940   Ho sey contraly, I cast heym in carys cold,   *Whoever speaks contrarily*
    And he shall bey the bargayn wondyr dere!   *extremely*
    I have a favorows fode and fresse as the fakown,[5]
    She is full fayur in hyr femynyté.
    Whan I loke on this lady, I am losty as the lyon.   *look upon; lusty*
945   In my syth   *sight [she is]*
    Of delycyté most delycyows,   *delight; delightful*
    Of felachyp most felecyows,   *companionship; happy*

---

[1] *Because of which you are made whole (healthy) in your souls*

[2] *Go away, go away, you unworthy wretches*

[3] *When I go eagerly and fiercely to the field [of battle]*

[4] Lines 934–35: *When banners begin to wave and trumpets begin to blow / I am considered the head, the highest among all heathens*

[5] *I have a pleasing young woman who is fresh as the falcon*

Of alle fodys most favarows —   *young ladies; pleasing*
O, my blysse, in beuteus bryght!   *beauteous brightness*

REGINA   O of condycyons and most onorabyll,[1]   ***[fol. 117r]; Queen***
951   Lowly I thank yow for this recummendacyon —   *Humbly*
      The bounteest and the boldest ondyr baner bryth,   *most bountiful*
      No creatur so coroscant to my consolacyon.[2]
      Whan the regent be resydent, itt is my refeccyon.   *refreshment (nourishment)*
955   Yower dilectabyll dedys devydytt me from dyversyté.
      In my person I privyde to put me from polucyon,[3]
      To be plesant to yower person, itt is my prosperyté.

REX   Now, godamercy, berel brytest of bewté!   ***King**; thank you; beryl brightest*
      Godamercy, ruby, rody as the rose.   *ruddy*
960   Ye be so plesaunt to my pay, ye put me from peyn.   *to my liking; keep me*
      Now, comly knygthys, loke that ye forth dresse   *see to it; arrange*
      Both spycys and wyn here in hast!   *spices*

          Here shall the knygtys gete spycys and wynne, and here
          shall entyr a dylle in orebyll aray, thus seyyng: *devil horribly attired*

[Hell]

[DYLLE]   Owt, owt, harrow! I may crye and yelle,   ***Devil***
      For lost is all ower labor, wherfor I sey alas!
965   For of all holddys that evyr hort, non so as hell![4]
      Owur barrys of iron ar all to-brost, stronge gatys of brasse!   *bars; broken up*
      The Kyng of Joy entyryd in therat, as bryth as fyrys blase!
      For fray of hys ferfull banere, ower felashep fled asondyr.
      Whan he towcheyd it wyth hys toukkyng, they brast as ony glase,
970   And rofe asondyr, as it byn wyth thondore![5]
fol. 117v   Now ar we thrall that frest wher fre,   *slaves; once were free*
      Be the passon of hys manhede.   *Because of; human nature*
      On a crosce on hye hangyd was he,
      Whyche hath dystroyd ower labor and alle ower dede.   *destroyed; deeds*
975   He hath lytynnyd lymbo and to paradyse yede!   *lightened; is gone to*
      That wondyrfull worke werkytt us wrake: *does us harm*

---

[1] *Most to be honored for your conditions (circumstances)*

[2] *No person gleams as you do, to my comfort and well-being*

[3] *Lines 955–56: Your admirable deeds separate (protect) me from adversity / I am careful to keep my person from impurity*

[4] *For of all prisons that were ever harmful, none [is as harmful] as hell*

[5] *Lines 967–70: The King of Joy entered therein, as bright as a blazing fire! / Because of the terror of his frightening banner, our fellowship fled in every direction. / When he touched it [the gates] with his touch, they broke like glass, / And split asunder, as if [his touch] had been thunder*

	Adam and Abram and alle hyre kynred,	*Abraham; their kindred*
	Owt of ower preson to joy were they take!	*prison*
	All this hath byn wrowth syn Freyday at none.	*done; noon*
980	Brostyn don ower gatys that hangyd were full hye!	*Broken*
	Now is he resyn. Hys resurreccyon is don,	*risen*
	And is procedyd into Galelye.	*He is gone*
	Wyth many a temptacyon we tochyd hym to atrey,	*tried to test him*
	To know whether he was god ore non.	*or not*
985	Yet, for all ower besynes, bleryd is ower eye,	*busyness (labor); bleared*
	For wyth hys wyld werke he hath wonne hem everychon![1]	
	Now, for the tyme to come,	*in times to come*
	Ther shall non falle to ower chanse	*to our fortunes*
	But at hys deleverans.	*Except by his (Christ's) judgment*
990	And weyyd be rythfull balans,	
	And yowyn be rythfull domme.[2]	
	I telle yow alle, *in fine*, to helle wyll I gonne!	*in conclusion*

| fol. 118r | *Here shall entyr the thre Mariis, arayyd as chast women, wyth sygnis of the passon pryntyd upon ther brest, thus seyyng Mawdlyn:*[3] | |

[Place of the Crucifixion]

[MARY MAUDLEYN]	Alas, alas, for that ryall bem!	*beam (cross)*
	A, this percytt my hartt worst of all!	*pierces*
995	For here he turnyd agen to the woman of Jerusalem,	
	And for wherynesse lett the crosse falle.	*because of weariness*

MARY JACOBE	Thys sorow is beytterare than ony galle,	*more bitter*
	For here the Jewys spornyd hym to make hym goo,	*kicked*
	And they dysspyttyd ther kyng ryall,	*scorned; royal*
1000	That clyvytt myn hart and makett me woo.	*rends; sorrowful*

MARY SALOME	Yt ys intollerabyll to se or to tell,	
	For ony creature that stronkg tormentry.	*forceful torment*
	O Lord, thou haddyst a mervelows mell!	*horrible struggle*
	Yt is to hedyows to dyscry.	*too hideous to tell*

| | *Al the Maryys with on voyce sey this folowyng:* | *one* |

---

[1] *For with his (Christ's) wild work (his death, harrowing of hell, and resurrection), he has redeemed all of them*

[2] Lines 990–91: *And [it (Christ's judgment) shall be] weighed by judicious balance / And [shall be] given by lawful judgment*

[3] *Here shall enter the three Marys, dressed as chaste women, with signs of the Passion printed (represented) on their breasts, thus saying Magdalene*

[THREE MARYS] Heylle, gloryows crosse! Thou baryst that Lord on hye,   *bore (carried)*
1006   Whych be thi myght deddyst lowly bowe doun,[1]
    Mannys sowle to bye from all thraldam,   *redeem; slavery*
    That evyrmore in peyne shold a-be,[2]
    Be record of Davyt wyth myld stevyn: *David; voice*
1010   "*Domine, inclina celos tuos et dessende!*"[3]

MARY MAUDLEYN   Now to the monument lett us gon,   *[fol. 118v]*
    Wheras ower Lord and savyower layd was,   *Where*
    To anoynt hym body and bone,
    To make amendys for ower trespas.

[The Sepulchre]

[MARY JACOBE]   Ho shall putt doun the led of the monument,   *Who; remove; lid*
1016   Thatt we may anoytt hys gracyus woundys,   *anoint*
    Wyth hartt and mynd to do ower intentt
    With precyus bamys, this same stounddys?   *at this time*

MARY SALOME   Thatt blyssyd body wythin this boundys,   *space*
1020   Here was layd wyth rufull monys.   *rueful moans*
    Nevyr creature was borne upon gronddys   *earth*
    That myght sofere so hediows a peyne at onys.[4]

    Here shall apere to angelys in whyte at the grave: *appear two*

ANGELUS   Ye women presentt, dredytt yow ryth nowth!   **Angel**; *fear*
    Jhesus is resun and is natt here.   *risen*
1025   Loo, here is the place that he was in browth.   *into which he was brought*
    Go, sey to hys dysypyllys and to Petur he shall apere.

SECUNDUS ANGELUS   In Galelye, wythowtyn ony wyre,   *doubt*
    Ther shall ye se hym lyke as he sayd.   *just as*
    Goo yower way, and take comfortt and chyr,   *cheer*
1030   For that he sayd shall natt be delayyd.   *what*

    Here shall the Maryys mete with Petyr and Jhon.   *meet*

MARY MAUDLEYN   O, Petyr and John, we be begylyd!   *[fol. 119r]; are beguiled (deceived)*
    Ower Lordys body is borne away!

---

[1] *Who (Christ) through your power humbly bowed down*

[2] *That (man's soul) otherwise had been forever in pain*

[3] *Lord, incline (bow down) your heavens and descend (Psalms 143:5)*

[4] *Who could suffer such altogether hideous pains*

I am aferd itt is dyffylyd.   *afraid; defiled*
I am so carefull, I wott natt whatt to saye.   *full of care*

PETYR Of thes tydynggys gretly I dysmay!
1036   I woll me thethere hye wyth all my myth.   *will hurry there*
Now, Lord defend us as he best may.   *protect us as only he can*
Of the sepulture we woll have a syth.   *sepulcher; sight*

JHON A, myn inward sowle stondyng in dystresse —
1040   The weche of my body shuld have a gyde —
For my lord stondyng in hevynesse,[1]
Whan I remembyr hys woundys wyde.

PETYR The sorow and peyne that he ded drye   *endure*
For ower offens and abomynacyon!   *offences*
1045   And also I forsoke hym in hys turmentry;   *torment*
I toke no hede to hys techeyng and exortacyon.   *paid no attention*

     Here Petyr and Jhon go to the sepulcur and the Maryys folowyng.

[PETYR] A, now I se and know the sothe!   *truth*
But, gracyus Lord, be ower protexcyon!
Here is nothyng left butt a sudare cloth,   *winding sheet*
1050   That of thi beryyng shuld make mencyon.   *burying gives evidence*

JHON I am aferd of wykkytt opressyon.   *wicked (evil)*
Where he is becum, it can natt be devysyd.[2]
Butt he seyd aftyr the third day he shuld have resurrexon.
fol. 119v Long beforn, thys was promysyd.   *ago*

MARY MAUDLEYN Alas, I may no lengar abyde,   *longer endure*
1056   For dolour and dyssese that in my hartt doth dwell.   *distress*

PRIMUS ANGELUS Woman, woman, wy wepest thou?   *why do you weep*
Wom sekest thou with dolare thus?   *Whom; dolor (grief)*

MARY MAUDLEYN A, fayn wold I wete, and I wyst how,[3]
1060   Wo hath born away my Lord Jhesus.   *Who; carried*

     Hic aparuit Jhesus.   *Here Jesus appears*

---

[1] Lines 1039–41: *Ah, distressed is my inward soul, / Which should guide my body, / Because of my Lord's heaviness (suffering)*

[2] *Whatever has become of him (where he has gone) cannot be explained*

[3] *Gladly would I learn, if I knew how*

[JHESUS] Woman, woman, wy syest thow? *why do you sigh*
Wom sekest thou? Tell me this.

MARY MAUDLEYN A, good syr, tell me now,
Yf thou have born awey my Lord Jhesus.
1065 For I have porposyd in eche degré, *resolved in every way*
To have hym wyth me verely, *truly*
The wyche my specyall Lord hath be, *Who; has been*
And I hys lover and cause wyll phy. *I [am]; trust*

JHESUS O, O, Mari!

MARY MAUDLEYN A, gracyus Mastyr and Lord, yow it is that I seke!
1071 Lett me anoynt yow wyth this bamys sote. *sweet*
Lord, long hast thou hyd thee from my spece, *hidden; speech*
Butt now wyll I kesse thou for my hartys bote! *kiss; remedy*

JHESUS Towche me natt, Mary! I ded natt asend *have not ascended*
1075 To my Father in deyyté and onto yowers. *deity*
fol. 120r Butt go sey to my brotheryn I wyll pretende *intend*
To stey to my Father in hevnly towyrs. *ascend*

MARY MAUDLEYN Whan I sye yow fyrst, Lord, verely, *saw*
I wentt ye had byn Symoud the gardenyr. *thought; gardener*

JHESUS So I am for sothe, Mary.
1081 Mannys hartt is my gardyn here.
Therin I sow sedys of vertu all the yere. *seeds*
The fowle wedys and vycys I reynd up be the rote. *weeds; tear; root*
Whan that gardyn is watteryd wyth terys clere,
1085 Than spryng vertuus and smelle full sote. *very sweet smells*

MARY MAUDLEYN O thou dereworthy Emperowere, thou hye devyne![1]
To me this is a joyfull tydyng,
And onto all pepull that aftyr us shall reyngne, *rule*
Thys knowlege of thi deyyté,
1090 To all pepull that shall obteyne,
And know this be posybylyté.[2]

JHESUS I wol show to synnars as I do to thee *sinners*
Yf they woll wyth vervens of love me seke. *fervor*

---

[1] *Oh, thou precious Emperor, thou high divine [one]*

[2] Lines 1089–91: *This knowledge of your deity (divinity) [is a joyful tiding] / To all people who shall possess [it] / And know it to be possible*

Be stedfast, and I shall evyr wyth thee be,

1095   And wyth all tho that to me byn meke.   *those*

Here avoydyd Jhesus sodenly, thus seyyng Mary M: *departs*

[MARY MAUDLEYN] O systyrs, thus the hey and nobyll influentt grace   *flowing*

fol. 120v Of my most blessyd Lord Jhesus, Jhesus, Jhesus!

He aperyd onto me at the sepulcur ther I was!   *appeared; where*

That hath relevyd my woo and moryd my blysche.   *relieved; increased*

1100   Itt is innumerabyll to expresse,   *too great*

Or for ony tong for to tell,

Of my joye how myche itt is,   *much*

So myche my peynnys itt doth excelle!   *pains; exceed*

MARY SALOME Now less us go to the setté, to ower lady dere,   *city*

1105   Hyr to shew of hys wellfare,   *make known*

And also to dyssypyllys that we have syn here,   *what; seen*

The more yt shall rejoyse them from care.   *gladden*

MARY JACOBE Now, systyr Magdleyn, wyth glad chyr.

So wold that good Lord we myth wyth hym mete![1]

JHESUS To shew desyrows hartys I am full nere,   *desirous; very*

1111   Women, I apere to yow and sey *"Awete!"*   *Hail*

MARY SALOME Now, gracyus Lord, of yowur nymyos charyté,   *beyond measure*

Wyth hombyll hartys to thi presens complayne,   *[We who] with*

Grauntt us thi blyssyng of thi hye deyté,

1115   Gostly ower sowlys for to sosteynne.   *Spiritually; sustain*

JHESUS Alle tho byn blyssyd that sore refreynne.[2]

We blysch yow, Father and Son and Holy Gost,

fol. 121r All sorow and care to constryne   *constrain (control)*

Be ower power, of mytys most.   *greatest in might*

1120   *In nomine Patrys, ett Felii ett Spiritus Sancti, amen!* [3]

Goo ye to my brethryn and sey to hem ther,

That they procede and go into Gallelye,

And ther shall they se me as I seyd before,

Bodyly, wyth here carnall yye.   *their physical eye*

Here Jhesus devoydytt agen.   *departs*

---

[1] *Would that we might meet with that good Lord*

[2] *All those are blessed who sorrowfully abstain*

[3] *In the name of the Father, and of the Son, and of the Holy Spirit, amen* (Matthew 28:19)

MARY MAUDLEYN   O thou gloryus Lord of heven regyon,
1126   Now blyssyd be thi hye devynyté,
       Thatt evyr thow tokest incarnacyon,
       Thus for to vesyte thi pore servantys thre.   *visit*
       Thi wyll, gracyows Lord, fulfyllyd shall be.
1130   As thou commaundyst us in all thyng,
       Ower gracyows brethryn we woll go se
       Wyth hem to seyn all ower lekeyng.   *speak of; liking (pleasure)*

          Here devoyd all the thre Maryys, and the King
          of Marcyll shall begynne a sacryfyce.

REX MARCYLL   Now, lorddys and ladyys of grett aprise,   **King**; *worth*
       A mater to meve yow is in my memoryall:[1]
1135   This day to do a sacryfyce,
       Wyth multetude of myrth before ower goddys all,   *great mirth*
       Wyth preors in aspecyall before hys presens,   *special prayers*
       Eche creature wyth hartt demure.   *demure (sober)*

REGINA   To that lord curteys and kynd,   *[fol. 121v];* **Queen***; courteous*
1140   Mahond, that is so mykyll of myth,   *great*
       Wyth mynstrelly and myrth in mynd,   *music*
       Lett us gon ofer in that hye kyngis syth.   *go offer; sight*

          Here shall entyr an hethen prest and hys boye.   *heathen*

PRESBYTYR   Now, my clerke Hawkyn, for love of me,   **Priest**
       Loke fast myn awter wer arayd![2]
1145   Goo ryng a bell, to or thre.   *two or three*
       Lythly, chyld, it be natt delayd,   *Quickly; delayed*
       For here shall be a grett solemnyté,
       Loke, boy, thou do it wyth a brayd!   *in haste*

CLERICUS   Whatt, mastyr! Woldyst thou have thi lemman to thi beddys syde?[3]   **Clerk**
1150   Thow shall abyde tyll my servyse is sayd.   *wait; divine office*

PRESBYTYR   Boy! I sey, be Sentt Coppyn,   *by*
       No swyche wordys to thee I spake!

BOY   Wether thou ded or natt, the fryst jorny shall be myn,   *first undertaking*
       For, be my feyth, thou beryst Wattys pakke![4]

---

[1] *I have in mind a matter (business) to move (affect) you*

[2] *See to it that my altar is arrayed (prepared)*

[3] *What, master! Would you have your lover [brought] to your bed*

[4] *For, by my faith, you bear (carry) Watt's pack (a paunch)*

1155	But, syr, my mastyr, grett Morell,	
	Ye have so fellyd yower bylly with growell,	*filled; belly; gruel*
	That it growit grett as the dywll of hell.	*grows; devil*
	Onshapli thou art to see!	*Ill-shapen*
	Whan women comme to here thi sermon,	
1160	Pratyly wyth hem I can houkkyn,	*Cunningly; hook (fornicate)*
fol. 122r	Wyth Kyrchon and fayer Maryon,	
	They love me bettyr than thee,	
	I dare sey. And thou shulddys ryde,	*if you should ride*
	Thi body is so grett and wyde,	
1165	That nevyr horse may thee abyde,	*no horse can abide (carry) you*
	Exseptt thou breke hys bakk asoundyre!	*Unless; back asunder*

PRESBYTYR	A, thou lyyst, boy, be the dyvll of hell!	*by*
	I pray god, Mahond mott thee quell.	*may kill you*
	I shall whyp thee tyll thi ars shall belle!	*whip; until; ass; swell*
1170	On thi ars com mych wondyre!	*many wonders*

BOY	A fartt, mastyr, and kysse my grenne!	*groin*
	The dyvll of hell was thi emme.	*uncle*
	Loo, mastyrs, of swyche a stokke he cam;	*stock (lineage)*
	This kenred is asprongyn late.	*kindred is lately sprung (risen up)*

PRESBYTYR	Mahoundys blod, precyows knave!	*precious*
1176	Stryppys on thi ars thou shall have,	*Stripes*
	And rappys on thi pate!	*blows; head*

	Bete hym. Rex diciit:	*The king says*

[**REX**]	Now, prystys and clerkys of this tempyll cler,	*pure*
	Yower servyse to sey, lett me se.	*say*

PRESBYTYR	A, soveryn Lord, we shall don ower devyr.	*do our duty*
1181	Boy, a boke anon thou bryng me!	
	Now, boy, to my awter I wyll me dresse;	
	On shall my vestment and myn aray.[1]	

BOY	Now than, the lesson I woll expresse,	*read*
1185	Lyke as longytt for the servyse of this day:	*Such as belongs to*

	Leccyo mahowndys viri fortissimi sarasenorum:
fol. 122v	*Glabriosum ad glumandum glumardinorum,*
	Gormoerdorum alocorum, stampatinantum cursorum,
	Cownthtys fulcatum, congruryandum tersorum,

---

[1] Lines 1182–83: *Now, boy, to my altar I will go / And put on my [liturgical] vestments and my array*

1190 *Mursum malgorum, mararagorum,*
   Skartum sialporum, fartum cardiculorum,
   Slaundri stroumppum, corbolcorum,
   Snyguer snagoer werwolfforum,
   Standgardum lamba beffettorum,
1195 *Strowtum stardy strangolcorum,*
   Rygour dagour flapporum,
   Castratum raty rybaldorum.

   Howndys and hoggys, in heggys and hellys,   *Hounds; hogs; hedges; hells*
   Snakys and toddys mott be yower bellys![1]
1200 Ragnell and Roffyn, and other in the wavys,   *waves*
   Grauntt yow grace to dye on the galows!   *gallows*

PRESBYTYR Now, lordys and ladyys, lesse and more,
   Knele all don wyth good devocyon.
   Yonge and old, rych and pore,
1205 Do yower oferyng to Sentt Mahownde,   *Make; Saint*
   And ye shall have grett pardon,
   That longytt to this holy place,   *belongs*
   And receyve ye shall my benesown,   *blessing*
fol. 123r And stond in Mahowndys grace.

   Rex dicitt.   *The king says*

[REX OF MARCYLLE] Mahownd, thou art of mytys most,   *greatest in power*
1211 In my syth a gloryus gost.   *sight; spirit*
   Thou comfortyst me both in contré and cost,   *country; coast*
   Wyth thi wesdom and thi wytt,   *wisdom*
   For truly, lord, in thee is my trost.   *trust*
1215 Good Lord, lett natt my sowle be lost.
   All my cownsell well thou wotst,   *you well know*
   Here in thi presens as I sett   *set*
   Thys besawnt of gold, rych and rownd,   *coin*
   I ofer ytt for my lady and me,
1220 That thou mayst be ower counfortys in this stownd,   *at this time*
   Sweth Mahound, remembyr me!   *Sweet*

PRESBYTYR Now, boy, I pray thee, lett us have a song!
   Ower servyse be note, lett us syng, I say.[2]
   Cowff up thi brest, stand natt to long.   *Clear your throat; too*
1225 Begynne the offyse of this day.   *office (service)*

---

[1] *May snakes and toads be your bells (or, in your bellies)*

[2] *Let us sing our [religious] service musically (by note), I say*

BOY   I home and I hast, I do that I may,[1]
             Wyth mery tune the trebyll to syng.   *treble*

             Syng both.   *They both sing*

PRESBYTYR Hold up! The dyvll mote thee afray,[2]
             For all owt of rule thou dost me bryng!   *order*
1230   Butt now, syr, kyng, quene, and knyth,   *knight*
             Be mery in hartt everychon!   *everybody*
             For here may ye se relykys brygth —   *bright relics*
             Mahowndys own nekke bon!   *neck bone*
fol. 123v   And ye shall se er ever ye gon,   *before you go*
1235   Whattsomever yow betyde.   *Whatever happens to you*
             And ye shall kesse all this holy bon,   *kiss*
             Mahowndys own yeelyd!   *eyelid*
             Ye may have of this grett store —   *benefit*
             And ye know the cause wherfor —   *If you would know the reason why*
1240   Ytt woll make yow blynd forevyr more,
             This same holy bede.   *prayer*
             Lorddys and ladyys, old and ynge,   *young*
             Mahownd the holy and Dragon the dere,
             Golyas so good to blysse may yow bryng,
1245   Wyth Belyall, in blysse everlastyng,[3]
             That ye may ther in joy syng,
             Before that comly kyng
             That is ower god in fere.   *in common*

[Jerusalem]

PYLATT   Now, ye serjauntys semly, what sey ye?
1250   Ye be full wetty men in the law.   *prudent*
             Of the dethe of Jhesu I woll avysyd be —   *will be advised*
             Ower soferyn Sesar the soth must nedys know.[4]
             Thys Jhesu was a man of grett vertu,
             And many wondyrs in hys tyme he wrowth.   *miracles; worked*
1255   He was put to deth be cawsys ontru,   *for reasons untrue*
fol. 124r   Wheche matyr stekytt in my thowth.   *sticks; thought*
             And ye know well how he was to the erth browth,   *brought*
             Wacchyd wyth knygths of grett aray.   *Guarded by; armaments*

---

[1] *I hum and I hurry, I do what I can*

[2] *Stop! May the devil frighten you*

[3] Lines 1243–45: *[May] the holy Mahound and the dear Dragon, / [and] the good Golyas bring you to bliss / With Belial, [to remain] in everlasting bliss*

[4] *Caesar, our sovereign, must know the truth*

He is resyn agayn, as before he tawth,   *he previously taught*
1260   And Joseph of Baramathye he hath takyn awey.[1]

SERJANTT   Soferyn juge, all this is soth that ye sey,
But all this must be curyd be sotylté,   *taken care of by cunning*
And sey how hys dysypyllys stollyn hym away —   *[we must] say; have stolen*
And this shall be the answer, be the asentt of me.   *assent*

SECUNDUS SERJANTT   So it is most lylly for to be!   *likely*
1266   Yower councell is good and commendabyll.
So wryte hym a pystyll of specyallté,   *special epistle (letter)*
And that for us shall be most prophytabyll.

PYLATT   Now, masengyr, in hast hether thou com!   *hither*
1270   On masage thou must, wyth ower wrytyng,[2]
To the soferyn emperower of Rome.
But fryst thu shall go to Herodys the kyng,   *first*
And sey how that I send hym knowyng   *knowledge*
Of Crystys deth, how it hath byn wrowth.   *brought about*
1275   I charge thee, make no lettyng,   *delay*
Tyll this lettyr to the emperower be browth!   *Until*

NUNCYUS PYLATTI   My lord, in hast yower masage to spede   *[fol. 124v]; Pilate's messenger*
Onto that lordys of ryall renown,
Dowth ye nat, my lord, it shall be don indede.   *Doubt*
1280   Now hens woll I fast owt of this town!   *hence will I [go]*

Her goth the masengyr to Herodys.

NUNCYUS   Heyll, soferyn kyng ondyr crown!
The prynsys of the law recummende to yower heynesse,   *commend themselves*
And sendytt yow tydyngys of Crystys passon,   *passion*
As in this wrytyng doth expresse.[3]

HERODYS   A, be my trowth, now am I full of blyss!
1286   Thes be mery tydyngys that they have thus don.
Now certys I am glad of this,
For now ar we frendys that afore wher fon.   *friends; before; foes*
Hold a reward, masengyr, that thow were gon,[4]
1290   And recummend me to my soferens grace.   *sovereign's*

---

[1] *Joseph of Arimathea has taken him away*

[2] *One message, of our writing, you must [carry]*

[3] *As this writing does relate*

[4] *Claim your reward, messenger, and be gone*

Shew hym I woll be as stedfast as ston,
Fere and nere and in every place.   *Far and near*

Here goth the masengyr to the emperower.

[Rome]

NUNCYUS Heyll be yow, sofereyn, settyng in solas!
    Heyll, worthy wythowtyn pere!   *peer*
1295 Heyll, goodly to grauntt all grace![1]
    Heyll, emperower of the world, ferr and nere!
    Soferyn, and it plese yower hye empyre,   *and [if] it; imperial majesty*
fol. 125r I have browth yow wrytyng of grett aprise,   *worth*
    Wych shall be pleseyng to yower desyre,
1300 From Pylatt, yower hye justyce.
    He sentt yow word wyth lowly intentt.   *humble*
    In every place he kepytt yower cummaundement,
    As he is bound be hys ofyce.   *office (position)*

INPERATOR A, welcum, masengyr of grett pleseauns!
1305 Thi wrytyng anon lett me se.   *at once*
    My juggys, anon gyffe atendans,   *give [your] attention*
    To ondyrstond whatt this wrytyng may be,
    Wethyr it be good are ony deversyté,   *or anything malicious*
    Or ellys natt for myn avayll.   *profit*
1310 Declare me this in all the hast!   *haste*

PROVOST Syr, the sentens we woll dyscus,   *meaning*
    And it plese yowere hye exseleyns.   *excellency*
    The intentt of this pystull is thus: *epistle*
    Pylatt recummendytt to yower presens,   *commends himself*
1315 And of a prophett is the sentens,[2]
    Whos name was callyd Jhesus.
    He is putt to dethe wyth vyolens,   *violence*
    For he chalyngyd to be kyng of Jewys.   *claimed*
    Therfor he was crucyfyed to ded,   *death*
1320 And syn was beryyd, as they thowth reson.[3]
    Also, he cleymyd hymsylf son of the Godhed.
fol. 125v The therd nyght he was stollyn away wyth treson,   *third*
    Wyth hys desypyllys that to hym had dyleccyon;[4]
    So wyth hym away they yode.   *went*

---

[1] *Hail, goodly one, granter of all graces (favors)*

[2] Lines 1314–15: *Pilate recommends himself to you; / His letter concerns a prophet*

[3] *And afterward was buried, as seemed reasonable to them*

[4] *By his disciples who loved him*

1325   I mervayll how they ded, wyth the bodyys corupcyon;
        I trow they wer fed wyth a froward fode![1]

INPERATOR   Crafty was ther connyng, the soth for to seyn.
            Thys pystyll I wyll kepe wyth me yff I can;
            Also I wyll have cronekyllyd the yere and the reynne,
1330   That nevyr shall be forgott, whoso loke theron.[2]
            Masengyre, owt of this town wyth a rage!   *speed*
            Hold this gold to thi wage,   *Have; for*
            Mery for to make!

NUNCYUS   Farewell, my lord of grett renown,
1335   For owt of town my way I take.

                    Her entyr Mawdleyn wyth hyr dysypyll, thus seyyng:

[MARY MAUDLEYN]   A, now I remembyr my lord that put was to ded   *death*
            Wyth the Jewys, wythowtyn gyltt or treson.   *By; guilt*
            The therd nygth he ros be the myth of hys Godhed;   *third; arose*
            Upon the Sonday had hys gloryus resurrexcyon.
1340   And now is the tyme past of his gloryus asencyon;   *ascension*
            He steyyd to hevyn, and ther he is kyng.   *rose up*
            A, hys grett kendness may natt fro my mencyon.[3]
            Of alle manyr tonggys he gaf us knowyng,   *many languages; knowledge*
            For to undyrstond every langwage.
fol. 126r Now have the dysyllpyllys take ther passage,   *their journeys*
1346   To dyvers contreys her and yondyr;   *countries here*
            To prech and teche of hys hye damage,   *injury (the Passion)*
            Full ferr ar my brothyrn departyd asondyr.   *Very far; separated*

                    Her shall hevyn opyn, and Jhesus shall shew.   *appear*

JHESUS   O, the onclypsyd sonne, tempyll of Salamon!   *un-eclipsed sun*
1350   In the mone I restyd, that nevyr chonggyd goodnesse;[4]
            In the shep of Noee, fles of Judeon.   *ship; Noah, fleece; Gideon*
            She was my tapyrnakyll of grett nobyllnesse;   *tabernacle*
            She was the paleys of Phebus brygthnesse;   *palace; Phoebus'*
            She was the vessell of puere clennesse,
1355   Wher my Godhed gaff my manhod myth: *gave; manhood might*

---

[1] Lines 1325–26: *I marvel how they did [steal away with the body], considering the body's corruption; / I bet they were fed an unsatisfactory food*

[2] Lines 1329–30: *Also I will have chronicled the year and reign [of this event] / So that [it] shall never be forgotten, whosoever looks thereupon [the chronicle]*

[3] *Ah, his great kindness may not [depart] from my memory*

[4] *In the moon, unchanging in goodness, I rested (took my place)*

My blyssyd mother, of demure femynyté,

For mankynd, the feynddys defens,[1]

Quewne of Jherusalem, that hevnly ceté,   *city*

Empresse of hell, to make resystens.[2]

1360 She is the precyus pyn, full of ensens,   *pine; incense*

The precyus synamvyr, the body thorow to seche.

She is the muske agens the hertys of vyolens,

The jentyll jelopher agens the cardyakyllys wrech.[3]

The goodnesse of my mothere no tong can expresse,

1365 Nere no clerke of hyre, hyre joyys can wryth.[4]

Butt now of my servantt I remembyr the kendnesse;   *kindness*

fol. 126v With hevenly masage I cast me to vesyte.[5]

Raphaell, myn angell in my syte,   *sight*

To Mary Maudleyn decende in a whyle,   *descend*

1370 Byd here passe the se be my myth,   *Bid her cross the sea by my power*

And sey she shall converte the land of Marcyll.   *say*

ANGELUS   O gloryus Lord, I woll resortt   *proceed*

To shew your servant of yower grace.

She shall labor for that londys comfortt,   *land's*

1375 From hevynesse them to porchasse.   *deliver them from sadness*

Tunc decendet angelus.   *Then the angel will descend*

Abasse thee noutt, Mary, in this place!   *Fear not*

Ower lordys preceptt thou must fullfyll.   *precept (command)*

To passe the see in shortt space,   *cross; time*

Onto the lond of Marcyll.

1380 Kyng and quene converte shall ye,

And byn amyttyd as an holy apostylesse.[6]

Alle the lond shall be techyd alonly be thee,   *taught solely by*

Goddys lawys onto hem ye shall expresse.

Therfore hast yow forth wyth gladnesse,   *hurry*

1385 Goddys commaunddement for to fullfylle.

---

[1] *For mankind, the defense against the fiend (devil)*

[2] *Empress of hell, who makes resistance [against it]*

[3] Lines 1361–63: *[She is] the precious cinnabar (a purgative), that makes its way through the body. / She is the musk, [medicinal] against the heart's extreme reactions, / The gentle gillyflower against the heart's sickness*

[4] *Nor can any of her [his mother's] clerks (learned men) write about her joys [fully and adequately]*

[5] *With heavenly message I intend now to visit [her]*

[6] *And you shall be accepted as a holy apostoless*

MARY MAUDLEYN   He that from my person seven dewllys mad to fle,[1]   *[fol. 127r]*
        Be vertu of hym alle thyng was wrowth;   *created*
        To seke thoys pepull I woll rydy be,   *those; ready*
        As thu hast comaunddytt, in vertu they shall be browth.
1390   Wyth thi grace, good Lord in deité,
        Now to the see I wyll me hy,   *sea; hie (go quickly)*
        Sum sheppyng to asspy.   *Some ship; see*
        Now spede me, Lord, in etyrnall glory!   *hasten*
        Now be my spede, allmyty Trenité!   *success*

       Here shall entyre a shyp with a mery song.

[Jerusalem — The Coast]

SHEPMAN   Stryke! Stryke! Lett fall an ankyr to grownd.[2]
1396   Her is a fayer haven to se!   *Here; port*
        Connyngly in, loke that ye sownd![3]
        I hope good harborow have shal wee.   *harbor*
        Loke that we have drynke, boy thou!   *See to it*

BOY   I may natt for slep, I make god a vow!
1401   Thou shall abyde ytte, and thou were my syere.[4]

SHEPMAN   Why, boy, we are rydy to go to dynere!
        Shall we no mete have?   *food*

BOY   Natt for me, be of good chyr,   *[fol. 127v]*
1405   Thowe ye be forhongord tyll ye rave,   *made very hungry; rave*
        I tell yow plenly beforn!   *I told you plainly before*
        For swyche a cramp on me sett is,   *has come upon me*
        I am a poynt to fare the worse.   *likely to*
        I ly and wryng tyll I pysse,   *twist and turn*
1410   And am a poyntt to be forlorn!   *about; destroyed*

THE MASTYR   Now, boy, whatt woll ye this seyll?[5]

BOY   Nothyng butt a fayer damsell!
        She shold help me, I know it well,
        Ar ellys I may rue the tyme that I was born!   *Or else; regret*

---

[1] *He who caused seven devils to flee from my person (body)*

[2] *Lower the sails! Let the anchor fall to the ground*

[3] *Skillfully in [to the harbor]; be sure to measure the depth*

[4] *I cannot because I'm too sleepy, I swear to God! / You shall endure it [the boy's refusal], even if you were my sire (father)*

[5] *What do you want this time?*

THE MASTYR Be my trowth, syr boye, ye shal be sped!   *helped*
1416   I wyll hyr bryng onto yower bed!
        Now shall thou lern a damsell to wed —
        She wyll nat kysse thee on skorn!¹

                Bete hym.

THE BOY A skorn! No, no, I fynd it hernest!   *In jest; earnest*
1420   The dewlle of hell motte the brest,   *May the devil of hell break you*
        For all my corage is now cast.   *vigor; overthrown*
        Alasse, I am forlorn!   *forsaken*

MARY MAUDLEYN Mastyr of the shepe, a word with thee.   *ship*

MASTYR All redy, fayer woman! Whatt wol ye?   **[fol. 128r]**

MARY MAUDLEYN Of whense is thys shep? Tell ye me,   *From where*
1426   And yf ye seyle wythin a whyle.   *sail; soon*

MASTYR We woll seyle this same day,
        Yf the wynd be to ower pay.   *advantage*
        This shep that I of sey,   *of which I speak*
1430   Is of the lond of Marcyll.

MARY MAUDLEYN Syr, may I natt wyth yow sayle?
        And ye shall have for yower avayle.²

MASTYR Of sheppyng ye shall natt faylle,³
        For us the wynd is good and saffe.   *safe*
1435   Yondyr is the lond of Torke,   *Turkey*
        I wher full loth for to lye!   *would be; tell a lie*
        Yendyr is the lond of Satyllye —   *Antalya (southern Turkey)*
        Of this cors we thar nat abaffe.   *From; course; need not go back*

                Now shall the shepmen syng.

        Stryk! Beware of sond!   *Lower the sails; land*
1440   Cast a led and in us gyde!   *Take a sounding; guide*
        Of Marcyll this is the kynggys lond.
        Go a lond, thow fayer woman, this tyde,   *time*
        To the kynggys place. Yondyr may ye se.
        Sett off! Sett off from lond!

---

¹ Lines 1417–18: *Now you shall learn [how to] wed a damsel / She [the whip] will not kiss you in jest*

² *And you shall have [something] for your profit (i.e., I will pay you)*

³ *You shall not want for passage by ship*

THE BOY All redy, mastyr, at thyn hand.   *[fol. 128v]*

    Her goth the shep owt of the place.

[Marseilles]

MARY MAUDLEYN O Jhesu, thi mellyfluos name   *sweetly flowing*
1447   Mott be worcheppyd wyth reverens!   *May it be*
    Lord, graunt me vyctoré agens the fyndys flame,   *fiend's*
    And yn thi lawys gyf this pepyll credens.   *give; people credence (belief)*
1450   I wyll resortt be grett convenyens;   *proceed expeditiously*
    On hys presens I wyll draw nere,   *Onto his (the king's)*
    Of my Lordys lawys to shew the sentens,   *meaning*
    Bothe of hys Godhed and of hys powere.

    Here shall Mary entyr before the kyng.

    Now, the hye kyng Crist, mannys redempcyon,
1455   Mote save yow, syr kyng, regnyng in equité,   *May; justice*
    And mote gydde yow the way toward savasyon.   *guide; salvation*
    Jhesu, the Son of the mythty Trenité,
    That was, and is, and evyr shall be,
    For mannys sowle the reformacyon,   *soul [is]*
1460   In hys name, lord, I beseche thee,
    Wythin thi lond to have my mancyon.   *dwelling*

REX Jhesu? Jhesu? What deylle is hym that?   *[fol. 129r]; What the devil is he?*
    I defye thee and thyn apenyon!   *opinion*
    Thow false lordeyn, I shal fell thee flatt!   *wretch; knock you down*
1465   Who made thee so hardy to make swych rebon?   *daring; answer*

MARY MAUDLEYN Syr, I com natt to thee for no decepcyon,
    But that good Lord Crist hether me compassyd.   *hither; directed*
    To receyve hys name, itt is yower refeccyon,   *refreshment*
    And thi forme of mysbelef be hym may be losyd.   *by; undone*

REX And whatt is that lord that thow speke of her?

MARY MAUDLEYN *Id est salvator,* yf thow wyll lere,   *It is the Savior; learn*
1472   The Secunde Person, that hell ded conquare,   *who; conquer*
    And the son of the Father in Trenyté.

REX And of whatt power is that god that ye reherse to me?   *recount*

MARY MAUDLEYN He mad hevyn and erth, lond and see,
1476   And all this he mad of nowth.   *from nought (nothing)*

REX   Woman, I pray thee, answer me!
             Whatt mad God at the fyrst begynnyng?
             Thys processe ondyrstond wol we,[1]
1480   That wold I lerne; itt is my plesyng.   *pleasure*

MARY MAUDLEYN   Syr, I wyll declare al and sum,   *[fol. 129v]*
             What from God fryst ded procede.   *first did*
             He seyd, "*In principio erat verbum*,"   *In the beginning was the Word*
             And wyth that he provyd hys grett Godhed.   *demonstrated*
1485   He mad heven for ower spede,   *our help*
             Wheras he syth in tronys hyee;   *Where he sits on high thrones*
             Hys mynystyrs next, as he save nede,   *as he saw the need*
             Hys angelus and archangyllys, all the compeny.
             Upon the fryst day God mad all this,   *made*
1490   As it was plesyng to hys intent.
             On the Munday, he wold natt mys,   *fail*
             To make sonne, mone, and sterrys and the fyrmament,   *stars*
             The sonne to begynne hys cors in the oryent,   *sun; course; east*
             And evyr labor wythowtyn werynesse,[2]
1495   And kepytt hys cours into the occedentt.   *keep; west*
             The Twysday, as I ondyrstond this,
             Grett grace for us he gan to incresse.
             That day he satt upon watyris,   *the waters*
             As was lykyng to hys goodnesse,   *pleasing*
1500   As holy wrytt berytt wettnesse.   *bears witness*
             That tyme he made both see and lond,
             All that werke of grett nobyllnesse,
             As it was plesyng to hys gracyus sond.   *intention*
fol. 130r   On the Weddysday, ower lord of mythe,
1505   Made more at hys plesyng,
             Fysche in flod and fowle in flyth,   *Fish; birds; flight*
             And all this was for ower hellpyng.   *help*
             On the Thorsday, that nobyll kyng
             Mad dyverse bestys, grett and smale.   *beasts*
1510   He gaff hem erth to ther fedyng,   *gave; to feed them*
             And bad hem cressyn be hylle and dale.   *to increase*
             And on the Fryday, God mad man,
             As it plesett hys hynesse most,   *pleased; highness*
             Aftyr hys own semelytude than,   *similitude (likeness)*
1515   And gaf hem lyfe of the Holy Gost.   *gave; through the*
             On the Satyrday, as I tell can,
             All hys werkys he gan to blysse.   *bless*
             He bad them multyply and incresse than,

---

[1] *This design we would (wish to) understand*

[2] *And labor constantly without growing weary*

As it was plesyng to hys worthynesse.

1520 And on the Sonday, he gan rest take,   *he rested*

As skryptur declarytt pleyn,

That al shold reverens make[1]

To hyr makar that hem doth susteyn —   *their maker; sustains them*

Upon the Sonday to leven in hys servyse,   *live*

1525 And hym alonly, to serve I tell yow pleyn.   *serve him alone; clearly*

REX   Herke, woman, thow hast many resonnys grett!   *great words*

I thyngk onto my goddys aperteynyng they beth.[2]

But thou make me answer son, I shall thee frett,   *Unless; soon; harm*

And cut the tong owt of thi hed!

MARY MAUDLEYN   Syr, yf I seyd amys, I woll return agayn.[3]   *[fol. 130v]*

1531 Leve yower encomberowns of perturbacyon,   *burdens of worry*

And lett me know what yower goddys byn,   *are*

And how they may save us from treubelacyon.   *tribulation*

REX   Hens to the tempyll that we ware,[4]

1535 And ther shall thow se a solom syth.   *solemn sight*

Come on all, both lesse and more,

Thys day to se my goddys myth!

Here goth the kyng wyth all hys atendaunt to the tempyll.   *attendants*

Loke now, what seyyst thow be this syth?   *about*

How pleseaunttly they stond, se thow how?[5]

1540 Lord, I besech thi grett myth,   *beseech*

Speke to this Chrisetyn that here sestt thou!   *Christian; you see here*

Speke, god lord, speke! Se how I do bow!

Herke, thou pryst! What menytt all this?   *priest; means*

What? Speke, good lord, speke! What eylytt thee now?   *ails*

1545 Speke, as thow artt bote of all blysse!   *reward*

PRESBYTYR   Lord, he woll natt speke whyle Chriseten here is.

MARY MAUDLEYN   Syr kyng, and it plese yower gentyllnesse,   *if it*

Gyff me lycens my prayors to make   *license*

---

[1] *So that (i.e., as an example that) all should show reverence*

[2] *I think they pertain to my gods*

[3] *Sir, if I said [anything] amiss, I will go back (i.e., revisit what I said)*

[4] *Hence to the temple let us go*

[5] *Don't you see how pleasantly they (the gods) stand*

| | Onto my God in heven blysch, | *heaven's bliss* |
| 1550 | Sum merakyll to shewyn for yower sake. | *miracle* |

| **REX** | Pray thi fylle tyll then knees ake! | *your; ache* |

MARY MAUDLEYN   *Dominus, illuminacio mea, quem timbeo?*
fol. 131r *Dominus, protecctor vite mee, a quo trepedabo?*[1]

Here shal the mament tremyll and quake. — *idol; tremble*

	Now Lord of lordys, to thi blyssyd name sanctificatt,	*sanctified*
1555	Most mekely my feyth I recummend.	*meekly; commit*
	Pott don the pryd of mamentys violatt![2]	
	Lord, to thi lover thi goodnesse descend;	*send down*
	Lett natt ther pryd to thi posté pretend,[3]	
	Wheras is rehersyd thy hye name Jhesus![4]	
1560	Good Lord, my preor I feythfully send;	*prayer*
	Lord, thi rythwysnesse here dyscus!	*righteousness; demonstrate*

*Here shall come a clowd from heven and sett the tempyl
on a fyre, and the pryst and the clerk shall synke, and the
kyng gothe hom, thus seyyng:*

[**REX**]	A, owt! For angur I am thus deludyd![5]	
	I wyll bewreke my cruell tene!	*revenge; misfortune*
	Alas, wythin mysylfe I am concludytt!	*have made up my mind*
1565	Thou woman, comme hether and wete whatt I mene.	*know*
	My wyff and I together many yerys have byn,	
	And nevyr myth be conceyvyd wyth chyld.	
	Yf thou for this canst fynd a mene,	*means*
	I wyll abey thi god and to hym be meke and myld.	*obey*

MARY MAUDLEYN	Now, syr, syn thou seyst so,	*since*
1571	To my Lord I prye wyth reythfull bone.	*pray; worthy boon (request)*
	Beleve in hym and in no mo,	*no others*
	And I hope she shall be conceyvyd sone.	

| **REX** | Avoyd, avoyd! I wax all seke! | *Go away; sick* |
| 1575 | I wyll to bed this same tyde. | *[go] to; right now* |

---

[1] Lines 1552–53: *The Lord [is] my light; whom shall I fear? / The Lord [is] protector of my life; of whom should I be afraid?* (Psalms 26:1)

[2] *Subdue the pride of impure idols*

[3] *Let not their pride lay claim to your power*

[4] *Wherever the high name Jesus is spoken*

[5] *Ah, out! How angry I am to be deluded thus*

fol. 131v I am so wexyd wyth yen suek,[1]
　　　　That hath nere to deth me dyth!   *nearly brought me to death*

　　　　　Here the kyng goth to bed in hast, and Mary goth in to
　　　　　an old logge wythowt the gate, thus seyyng: *lodging outside*

[MARY MAUDLEYN]   Now Cryst, my creatur, me conserve and kepe,   *creator*
　　　　That I be natt confunddyd wyth this reddure.   *defeated; harshness*
1580　　For hungore and thurst to thee I wepe!   *Because of*
　　　　Lord, demene me wyth mesuer.   *treat; measure (moderation)*
　　　　As thou savydyst Daniell from the lyounys rigur,   *lion's severity*
　　　　Be Abacuk thi masengyre, relevyd wyth sustynouns,[2]
　　　　Good Lord, so hellpe me and sokore,   *aid*
1585　　Lord, as itt is thi hye pleseawns!   *high pleasure*

[Heaven]

JHESUS   My grace shall grow and don decend   *descend*
　　　　To Mary my lover, that to me doth call,
　　　　Hyr asstatt for to amend.   *estate (condition)*
　　　　She shall be relevyd with sustinons corporall.   *bodily sustenance*
1590　　Now, awngelys, dyssend to hyr in especyall,   *especially*
　　　　And lede hyr to the prynssys chambyr ryth.   *lead her directly*
　　　　Bed hyre axke of hys good be weyys pacyfycal.[3]
　　　　And goo yow before hyr wyth reverent lyth.   *light*

PRIMUS ANGELUS   Blyssyd Lord, in thi syth   ***First Angel***
1595　　We dyssend onto Mary.

SECUNDUS ANGELUS   We dyssend from yower blysse bryth;   ***Second Angel***; *bright*
　　　　Onto yower cummaundement we aplye.   *comply*

fol. 132r　　　*Tunc dissenditt angelus. Primus dyxit:*[4]

[PRIMUS ANGELUS]   Mary, ower Lord wyll comfortt yow send!
　　　　He bad, to the kyng ye shuld take the waye,
1600　　Hym to asay, yf he woll condesend,[5]
　　　　As he is slepyng, hem to asaye.   *While; to test them*

---

[1] *I have become so sick with that illness*

[2] *Who (Daniel) was relieved with sustenance by Habakkuk, your messenger*

[3] *Bid her to ask for some his goods (riches) in a peaceful manner*

[4] *Then the angel descends. The first says*

[5] Lines 1599–1600: *He bids you to make your way to the king / to assay if he will condescend [to help you]*

SECUNDUS ANGELUS   Byd hym releve yow, to goddys pay,[1]
       And we shal go before yow wyth solem lyth;   *light*
       In a mentyll of whyte shall be ower araye.   *mantle; white; array*
1605   The dorys shall opyn agens us be ryth.   *doors; toward; right*

MARY MAUDLEYN   O gracyus God, now I undyrstond!
       Thys clothyng of whyte is tokenyng of mekenesse.   *token (sign)*
       Now gracyus Lord, I woll natt wond,   *hesitate*
       Yower preseptt to obbey wyth lowlynesse.   *humility*

      Here goth Mary, wyth the angelys before hyre to the kynggys
      bed, wyth lythys beryng, thus seyyng Mary:[2]

1610   Thow froward kyng, trobelows and wood,   *hostile; troublous and mad*
       That hast at thi wyll all worlddys wele,[3]
       Departe wyth me wyth sum of thi good,   *Distribute to; some; riches*
       That am in hongor, threst, and cold.   *Who is; thirst*
       God hath thee sent warnygys felle.   *many*
1615   I rede thee, torne, and amend thi mood.[4]
       Beware of thi lewdnesse for thi own hele,   *ignorance; spiritual health*
       And thow, qwen, turne from thi good.   *queen; your possessions*

      Here Mari voydyt, and the angyll and Mary chongg hyr
      clotheyng, thus seyyng the kyng:[5]

[REX]   A, this day is com! I am mery and glad!
fol. 132v   The son is up and shynyth bryth.   *sun*
1620   A mervelows shewyng in my slep I had,   *showing (vision)*
       That sore me trobelyd this same nyth: *greatly troubled me; night*
       A fayer woman I saw in my syth,
       All in whyte was she cladd;
       Led she was wyth an angyll bryth,   *by a bright angel*
1625   To me she spake wyth wordys sad.   *serious*

REGINA   I trow from good that they were sentt!   **Queen**; *believe*
       In ower hartys we may have dowte.   *fear*
       I wentt ower chambyr sholld a brentt,   *thought; should have burned*
       For the lyth that ther was all abowth.   *Because of*
1630   To us she spake wordys of dred,   *spoke; authority*

---

[1] *Command him to relieve you, to God's satisfaction*

[2] *Here, with the angels bearing lights before her, Mary goes to the king's bed*

[3] *You have at your disposal all the world's wealth*

[4] *I counsel you to turn [from your current thinking] and amend your disposition*

[5] *Here Mary departs, and the angel and Mary change their clothing, and the king says*

That we shuld help them that have nede,
Wyth ower godys, so God ded byd,   *goods; as; did bid*
I tell yow, wythowtyn dowthe.   *doubt*

REX   Now, semely wyff, ye sey ryth well.   *speak very*
1635   A, knyth, anon, wythowtyn delay!   *knight*
            Now, as thou hast byn trew as stylle,   *steel*
            Goo fett that woman before me this daye!   *fetch*

MILES   My sovereyn lord, I take the waye.
            She shall com at yower pleseawns.
1640   Yower soveryn wyll I wyll goo saye,   *declare [to her]*
            Itt is almesse hyr to avawns.   *alms; advance (assist)*

fol. 133r   *Thunc transit miles ad Mariam.*[1]

            Sped well, good woman! I am to thee sentt,   *May you prosper*
            Yow for to speke wyth the kyng.   *[in order] for you*

MARY MAUDLEYN   Gladly, syr, at hys intentt,
1645   I comme at hys own pleseyng.

                Tunc transytt Maria ad regem.[2]

            The mythe and the powere of the heye Trenyté,
            The wysdom of the Son, mott governe yow in ryth!   *may (they); right*
            The Holy Gost mott wyth yow be.
            What is yowre wyll? Sey me in sythe.   *Tell me now*

REX   Thow fayer woman, itt is my delyth,   *delight*
1651   Thee to refresch is myn intentt,[3]
            Wyth mete and mony, and clothys for the nyth,   *night*
            And wyth swych grace as God hathe me lentt.   *lent me*

MARY MAUDLEYN   Than fullfylle ye Goddys cummaundement,
1655   Pore folk in myschef them to susteyn.   *misfortune*

REX   Now, blyssyd woman, reherse here presentt,   *relate*
            The joyys of yower lord in heven.

MARY MAUDLEYN   A, blyssyd the ower and blyssyd be the tyme, *hour*
            That to Goddys lawys ye wyll gyff credens!   *give credence*

---

[1] *Then the soldier goes over to Mary*

[2] *Then Mary goes over to the king*

[3] *It is my intention to refresh (provide support for) you*

1660	To yowerselfe ye make a glad pryme	*beginning*
	Agens the fenddys malycyows violens.	*fiend's malicious*
fol. 133v	From God above comit the influens,	*comes; spiritual power*
	Be the Holy Gost into thi brest sentt down,	*breast*
	For to restore thi offens,	*atone for*
1665	Thi sowle to bryng to evyrlastyng salvacyon.	
	Thy wyffe, she is grett wyth chyld!	
	Lyke as thou desyerst, thou hast thi bone!	*Just as; desire; request*

REGINA   A, ye! I fel ytt ster in my wombe up and down!   *feel; stir*
I am glad I have thee in presens.[1]
1670   O blyssyd woman, rote of ower savacyon,   *root*
Thi God woll I worchep with dew reverens.   *due*

REX   Now fayer woman, sey me the sentens,   *tell me*
I beseche thee, whatt is thi name?

MARY MAUDLEYN   Syr, agens that I make no resystens.   *against*
1675   Mary Maudleyn, wythowtyn blame.   *reproach*

REX   O blyssyd Mary, ryth well is me,
That ever I have abedyn this daye.   *lived until*
Now thanke I thi God, and specyally thee,
And so shall I do whyle I leve may.   *live*

MARY MAUDLEYN   Ye shall thankytt Petyr, my mastyr, wythowt delay.
1681   He is thi frend, stedfast and cler.
fol. 134r   To allmythy God he halp me pray,   *helped*
And he shall crestyn yow from the fynddys power,   *christen; fiend's*
In the syth of God an hye.   *sight*

REX   Now, suerly, ye answer me to my pay.   *surely; liking*
1686   I am ryth glad of this tyddyngys!
Butt, Mary, in all my goodys I sese yow this day,   *with all; endow*
For to byn at yower gydyng,   *under your control*
And them to rewlyn at yower pleseyng,   *rule*
1690   Tyll that I comme hom agayn.
I wyll axke of yow neythyr lond nore rekynyng,[2]
But I here delever yow powere pleyn.   *deliver; full*

REGINA   Now, worshepfull lord, of a bone I yow pray,   *request*
And it be pleseyng to yower hye dygnité.   *If it be*

---

[1] *I am glad to be in your presence*

[2] *I will ask of you neither land nor reckoning (payment) [in return for this endowment]*

REX	Madam, yower desyere onto me say.	*desire*
1696	What bone is that ye dysyere of me?	

REGINA	Now, worshepfull sovereyn, in eche degré,	*in every way*
	That I may wyth yow goo,	
	A Crestyn womman made to be.[1]	
1700	Gracyus lord, it may be soo.	*may it be so*

REX	Alas, the wyttys of wommen, how they byn wylld!	*wits; wild*
fol. 134v	And therof fallytt many a chanse.[2]	
	A, why desyer it yow, and ar wyth chyld?	*since you are*

REGINA	A, my sovereyn, I am knett in care,	*knit (bound up)*
1705	But ye consedyr now that I crave,	*Unless; what I now*
	For all the lovys that ever ware,	*loves; were*
	Behynd yow that ye me not leve!	*Don't leave me behind*

REX	Wyff, syn that ye woll take this wey of pryse,	*since; special voyage*
	Therto can I no more seyn.	*say*
1710	Now Jhesu be ower gyd, that is hye justyce,	*guide*
	And this blyssyd womman, Mary Maugleyn!	

MARY MAUDLEYN	Syth ye ar consentyd to that dede,	*Since; deed*
	The blyssyng of God gyff to yow wyll I.	
	He shall save yow from all dred,	
1715	*In nomine Patrys, et Filii, et Spiritus Sancti. Amen.*[3]	

Ett tunc navis venit in placeam et nauta dicit:[4]

[NAUTA]	Loke forth, Grobbe, my knave,	**Sailor**
	And tell me what tydyngys thou have,	*tidings (information)*
	And yf thou aspye ony lond.	*see*

BOY	Into the shrowdys I woll me hye.	*ship's rigging; go quickly*
1720	Be my fythe, a castell I aspye,	*faith*
	And as I ondyrstond!	

---

[1] Lines 1698–99: *Let me go with you / And be made a Christian woman*

[2] *And from that befalls many an unexpected circumstance*

[3] *In the name of the Father, the Son, and the Holy Spirit. Amen*

[4] *And then the ship comes into the platea (place), and the sailor says*

NAUTA Sett therwyth, yf we mown,[1]
     For I wott itt is a havyn town   *haven (harbor)*
     That stondyt upon a strond.   *shore*

     Ett tuncc transitt rex ad navem, et dicit rex:[2]

[REX] How, good man, of whens is that shep?   *[fol. 135r]; from where does that ship come*
1726   I pray thee, syr, tell thou me.

NAUTA Syr, as for that, I take no kepe.   *heed*
     For what cause enquire ye?   *reason*

REX For causys of nede, seyle wold we,   *need sail*
1730   Ryth fayn we wold over byn.[3]

NAUTA Yee, butt me thynkytt, so mote I thee,
     So hastely to passe, yower spendyng is thyn.[4]
     I trow, be my lyfe,
     Thou hast stollyn sum mannys wyffe;   *stolen*
1735   Thou woldyst ledd hyr owt of lond![5]
     Neveretheles, so God me save,
     Lett se whatt I shall have,   *Let [me] see*
     Or ellys I woll nat wend!   *else; go*

REX Ten marke I wyll thee gyff,   *marks (in currency)*
1740   Yf thou wylt set me up at the cleyff   *deliver; cliff*
     In the Holy Lond.

NAUTA Set off, boy, into the flod!   *sea*

BOY I shall, mastyr! The wynd is good.
     Hens that we were!   *That we were hence (let's go)*

     Lamentando regina.   *The queen lamenting*

[REGINA] A, lady, hellp in this nede,   *distress*
1746   That in this flod we drench natt!   *drown*
     A, Mary, Mary, flower of wommanned!   *womanhood*
     O blyssyd lady, foryete me nowth!   *do not forget me*

---

[1] *Set [the ship's course] there, if we may (are able)*

[2] *And then the king goes over to the ship, and the king says*

[3] *We would [be] very glad to cross over [the sea]*

[4] Lines 1731–32: *Yes, but so may I thrive, I suppose / your payment will be meager, given your hasty passage*

[5] *You want to take her out of the country*

REX	A, my dere wyffe, no dred ye have,	*[fol. 135v]; do not fear*
1750	Butt trost in Mary Maudleyn,	*trust*
	And she from perellys shall us save,	*perils*
	To God for us she woll prayyn.	*pray*

REGINA	A, dere hosbond, thynk on me,	
	And save yowersylfe as long as ye may,	*while you can*

1755	For trewly itt wyll no otherwyse be,	
	Full sor my hart it makytt this day.[1]	
	A, the chyld that betwyx my sydys lay —	*lies between my sides*
	The wyche was conseyvyd on me be ryth —	*Which; by right*
	Alas, that wommannys help is away!	*woman's; not here*
1760	An hevy departyng is betwyx us in syth,[2]	
	Fore now departe wee!	
	For defawte of wommen here in my nede,	*Because of default (lack)*
	Deth my body makyth to sprede.	*spreads throughout*
	Now, Mary Maudleyn, my sowle lede!	*lead*
1765	*In manus tuas, Domine!*	*Into your hands, Lord*

REX	Alas, my wyff is ded!	
	Alas, this is a carefull chans!	*sorrowful chance (fortune)*
	So shall my chyld, I am adred,[3]	
	And for defawth of sustynons.	*lack of nourishment*
1770	Good Lord, thi grace graunte to me	*granted*
fol. 136r	A chyld betwen us of increse,[4]	
	An it is motherles!	
	Help me my sorow for to relesse,	*release*
	Yf thi wyl it be!	

NAUTA	*Benedicité, benedicité!*	*Bless us*
1776	What wethyr may this be?	*weather*
	Ower mast woll all asondyr!	*Our mast will break asunder*

BOY	Mastyr, I therto ley myn ere,	*bet my ear*
	It is for this ded body that we bere.	*because of*
1780	Cast hyr owt, or ellys we synke ondyr.	

Make redy for to cast hyr owt.

---

[1] Lines 1755–56: *For truly it [my dire situation] will not be otherwise / It [the situation] makes my heart very sorrowful this day*

[2] *Between us a sad parting comes at this time*

[3] *So shall my child [be dead], I fear*

[4] *A child, the offspring of the two of us*

REX	Nay, for Goddys sake, do natt so!	
	And ye wyll hyr into the se cast,	*If; sea*
	Gyntyll serys, for my love do.	*do [otherwise]*
	Yender is a roch in the west,	*Yonder; rock*
1785	As ley hyr theron all above,	*upon it*
	And my chyld hyr by.	*beside her*

NAUTA	As therto I asent well.	*assent*
	And she were owt of the vessell,	*If*
	All we shuld stond the more in hele,[1]	
1790	I sey yow, verely.	

Tunc remigant ad montem, et dicit rex:[2]

REX	Ly here, wyff, and chyld thee by.	
	Blyssyd Maudleyn be hyr rede!	*counselor*
	Wyth terys wepyng, and grett cause why,	*great reason for it*
	I kysse yow both in this sted.	*place*
1795	Now woll I pray to Mary myld	
	To be ther gyde here.	*their guide*

Tunc remigant a monte, et nauta dicit:[3]

NAUTA	Pay now, syr, and goo to lond,	*[fol. 136v]*
	For here is the portt Zaf, I ondyrstond;	*Jaffa*
	Ley down my pay in my hand,	
1800	And belyve go me fro!	*quickly go from me*

REX	I graunt thee, syr, so God me save!	
	Lo, here is all thi connownt.	*covenant (agreed sum)*
	All redy thou shall it have,	*Promptly*
	And a marke more than thi graunt,	*mark (in currency); what is due*
1805	And thou, page, for thi good obedyentt;	*obedience*
	I gyff yow besyde yower styntt,	*in addition to your allotted income*
	Eche of yow a marke for yower wage!	

NAUTA	Now he that mad bothe day and nyth,	
	He sped yow in yower ryth,	*[May] he help*
1810	Well to go on yower passage!	*voyage*

---

[1] *We should all have greater well being*

[2] *Then they row to the mountain, and the king says*

[3] *Then they row from the mountain, and the sailor says*

[Jerusalem]

PETYR	Now all creaturs upon mold,	*earth*
	That byn of Crystys creacyon,	*are*
	To worchep Jhesu they are behold,	*beholden (obliged)*
	Nore nevyr agens hym to make varyacyon.[1]	

REX	Syr, feythfully I beseche yow this daye,	
1816	Wher Petyr the apostull is, wete wold I.	*know*

PETYR	Itt is I, syr, wythowt delay.	
	Of yower askyng tell me why.	

REX	Syr, the soth I shall yow seyn,	*truth*
fol. 137r	And tell yow myn intentt wythin a whyle.	
1821	Ther is a woman hyth Mary Maudleyn,	*named*
	That hether hath laberyd me owt of Mercyll —	*hither; brought*
	Onto the wyche woman I thynke no gyle —[2]	
	And this pylgramage causyd me to take —	*pilgrimage*
1825	I woll tell you more of the stylle —	*circumstances*
	For to crestyn me from wo and wrake.	*christen; woe; harm*

PETYR	O, blyssyd be the tyme that ye are falle to grace,	*fallen (come)*
	And ye wyll kepe yower beleve aftyr my techeyng,[3]	
	And alle-only forsake the fynd Satyrnas,	*completely; fiend Satanas*
1830	The commaundmenttys of God to have in kepyng.	

REX	Forsoth, I beleve in the Father that is of all wyldyng,	*power*
	And in the son, Jhesu Cryst,	
	Also in the Holy Gost, hys grace to us spredyng;	*extending*
1834	I beleve in Crystys deth and hys uprysyng.	*Christ's; Resurrection*

PETYR	Syr, than whatt axke ye?	*ask*

REX	Holy father, baptym, for charyté,	*baptism*
	Me to save in eche degré	*in every way*
	From the fyndys bond.	*bondage*

PETYR	In the name of the Trenité,	
1840	Wyth this watyr I baptysse thee,	
	That thou mayst strong be	
	Agens the fynd to stond.	*Against*

---

[1] *[And they are obliged] never to oppose him*

[2] *Of whom [Mary Magdalene] I suspect no guile*

[3] *If you will maintain your belief after (according to) my teaching*

Tunc aspargit illum cum aqua.[1]

REX	A, holy fathyr, how my hart wyll be sor	*[fol. 137v]*
	Of cummaunddementt, and ye declare nat the sentens![2]	

PETYR	Syr, dayly ye shall lobor more and more,	*daily; labor*
1846	Tyll that ye have very experyens.	*Until; true experience*
	Wyth me shall ye dwall to have more eloquens,	*dwell*
	And goo vesyte the stacyons by and by;	*visit; holy places*
	To Nazareth and Bedlem, goo wyth delygens,	*Bethlehem; diligently*
1850	And be yower own inspeccyon, yower feyth to edyfy.[3]	

REX	Now, holy father, dereworthy and dere,	*precious; dear*
	Myn intent now know ye.	
	Itt is gon full to yere	*two years*
	That I cam to yow overe the se,	
1855	Crystys servont and yower to be,	*servant; yours*
	And the lawe of hym evyr to fulfyll.	*always*
	Now woll I hom into my contré.	*will I [go]; country*
	Yower puere blyssynd graunt us tylle —[4]	
	That feythfully I crave!	

PETRUS	Now in the name of Jhesu,	*Peter*
1861	*Cum Patre et Sancto Speritu*	*With the Father and the Holy Spirit*
	He kepe thee and save.	

Et tunc rex transit ad navem et dicit:[5]

REX	Hold ner, shepman, hold, hold!	*Come near*

BOY	Sir, yendyr is on callyd aftyr cold.	*yonder; one [who]*

NAUTA	A, syr! I ken yow of old.	*know; from earlier times*
1866	Be my trowth, ye be welcum to me!	*By*

REX	Now, gentyll marranere, I thee pray,	*[fol. 138r]; mariner*
	Whatsoever that I pay,	*Whatever the payment*
	In all the hast that ye may,	*haste*
1870	Help me over the se!	*sea*

---

[1] *Then he sprinkles him with water*

[2] Lines 1843–44: *Ah, holy father, how my heart will find instruction painful unless you explain the doctrine [of my new faith]*

[3] *And edify (strengthen) your faith by seeing them (the holy places) for yourself*

[4] *Grant us your pure blessing*

[5] *And then the king crosses to the ship and says*

NAUTA   In good soth, we byn atenddawntt;   *Truly; on duty*
         Gladly ye shall have yower graunt,   *request*
         Wythowtyn ony connownt.   *any covenant*
         Comme in, in Goddys name!
1875   Grobbe, boy, the wynd is nor-west;
         Fast abowth the seyle cast![1]
         Rere up the seyll in all the hast,   *Raise*
         As well as thou can!

Et tunc navis venit ad circa placeam. Rex dicit:[2]

[REX]   Mastyr of the shyp, cast forth yower yee!   *eye (i.e., look out there)*
1880   Me thynkyt the rokke I gyn to aspye![3]
         Gentyll mastyr, thether us gye;   *guide us thither*
         I shall qwyt yower mede.   *pay; reward*

NAUTA   In feyth, it is the same ston   *stone*
         That yower wyff lyeth upon!   *On which your wife lay*
1885   Ye shall be ther even anon,   *at once*
         Verely, indeed!

REX   O thou myty Lord of heven region,
         Yendyr is my babe of myn own nature,   *Yonder*
         Preservyd and keptt from all corrupcyon!
1890   Blyssyd be that Lord that thee doth socure!   *succors (aids) you*
         And my wyff lyeth here fayer and puer!   *lies*
         Fayere and clere is hur colour to se!   *clear; see*
         A, good Lord, yower grace wyth us indure,[4]
fol. 138v My wyvys lyfe for to illumyn.   *kindle*
1895   A, blyssyd be that puer vergyn!   *virgin*
         From grevos slepe she gynnyt revyve![5]
         A, the sonne of grace on us doth shynne.   *shine*
         Now blyssyd be God, I se my wyff alyve!

REGINA   O *virgo salutata*, for ower savacyon!
1900   O *pulcra et casta*, cum of nobyll alyauns![6]
         O almyty maydyn, ower sowlys confortacyon!   *almighty; consolation*

---

[1] *Quickly cast the sail around*

[2] *And then the ship goes around the platea. The king says*

[3] *I think I begin to see the rock*

[4] *Ah, good Lord, may your grace strengthen us*

[5] *From grievous sleep she (the queen) begins to be revived*

[6] Lines 1899–1900: *O worshipful virgin, for our salvation / O beautiful and chaste one, come from a noble lineage*

O demur Maudlyn, my bodyys sustynauns!   *modest; body's sustenance*
Thou hast wrappyd us in wele from all varyawns,[1]
And led me wyth my lord into the Holy Land.
1905   I am baptysyd as ye are, be Maryus gyddauns,   *Mary's guidance*
Of Sent Petyrys holy hand.   *By*
I sye the blyssyd crosse that Cryst shed on hys precyus blod;   *saw; on which*
Hys blyssyd sepulcur also se I.
Wherfor, good hosbond, be mery in mode,   *mood*
1910   For I have gon the stacyonnys, by and by.[2]

REX   I thanke it, Jhesu, with hart on hye,   *high*
Now have I my wyf and my chyld both!
I thank ytt Maudleyn and ower lady,   *for it*
And ever shall do, wythowtyn othe.   *oath*

            Et tunc remigant a monte, et nauta dicit:[3]

[NAUTA]   Now are ye past all perelle;   *[fol. 139r]; peril*
1916   Her is the lond of Mercylle.
Now goo a lond, syr, whan ye wyll,
I prye yow for my sake.   *pray (ask)*

REX   Godamercy, jentyll marraner!   *gentle mariner*
1920   Here is ten pounds of nobyllys cler.   *nobles (a currency)*
And ever thi frynd both ferre and nere.[4]
Cryst save thee from wo and wrake!   *harm*

            Here goth the shep owt of the place and Maud seyth:

[Marseilles]

[MARY MAUDLEYN]   O dere fryndys, be in hart stabyll,
And think how dere Cryst hathe yow bowth.   *bought (redeemed)*
1925   Agens God be nothyng vereabyll;[5]
Thynk how he mad all thyng of nowth.   *from nothing*
Thow yow in poverté sumtyme be browth,   *brought*
Yitte be in charyté both nyth and day,   *Yet*
For they byn blyssyd that so byn sowth,[6]

---

[1] *You have wrapped (surrounded) us in well-being, protected from all change*

[2] *For I have visited the holy places, one by one*

[3] *And then they row from the mountain, and the sailor says*

[4] *And I [will] always [be] your friend [whether] far and near (i.e., wherever we may be)*

[5] *Be not at all inconstant towards God*

[6] *For they are blessed that are so true*

1930   For *paupertas est donum dei.*   *poverty is God's gift*
        God blyssyt alle tho that byn meke and good,   *those*
        And he blyssyd all tho that wepe for synne.
        They be blyssyd that the hungor and the thorsty gyff fode;[1]
        They be blyssyd that byn mercyfull agen wrecched men;   *toward*
1935   They byn blyssyd that byn dysstroccyon of synne;   *destruction of sin*
        These byn callyd the chyldyren of lyfe,
fol. 139v Onto the wyche blysse, bryng both yow and me,
        That for us dyyd on the rode tre. Amen.   *died; cross*

            Here shall the kyng and the qwuene knele doun. Rex dicit:

[**REX**]   Heyll be thou Mary, ower Lord is wyth thee!
1940   The helth of ower sowllys and repast contemplatyff!   *refreshment*
        Heyll, tabyrnakyll of the blysssyd Trenité!   *tabernacle*
        Heyll, counfortabyll sokore for man and wyff!

REGINA   Heyll, thou chosyn and chast of wommen alon![2]
        It passyt my wett to tell thi nobyllnesse!   *surpasses my wit*
1945   Thou relevyst me and my chyld on the rokke of ston,   *relieved*
        And also savyd us be thi hye holynessse.   *saved*

MARY MAUDLEYN   Welcum hom, prynse and prynsses bothe!
        Welcom hom, yong prynsse of dew and ryth!   *rightful prince*
        Welcom hom to your own erytage wythowt othe,   *heritage by natural right*
1950   And to alle yower pepyll present in syth!
        Now are ye becum Goddys own knyght,   *you have become*
        For sowle helth, salve ded ye seche,   *remedy did you seek*
        In hom the Holy Gost hath take resedens,   *whom; residence*
        And drevyn asyde all the desepcyon of wrech.[3]
1955   And now have ye a knowlege of the sentens,   *substantial knowledge*
        How ye shall com onto grace.
        But now in yower godys agen I do yow sese;   *goods again; endow*
fol. 140r I trost I have governyd them to yower hertys ese.   *trust; ease*
        Now woll I labor forth, God to plese,
1960   More gostly strenkth me to purchase.[4]

REX   O blyssyd Mary, to comprehend   *accomplish*
        Ower swete sokor, on us have peté!   *succor; pity*

---

[1] *They are blessed who give food to the hungry and the thirsty*

[2] *Hail, thou chosen and chaste [one], alone among women*

[3] *And has driven away all the deceptions of evil*

[4] *To obtain for myself more spiritual strength*

REGINA To departe from us, why should ye pretende? *part; venture*
O blyssyd lady, putt us natt to that poverté!¹

MARY MAUDLEYN Of yow and yowers I wyll have rememberauns,
1966 And dayly yower bede woman for to be,²
That alle wyckydnesse from yow may have deleverans,
In quiet and rest that leve may ye. *live*

REX Now thanne, yower puere blyssyng graunt us tylle. *to us*

MARY MAUDLEYN The blyssyn of God mott yow fulfyll. *May the blessing*
1971 *Ille vos benedicatt, qui sene fine vivit et regnat!*³

Her goth Mary into the wyldyrnesse, thus seyyng Rex: *goes*

[REX] A, we may syyn and wepyn also, *sigh; weep*
That we have forgon this lady fre — *Because; lost; excellent*
It brynggytt my hart in care and woo —
1975 The whech ower gydde and governor should a be. *Who; guide*

REGINA That doth perswade all my ble,
That swete sypresse that she wold so.⁴
In me restytt neyther game nor gle *remains; play; joy*
fol. 140v That she wold from owere presens goo.

REX Now of hyr goyng I am nothyng glad.
1981 But my londdys to gyddyn I must aplye, *rule; apply [myself]*
Lyke as Sancte Peter me badde. *commanded*
Chyrchys in cetyys I woll edyfye, *cities; edify (build)*
And whoso agens ower feyth woll replye, *whoever; complain*
1985 I woll ponysch swych personnys with perplyxcyon. *punish; distress*
Mahond and hys lawys I defye!
A, hys pryde owt of my love shall have polucyon,⁵
And holle onto Jhesu I me betake! *wholly; betake myself*

Mari in herimo. *Mary in the desert*

---

¹ *Oh blessed lady, do not impoverish us [with your absence]*

² *And everyday I shall be your bede woman (i.e., one who prays for you)*

³ *May he who lives and reigns without end bless you*

⁴ Lines 1976–77: *It (Mary Magdalene's leaving) alters my complexion, / That this sweet cyperus (an aromatic plant) would do so (depart)*

⁵ *From my love [for God] his (Mahond's) pride shall be profaned*

[The Desert]

[MARY MAUDLEYN] In this deserte abydyn wyll wee,		*remain*
1990	My sowle from synne for to save.	
	I wyll evyr abyte me wyth humelyté,	*always clothe myself*
	And put me in pacyens, my Lord for to love.	*patience*
	In charyté my werkys I wol grave,	*engrave*
	And in abstynens, all dayys of my lyfe.	
1995	Thus my concyens of me doth crave;[1]	
	Than why shold I wyth my consyens stryffe?	*Then; strive (contend)*
	And ferdarmore, I wyll leven in charyté,	*furthermore; live*
	At the reverens of ower blyssyd lady,	
	In goodnesse to be lyberall, my sowle to edyfye.	*generous; strengthen*
2000	Of worldly fodys I wyll leve all refeccyon,[2]	
	Be the fode that commyt from heven on hye,	
fol. 141r	Thatt God wyll me send, be contemplatyff.[3]	

[Heaven]

JHESUS O, the swettnesse of prayors sent onto me		
	Fro my wel-belovyd frynd wythowt varyouns.	*From; friend; variance (change)*
2005	With gostly fode relevyd shall she be.	*spiritual; relieved*
	Angellys, into the clowdys ye do hyr hauns,	*cause her to be raised up*
	Ther fede wyth manna to hyr systynouns.	*feed; sustenance*
	Wyth joy of angyllys, this lett hur receyve.	*enable her to*
	Byd hur injoye wyth all hur afyawns,	*Bid; enjoy; faith in us*
2010	For fynddys frawd shall hur non deseyve.	*fiend's fraud shall not deceive her*

PRIMUS ANGELUS O thou redulent rose that of a vergyn sprong!		*fragrant*
	O thou precyus palme of vytory!	*victory*
	O thou osanna, angellys song!	*hosanna*
	O precyus gemme, born of ower Lady!	*from*
2015	Lord, thi commaunddement we obeyy lowly!	*humbly*
	To thi servant that thou hast grauntyd blysse,	*to whom you*
	We angellys all obeyyn devowtly.	
	We woll desend to yen wyldyrnesse.	*descend; yon(der)*

> *Here shall to angyllys desend into wyldyrnesse, and*
> *other to shall bryng an oble, opynly aperyng aloft in the*

---

[1] *My conscience craves (requires) that I do thus*

[2] *Of worldly foods I will abandon all partaking*

[3] Lines 2001–02: *[And I will be nourished] by the food that comes from heaven on high, / By the contemplative food that God will send me*

clowddys; the to benethyn shall bryng Mari, and she shall
receyve the bred, and than go agen into wyldyrnesse.[1]

SECUNDUS ANGELUS   Mari, God gretyt thee wyth hevenly influens![2]

2020	He hath sent thee grace wyth hevenly synys.	*signs*
	Thou shall byn onoryd wyth joye and reverens,	*honored*
fol. 142v	Inhansyd in heven above vergynnys.	*Raised up; virgins*
	Thou hast byggyd thee here among spynys;	*settled; thorns*
	God woll send thee fode be revelacyon.	
2025	Thou shall be receyvyd into the clowddys,	
	Gostly fode to reseyve to thi savacyon.	*Spiritual food; for*

MARY MAUDLEYN   *Fiat voluntas tua* in heven and erth!   *Your will be done*

Now am I full of joye and blysse.
Laud and preyse to that blyssyd byrth![3]
2030   I am redy, as hys blyssyd wyll isse.   *according to*

Her shall she be halsyd wyth angyllys wyth reverent song:

Asumpta est Maria in nubibus. Celi gaudent, angeli
laudantes felium Dei.

Et dicit Mari:[4]

[MARY MAUDLEYN]   O, thou Lord of lorddys, of hye domenacyon!

	In heven and erth worsheppyd be thi name!	
	How thou devydyst me from houngure and vexacyon!	*separated; hunger*
	O, gloryus Lord, in thee is no frauddys nor no defame!	*fraud; dishonor*
2035	But I shuld serve my Lord, I were to blame,	*Unless*
	Wych fullfyllyt me wyth so gret feliceté,	*Who so fills; felicity*
	Wyth melody of angyllys shewit me gle and game,[5]	
	And have fed me wyth fode of most delycyté.	*has*

Her shall speke an holy prest in the same wyldyrnesse,
thus seyyng the prest:

---

[1] *Here shall two angels descend into the wilderness, and another two shall bring an oble (eucharistic wafer), openly appearing aloft in the clouds; the two beneath shall bring Mary [up to the clouds], and she shall receive the bread (the oble), and then go again into the wilderness*

[2] *Mary, God greets you with heavenly inspiration*

[3] *Honor and praise for that blessed birth (of Jesus)*

[4] *Here shall she be greeted by angels with reverent song: Mary has been assumed into the clouds. The heavens rejoice, the angels praising the son of God. And Mary says*

[5] *[Who] with melody of angels showed me joy and pleasure*

[The Desert]

[PREST] O Lord of lorddys! What may this be?		*Priest*
2040	So gret mesteryys shewyd from heven,	*mysteries*
	Wyth grett myrth and melody,	
fol. 143r	With angellys brygth as the levyn!	*bright; lightening*
	Lord Jhesu, for thi namys sevynne	*seven names*
	As graunt me grace that person to see!	

> *Her he shal go in the wyldyrnesse and spye Mari in hyr*   *observe*
> *devocyon, thus seyyng the prest:*

2045	Heyl, creature, Crystys delecceon!	*beloved*
	Heyl, swetter than sugur or cypresse!	*sweeter; cyperus*
	Mary is thi name be angyllys relacyon;	*report*
	Grett art thou wyth God for thi perfythnesse!	*because of your perfection*
	The joye of Jherusallem shewyd thee expresse —	
2050	The wych I nevyr save this thirty wyntyr and more —[1]	
	Wherfor I know well thou art of gret perfytnesse.	
	I woll pray yow hartely to shew me of yower Lord![2]	

MARY MAUDLEYN Be the grace of my Lord Jhesus,		
	This thirty wyntyr this hath byn my selle,	*cell*
2055	And thryys on the day enhansyd thus,	*thrice each day raised up*
	Wyth more joy than ony tong can telle.	
	Nevyr creature cam ther I dwelle,	*where*
	Tyme nor tyde, day nore nyth,	*At no time; nor*
	That I can wyth spece telle,	*With whom I can speak*
2060	But alonly wyth goddys angyllys brygth.	*Except*
	But thou ar wolcum onto my syth,	*welcome; sight*
	If thou be of good conversacyon.	*manner of living*
	As I thynk in my delyth,	*delight*
fol. 143v	Thow sholddyst be a man of devocyon.	*must be*

PREST In Crystys law I am sacryed a pryst,		*ordained priest*
2066	Mynystryyd be angelys at my masse.	*Served*
	I sakor the body of ower Lord Jhesu Cryst,	*consecrate*
	And be that holy manna, I leve in sowthfastnesse.[3]	

MARY MAUDLEYN Now I rejoyse of yower goodnesse,		
2070	But tyme is comme that I shall asende.	*time; ascend*

---

[1] Lines 2049–50: *The joy of [heavenly] Jerusalem has openly revealed you — / The which [joy] I never saw these thirty winters and more*

[2] *I pray (beseech) you sincerely to reveal to me [something about] your Lord*

[3] *And through that holy manna (the consecrated body of Christ), I live in truthfulness*

PREST	I recummend me wyth all umbylnesse;	*commend myself; humility*
	Onto my sell I woll pretend.	*cell; go*

Her shall the prest go to hys selle, thus seyyng Jhesus:

[Heaven]

[JHESUS]	Now shall Mary have possesson,	*possession*
	Be ryth enirytawns a crown to bere.	*By true inheritance; bear*
2075	She shall be fett to evyrlastyng savacyon,	*fetched (brought)*
	In joye to dwell wythowtyn fere.	*equal*
	Now, angelys, lythly that ye were ther!	*quickly*
	Onto the prystys sell apere this tyde.	*at this time*
	My body in forme of bred that he bere,	
2080	Hur for to hossell, byd hym provyde.[1]	

PRIMUS ANGELUS	O blyysyd Lord, we be redy	*are*
	Yower massage to do wythowtyn treson!	*deliver; betrayal*

SECUNDUS ANGELUS	To hyr I wyll goo and make reportur,	
	How she shall com to yower habytacyon.	*dwelling place*

Here shall to angyllys go to Mary and to the prest,   *two*
thus seyyng the angellys to the prest:

[ANGELLYS]	Syr pryst, God cummaundytt from heven region,	
2086	Ye shall go hosyll hys servont expresse,	*housel; with haste*
fol. 144r	And we wyth yow shall take mynystracyon,	*serve*
	To bere lyth before Hys body of worthynesse.	*light*

PREST	Angyllys, wyth all umbyllnesse,	*humility*
2090	In a vestment I wyll me aray,	*array myself*
	To mynystyr my Lord of gret hynesse.	*serve*
	Straytt therto I take the way.	*Straight*

In heremo.   *In the desert*

[The Desert]

SECUNDUS ANGELUS	Mary, be glad, and in hart strong	
	To reseyve the palme of grett vytory!	*receive; victory*
2095	This day ye shall be reseyvyd wyth angellys song!	*received*
	Yower sowle shall departe from yower body.	

---

[1] Lines 2079–80: *Bid him provide my body in the form of bread (the eucharist), / To housel (administer the sacrament to) her*

MARY MAUDLEYN   O good Lord, I thank thee withowt veryawns!   *steadfastly*
         This day I am groundyd all in goodnesse,   *fixed*
         Wyth hart and body concludyd in substawns.   *essentially brought to an end*
2100   I thanke thee, Lord, with speryt of perfythnesse!   *spirit of perfection*

         Hic aparuit angelus et presbityr cum corpus domenicum.[1]

[PREST]   Thou blyssyd woman, inure in mekenesse,   *practiced*
         I have browth thee the bred of lyf to thi syth,   *brought; sight*
         To make thee suere from all dystresse,   *sure (secure)*
         Thi sowle to bryng to evyrlastyng lyth.

MARY MAUDLEYN   O thou mythty Lord of hye magesté,
2106   This celestyall bred for to determyn,
         This tyme to reseyve it in me,
fol. 144v My sowle therwith to illumyn.

         Her she reseyvyt it.

         I thanke thee, Lord of ardent love![2]
2110   Now I know well I shall nat opprese.   *be overwhelmed*
         Lord, lett me se thi joyys above!
         I recummend my sowle onto thi blysse.   *commend*
         Lord, opyn thi blyssyd gatys!   *gates*
         Thys erth at this tyme fervenly I kysse!   *fervently*
2115   *In manus tuas, Domine.*   *Into your hands, Lord*
         Lord, wyth thi grace me wysse.   *direct*
         Commendo spiritum meum. Redemisti me,
         Dominus Deus veritatis.[3]

PRIMUS ANGELUS   Now reseyve we this sowle, as reson is,   *as is right*
2120   In heven to dwelle us among.

SECUNDUS ANGELUS   Wythowtyn end to be in blysse,
         Now lett us syng a mery song!

         Gaudent in celis.   *They rejoice in heaven*

PREST   O good God, grett is thi grace!
         O Jhesu, Jhesu, blessyd be thi name!
2125   A, Mary, Mary, mych is thi solas,   *much (great); solace*

---

[1] *Here appear the angel and the priest with the body of the Lord (the eucharist)*

[2] Lines 2106–09: *I thank you, Lord of ardent love, / For determining (deciding) that this celestial bread / I should receive at this time / [And] thereby illuminate my soul*

[3] Lines 2117–18: *I commend my spirit. You have redeemed me, Lord God of Truth* (Psalms 30:6)

        In heven blysse with glé and game.

        Thi body wyl I cure from alle manyr blame,[1]

        And I wyll passe to the bosshop of the seté,   *go; bishop; city*

        Thys body of Mary to berye be name,   *bury*

2130   Wyth all reverens and solemnyté.

fol. 145r Sufferens, of this processe, thus enddyt the sentens[2]

        That we have playyd in yower syth.

        Allemythty God, most of magnyfycens,

        Mote bryng yow to hys blysse so brygth,   *May [he]*

2135   In presens of that kyng.

        Now, frendys, thus endyt thys matere,   *matter*

        To blysse bryng tho that byn here.   *those; are*

        Now, clerkys, wyth voycys cler,   *voices*

        "*Te Deum laudamus*" lett us syng.   *We praise you, God*

        Explicit oreginale de Sancta Maria Magdalena.[3]

2140   Yff ony thyng amysse be,   *amiss*

        Blame connyng, and nat me.   *learning*

        I desyer the redars to be my frynd,   *desire; readers; friend*

        Yff ther be ony amysse, that to amend.[4]

---

[1] *This body will I care for (protect) from all manner of harm*

[2] *Sovereigns, thus ends the substance of this play*

[3] *Here ends the original of Saint Mary Magdalene*

[4] *If there be anything amiss, [may the reader] amend it*

EXPLANATORY NOTES

ABBREVIATIONS: *AND*: Anglo-Norman Dictionary; **B**: *Medieval Drama*, ed. Bevington; **BMH**: *Late Medieval Religious Plays*, ed. Baker, Murphy, and Hall; **C**: Coletti, "'Curtesy doth it yow lere': The Sociology of Transgression in the Digby *Mary Magdalene*"; **Chester**: *The Chester Mystery Cycle*, ed. Lumiansky and Mills; **CT**: Chaucer, *Canterbury Tales*, ed. Benson; **EETS**: Early English Text Society; **F**: Findon, *Lady, Hero, Saint*; **GL**: *Critical Edition of the Legend of Mary Magdalena,* ed. Mycoff; **LA**: Jacobus de Voragine, *Legenda Aurea*, ed. Ryan; **M**: Maltman, "Light In and On the Digby *Mary Magdalene*"; **ME**: Middle English; **MED**: *Middle English Dictionary*; **MDS**: Coletti, *Mary Magdalene and the Drama of Saints*; **MP**: *Macro Plays*, ed. Eccles; **NT**: *N-Town Play*, ed. Spector; **PDD**: Coletti, "'*Paupertas est donum Dei*'"; **s.d.**: stage direction; **Towneley**: *The Towneley Plays*, ed. Stevens and Cawley; **Whiting:** Whiting, *Proverbs, Sentences, and Proverbial Phrases*.

1	*forfetur. MED, forfeture* (n.), sense 2c. In phrases with "in," the phrase means "on pain of losing, under penalty of losing."
9	*Tyberyus Sesar.* Roman emperor (42 BCE–37 CE) during the life and ministry of Jesus. No other ME life of Mary Magdalene depicts Caesar as ruler. Velz ("Sovereignty in the Digby") argues that the appearance of Tiberius and his political functionaries Herod and Pilate establishes the play's focus on forms of sovereignty and subjection, just and unjust rule. Mitchell-Buck ("Tyrants, Tudors") notes an abundance of tyrants in the play.
20	*Serybyl* (speech heading). This unusual name appears to denote an official function. BMH (pp. 197–98) suggest possible echoes of the Sibyl and the similarity of Serybyl to the "skrybe" addressed in line 114. Serybyl is called "Syrybbe" at line 33.
21	*Belyall.* A biblical term, deriving from 2 Corinthians 6:15 and 3 Kings 21:10, and indicating the personification of evil, often used as a synonym of Satan.
24	*provost. MED, provost* (n.), sense a: "the representative of a king or emperor in a country or district; governor, administrator."
44, s.d.	*all the pepul.* This is the first of several scenes in the play indicating the presence of a group, implying even a small crowd, of non-speaking characters.
46	*wyn and spycys.* Wine sweetened and seasoned with spices was a regular feature of meals prepared for aristocrats and other prosperous medieval people. For recipes and commentary, see Freedman, *Out of the East*, pp. 22–23. Dugan (*Ephemeral History of Perfume*, p. 37) notes that the play's "many calls for 'wine

and spices' mimic structures of trade symbolism . . . [and provide] stage properties culled from medieval markets."

49   *Syrus* (speech heading). Medieval versions of Mary Magdalene's legendary life created a domestic backstory for her reputed career as a sinner by giving her a nuclear family. The Digby play amplifies her father Syrus' brief role in that story. The *Legenda Aurea*, Jacobus de Voragine's thirteenth-century collection of saints' lives, provided the best known and most influential version of Mary Magdalene's legendary acts and wanderings (*GL*, pp. 117–44). Textual commentary on the play in BMH include detailed extracts from Jacobus' vita, thereby enabling comparison with the Digby play's representation of these non-biblical elements.

51   *bower*. MED, *bour* (n.), sense 1a: "a dwelling, house, mansion, cottage."

55   *be cleffys so cold*. BMH (p. 198) note the playwright's use here of a common verse tag, citing an analogy in the *Croxton Play of the Sacrament*, "be the clyffys cold" (line 100).

71   *ful of femynyté*. Cyrus is the first to speak this important word in the play (see lines 423, 516, 943, 1356). T. Williams (*Inventing Womanhood*, pp. 149, 4) argues that "femininity" emerges as a new gendered term in late medieval English writing, calling attention to the "evolution of gendered language" in a period when "what it meant to be a woman . . . was very much an open question." Dixon ("'Thys Body of Mary'") discusses the bodily dimensions of femininity in the play and in late medieval women's spirituality.

71–74   *Here is Mary . . . . hart with consolacyon*. C (p. 5) notes that Cyrus' courtly language here anticipates the idiom employed by the King of Flesh (line 423) and the king of Marseilles (lines 942–49), as well as the entire verbal performance of Mary Magdalene's tempter, Curiosity. Such language also affirms the "jentyll" status claimed by Cyrus and his family (lines 105, 112–13). Cyrus' introduction of his children (see also lines 66–70) resembles the account of their many physical and social gifts in the thirteenth-century life of the saint sometimes attributed to Rabanus Maurus. See *Life of Saint Mary Magdalene*, ed. Mycoff, p. 29.

73   *merrorys*. MED, *mirour* (n.), sense 3a: "a model of good or virtuous conduct."

81   *thys castell*. When Cyrus identifies his bequest to daughter Mary Magdalene as *thys castell*, he both draws upon Jacobus de Voragine's idea that she derived her identity from the castle Magdalo, as Caxton's translation puts it (*GL*, p. 118), and situates his family within the social and economic matrix of the feudal world. See *PDD*, pp. 347–49. At the same time, medieval literary castles are potent and multivalent symbols, pointing to spiritual and material allegorical meanings. For example, as Riggio has shown ("Allegory of Feudal Acquisition"), in the East Anglian morality play *Castle of Perseverance*, the trope of the individual Christian soul's protective spiritual enclosure spills out onto the economic realities and pressures of feudal society. Mary Magdalene's castle merits attention in light of the proliferation of allegorical castles in medieval English and continental literature. See Cornelius, "Figurative Castle."

83–84   *Thes gyftes . . . . in good mynd.* Cyrus repeats the idiom of late medieval testators who similarly pledged that their bequests were made under such conditions: John Baret (1463), "I, John Baret . . . of good mynde and memorye"; and John Wastell (1515), "I, John Wastell . . . beyng of good and hool mynde." See Tymms, *Wills and Inventories*, pp. 15, 113.

87–88   *Ye have grauntyd swych a lyfelod . . . . from all nessesyté.* MED, *lif-lod(e* (n.), sense 2a; *MED, necessité* (n.), sense b. Lazarus invokes key terms from late medieval discourses on poverty and charity; Mary Magdalene explicitly refers to the "peynes of poverté" from which their father's gift frees her and her siblings (line 96). These terms signal the play's engagement with the relationship of economic discourses and social practices to construction of spiritual identities by the dominant classes in late medieval England. See *PDD*, pp. 347–49.

93–94   *Thatt God . . . . hony be kynd.* Mary Magdalene's reference to the "sweet" name of God anticipates the preoccupation with the name of Jesus expressed later in the play; see lines 761, 1446, 1468, 1555–62, 2031–32, 2124. From the thirteenth century, the Name of Jesus was the subject of a devotional cult that attracted monastic and lay participants. The Holy Name was honored in the Jesus mass and eventually in the new liturgical Feast of the Name of Jesus. The cult of the Holy Name was particularly popular in England. Declared official by the province of York in 1489, the Feast of the Holy Name appears frequently in liturgical service books of the late fifteenth and early sixteenth centuries, the period in which the Digby *Magdalene* was composed and copied in its single manuscript. See Pfaff, *New Liturgical Feasts*, pp. 62–83, and Renevey, "Name above Names." F (p. 58) suggests that Mary's reference to sweetness "introduces the first of many allusions in the play to the *Song of Songs.*"

97   *streytnes.* MED, *streitnes(se* (n.), sense 6a: "trouble, difficulty . . . hardship (esp. financial hardship), straitened circumstances; a state of impoverishment."

106   *So mekly.* MED, *mek* (adj.), sense 1b: "full of loving kindness, benevolent, kind, sweet"; and *MED, meke* (adv.): "humbly, submissively."

107–09   *Hey in heven . . . . shal hens passe.* Mary Magdalene and her siblings appear to be proto-Christians, all making reference to a singular God in this scene.

110   *mygthtys.* MED, *might* (n.), sense 3a: "ability, capability, capacity."

111   *enhanse.* MED, *enhauncen* (v.), sense 5: "to elevate or advance (someone to a high rank or station)."

112   *wyn and spycys.* Cyrus' call for wine and spices caps a scene in which he and his children declare their interest in the comfort afforded by material assets. On land-grabbing and conspicuous consumption by East Anglian gentry whom the play seems implicitly to address, see *PDD*, pp. 347–49. As Coletti notes ("Design of the Digby Play"), this is the first of many scenes associating Mary Magdalene with corporeal, heavenly, and sacramental food. See also note to line 46 above.

117   *Herowdys.* Among the several generations of the Herodian dynasty, scripture and traditions of biblical commentary attend to three important rulers: Herod the

Great (of Ascalon), his son Herod Antipas, and his grandson, Herod Agrippa. Writers of medieval English biblical drama follow traditions associated with Herod the Great, appointed by the Romans as King of the Jews in 37–34 BCE; but the sources they used sometimes conflated elements of the lives of these different Herods. For example, the Herod who was contemporary with the adult Jesus — and would be the historically accurate figure in the Digby play's scriptural narrative — was Herod Antipas. Nonetheless, the play gives him attributes that other English biblical dramas ascribed to Herod the Great, who was responsible for the Massacre of the Innocents (Matthew 2:13–18). See Coletti ("Story of Herod") for discussion of and extensive bibliography on this figure in medieval drama.

118   *Pylat.* Luke's gospel (3:1) names Pilate as governor of Judea in the reign of Tiberius Caesar. See note to lines 1255–56 below.

120–28 *Take hed . . . . make with malynacyon.* The syntax of the emperor's speech is convoluted and unclear: he commands Herod and Pilate either to do harm to any people in their respective realms who speak against Caesar himself and his laws and gods; or he warns them that such will be the fate of those persons. The reference at line 126 to the regent who holds "his croun" from Caesar by right pertains only to Herod.

120   *my precept wretyn be.* On the importance of writing and its attestation to complex influences of late medieval documentary culture, see Lim, "Pilate's Special Letter."

121   *owit wrech.* Literally, "to owe (or incur) harm." *MED, ouen* (v.), sense 2; and *MED, wrech(e* (n.), sense 2. See also the textual note on this line.

127   *harlettys. MED, harlot* (n.), sense 1b: "as term of abuse: scoundrel, knave, rogue, reprobate, base fellow, coward."

133   *So bere thes lettyrs.* Scherb (*Staging Faith*, p. 179) highlights the secular and spiritual importance of letters in the play. See also Lim, "Pilate's Special Letter." Northway ("It's All in the Delivery") discusses the relationship of letter-bearing to documentary practices and political culture in the early modern period, but with interesting implications for the Digby *Magdalene.*

136   *Nuncyus* (speech heading). Scherb (*Staging Faith*, pp. 172–73) notes the prevalence of messengers in large-scale East Anglian plays such as the Digby *Magdalene*, where they serve to link the occupants of various scaffolds. Messengers are also prominent in the *Castle of Perseverance* and the *N-Town Plays.*

140   *In the wyld, wanyng world. MED, waning(e* (ger.), sense 3c notes that this phrase "in a direct address" means "a curse upon you."

143   *Mahond.* Medieval English drama is replete with characters who profess devotion to Mohammed (Mahond, Mahowne, Mahowdys, etc.), the prophet of Islam whom they erroneously take for a god. Although dramatic invocations of Mohammed function differently from play to play, they generally denote a false god whose worship is contrasted to devotion to Christianity's true God. Appeals to Mahond/Mahowne in biblical plays are always anachronistic, since the

prophet of Islam was not born until the sixth century. The Digby Herod is not the only Jew in English biblical drama to pledge loyalty to Mahond; e.g., the Towneley manuscript's "Herod" play associates its main character with Mahowne (*Towneley*, 1:183–204); and the Jews of the *Croxton Play of the Sacrament* also invoke Machomet (see lines 149, 209, 332, 453). The Digby Herod's swearing by "Mahondys bonys" (line 142) echoes Christian oaths that anatomized the body of Christ, a practice that Chaucer's Pardoner excoriates (*CT* VI[C] 629–60), and demonstrates the tendency, in ME dramatic texts, for worship of Mahond to mimic that of the Christian god. See Chemers, "Anti-Semitism" and Leshock, "Representation of Islam."

156   *in dowt*. MED, *dout(e* (n.), sense 4: "a cause or reason for fear; something to be feared; danger, peril."

158–59   *Lord of Alapye . . . . Beryaby, and Bedlem*. BMH (pp. 283–84) modernize these names: Aleppo, Asia, Tyre, Hebron, Beersheba, Bethlehem. Similar geographical catalogs appear in the *Croxton Play of the Sacrament* (lines 94–116); the *Castle of Perseverance* (*MP*, p. 8, lines 170–78); and the *N-Town Play* (*NT*, 1: 218–19, lines 157–75).

163   *provostycacyon*. The word is a fine example of the playwright's ingenious creation of neologisms. BMH (p. 199) provide the gloss: "whom I serve in the office of provost."

167   *Phylysofyr* (speech heading). Herod's consultation with philosophers who interpret biblical prophecy in the play (lines 175–76, 184–85) is reminiscent of his conversations with the Magi and other wisdom figures in the Magi and Innocents plays of the English biblical cycle plays. The most extensive such discussion appears in play 8, "The Three Kings," of the Chester Cycle (*Chester*, 1:156–74).

171–76   *skreptour gevytt informacyon . . . . splendore ortus tui*. Lim notes that the reading practices of Herod and his philosophers rely on a mode of literal interpretation that "ignores the spiritual message of the Gospel" ("Pilate's Special Letter," p. 6).

172   *rehersse*. MED, *rehersen* (v.), sense 1a: "to narrate (a story, that something happened), report, tell; describe."

188   *fleyyng flappys*. MED, *fleing* (ger.1), sense 2a: "loss of skin by burning, scalding, tearing, etc.; an abrasion; an excoriation"; *MED*, *flappe* (n.), sense 2: "a device for slapping or striking; a flapper; a scourge."

190   *Ye langbaynnes! Loselles!* Herod's angry response to the interpretation of scriptural prophecy also echoes the name-calling, boasting, and cries for vengeance that characterize his performance in the English biblical cycles. See Coletti, "Story of Herod" and references therein.

194   *They ar but folys*. Primus Miles here refers to the philosophers who have advised Herod but implicitly also to the books that the wise men invoke.

202   *grettly rejoysyth to my sprytes indede.* In a typical twisting of grammar and syntax,
           the playwright (or scribe) adds the gratuitous preposition "to," which must take
           as its object "sprytes," the word that also acts as direct object of the verb
           "rejoysyth." The sense of lines 202–03 thus seems to be: "This [the soldier's
           announcement] is to me a gracious exhortation, one that brings great joy to my
           spirits."

204   *I woll suffer non to spryng of that kenred.* Herod declares his interest in halting the
           production of lineage by the genealogy ("kenred," or kindred) whose triumph
           is asserted in biblical prophecies. Plays on the Massacre of the Innocents in
           medieval English biblical drama represent this subject with imagination and
           creativity. Foundational to Herod's wrathful anxiety in these plays is the
           medieval account of his own tortured genealogical and familial crimes. In this
           account, Herod is motivated by political ambitions that sought to disavow his low
           birth as well as the derivative nature of power held not in his own right but by
           Roman sanction. Based on Josephus' *Jewish War* and *Jewish Antiquities* and
           developed by Eusebius' *Historia Ecclesiastica*, the medieval English story of Herod
           took shape in Peter Comestor's *Historia Scholastica*, Ranulph Higden's
           Polychronicon, and their translation and redaction in many historical and
           homiletic works. See Coletti, "Story of Herod," pp. 40–47; and "Saint Anne
           Dedication," pp. 34–36. In the *Killing of the Children* (BMH, p. 101, lines
           125–26), a play on the Massacre preserved in the same manuscript as *Mary
           Magdalene*, for example, Herod's dynastic ambitions are reinforced by a soldier
           who erroneously declares: "we hold you for chef regent, / By titelle of
           enheritaunce, as your auncetours beforn."

209–12   *Heyll . . . . in thi regensy.* The first of many moments of greeting and salutation in
           the play, the scene points to the wide ranging signifying capacities of the
           behavior and gestures that accompany them. Palmer ("Gestures of Greeting")
           provides a rich inventory of possibilities that invite application to such moments,
           e.g., Mary Magdalene's many angelic greetings.

213–14   *sofereyn . . . . soveren.* The spelling of the same word within the space of two lines
           highlights the scribe's inconsistencies, and possible haste.

217–24   *Be he sekyr . . . . thorow the hartt.* BMH (p. 200) note the strong resemblance to
           lines 97–104 in *The Killing of the Children* (also in BMH, pp. 98–115).

234   *pregedyse. MED, prejudice* (n.), sense 2c is a legal term meaning "detriment or
           damage caused to persons, organizations, or property by the disregarding or
           violation of a legal right."

237   *prommyssary and presedent. MED, procuratour* (n.), sense 1c: "the governor of a
           province; a viceroy, regent, or deputy"; *MED, president* (n.), sense 1a: "a ruler or
           head of either sovereign or subordinate status; often, one invested with judicial
           powers."

238   *inperrowpent.* See the textual note for this line.

253   *lover. MED, lover(e* (n.2), sense 1c: "one who loves his king, a loyal subject."

257   *Martes.* Pilate's invocation of Mars, the Roman god of war, affirms his aggressive persona even as it adds another detail to the play's allusions to Western classical antiquity.

264, s.d.   *Syrus takyt his deth.* Occurring without warning, Cyrus' demise exemplifies the horror of the *mors improvisa*, the unanticipated death that could catch body and soul unaware and unprepared, as underscored by "sodenly" at line 276, s.d. On *mors improvisa*, see Duffy, *Stripping of the Altars*, pp. 310–13; for this scene, see Coletti, "Social Contexts," pp. 294–95. Appleford's *Learning to Die* provides important insights that can inform the Digby play's representations of death and dying.

270   *help me to my bede.* Noting the proliferation of sleeping subjects and dead bodies in the play, M (p. 258) observes: "No medieval play makes such extensive use of beds as does the Digby *Mary Magdalene.*"

276, s.d.   *avoydyt. MED, avoiden* (v.), sense 5a: "to depart from or abandon (a place, a position); vacate (a dwelling); go away, withdraw." The Digby author uses this verb frequently in his stage directions.

285   *inwyttissymus God.* See *MED, witen* (v.1). The verb form, with its various meanings related to possession of knowledge, would seem to be the basis for one of the Digby playwright's experiments with aureate diction, in this instance affirming Mary Magdalene's elaboration of attributes of the deity. My reading departs from that of BMH (p. 200).

299   *Thys castell is owerys with all the fee.* See *MED, fe* (n.2). Lazarus' term unambiguously situates possession of the castle within the economy of late medieval inheritance practices.

304, s.d.   *Her shal entyr . . . thus seyyng the World.* The appearance of this evil cohort, presumably on separate scaffolds, marks the play's shift from the biblical historical world to an allegorical one. No other ME life of Mary Magdalene makes her the victim of colluding immoral forces. The World, the Flesh, the Devil, and the Seven Deadly Sins are not only frequent subjects but also organizing principles of anonymous medieval homiletic and catechetical writing and works by well known ME writers; e.g., among their many literary identities, Chaucer's Parson's Tale and Gower's *Confessio Amantis* are both penitential works structured by appeals to the Seven Deadly Sins. The Digby *Magdalene*'s cohort of tempters also appear together, though differently grouped, in the East Anglian *Castle of Perseverance.* BMH (pp. 200–01) compare the two plays' arrangement of these evil alliances.

306   *prymatt portature. MED, primate* (adj.): "highest in rank, chief"; *MED, portour* (n.), sense a ("a bearer") is probably used metaphorically here.

311   *recure. MED, recuren* (v.), sense 8a: "to acquire (something), obtain; achieve (peace, one's purpose)."

312   *whele of fortune.* World's alliance with the wheel of fortune is hardly surprising. The concept of Fortune and her wheel figures ubiquitously in medieval

reflections on the instability of human circumstances and fates, i.e. human existence in the material world. Boethius' adaptation of the Roman goddess Fortuna in *The Consolation of Philosophy* (523 CE) established the basic terms for representations of Fortune over the next millennium. For an overview, see Greene, "Fortune."

313–22   *In me restyt . . . . of so gret puernesse.* BMH (p. 201) cite Morton Bloomfield's classic study *The Seven Deadly Sins* (pp. 234 ff.) to affirm the traditional association of the seven sins with metals of the then seven planets, which here include the sun and moon (lines 315–16).

324   *seven prynsys of hell.* That is, the Seven Deadly Sins.

329   *mynystracyon.* MED, *ministracioun* (n.), sense 3: "governing service or management."

333, s.d. *Her shal entyr the Kyng of Flesch wyth Slowth, Gloteny, Lechery.* Appropriately, the King of Flesh is accompanied by the sins associated with bodily transgressions, such as Sloth's laziness, Gluttony's overindulgence in food and drink, and Lechery's overindulgence in sexual behaviors.

335   *deyntys.* MED, *deinte* (n.), sense 4: "a luxury; a precious thing."

338–44   *For I have comfortatywys . . . . delycyus use I.* Flesh's "deyntys delycyows" constitute a virtual catalog of the most popular medieval spices, including galingale, long pepper, and grains of paradise; their representation here introduces the aromatic balms that will become the penitent Magdalene's iconic emblem. As Freedman (*Out of the East*, pp. 1–75) notes, these and other spices attained widespread use in medieval cookery, but they were also understood to have medicinal properties, as were certain gemstones (Flesh also possesses "margaretton" or pearls in line 339). Dugan (*Ephemeral History of Perfume*, pp. 38–41) traces the unfolding of the olfactory sense in the play, noting its power to trespass bodily and other boundaries. BMH (p. 201) note that similar catalogs appear in *The Croxton Play of the Sacrament* (lines 173–88) and John Heywood's *Play Called the Four PP* (lines 604–43). Flesh's claim to jurisdiction over these pharmaceutical products makes him a sort of diabolical apothecary and a carnal foil to the *Christus medicus*, Christ the physician, appearing elsewhere in the play; see Coletti, "Social Contexts," pp. 292–93 and sources cited therein. The ubiquitous presence of spices in medieval food preparation and medicine suggests that Flesh's "comfortatywys" would likely be familiar to the dramatic audience. F (pp. 83–88) discusses the overlapping properties of culinary and medicinal herbs in the play.

352–55   *O ye prynse . . . . to your jentylnesse.* Lechery's appeal to the language of status echoes the interests of Cyrus and his family in the play's earlier scene (lines 49–113).

354   *aprowe.* MED, *ap(p)reven* (v.), sense 4: "to approve of (something); of an authority: approve, sanction, endorse, confirm formally."

356   *byrd.* MED, *birde* (n.1), sense 1: "a woman of noble birth; damsel, lady." See also the note to line 565 below.

357   *to halse.* MED, *halsen* (v.2), sense 1a: "to embrace or caress (somebody) as a sign
        of affection; embrace or fondle (somebody) sexually."

358–76 *Now I . . . . for my sake.* Devils play a decisive role in the Digby play. DiSalvo
        ("Unexpected Saints," pp. 70–75) states that the play's inclusion of
        "supernatural elements associated with . . . devils" enables the protagonist "to
        be" a "saint" (p. 70). DiSalvo compares the devils of *Mary Magdalene* with those
        of its companion play in Bodleian MS Digby 133, *The Conversion of St. Paul.* The
        play's devils also provide occasions for its most spectacular scenes.

358   *prykkyd in pryde.* See *MED, priken* (v.), sense 8a. BMH (p. 202) cite the appearance
        of this common tag of being 'pricked' or 'dressed up' in pride in the East
        Anglian *Castle of Perseverance* (*MP*, p. 8, line 159 and p. 9, line 209).

360   *atyred.* MED, *tiren* (v.3), sense 2a: "to equip (a knight) for battle, arm; also,
        prepare (oneself) for combat or a military expedition."

363   *bryng to abaye.* MED, *abai* (n.), sense 2 cites the phrase "at abai" to mean "in
        extreme difficulties, at the mercy of an enemy."

366–67 *For at hem . . . . for ther pryde.* Here the Devil explains his reasoning for
        instigating the fall of humankind and his continuing interest in tempting
        humanity, now represented by the vulnerable Mary Magdalene: he is jealous of
        the joy that Lucifer lost when he fell from heaven to hell, a joy that humanity
        somehow proleptically still experiences, even though Christ's death, and the
        redemption that accompanies it, have yet to occur in the world of the play.
        Nomenclature in this passage is confusing. The speaker self-identifies as Satan
        (line 359); whereas some accounts make Satan the fallen angel Lucifer, here
        Satan speaks as if Lucifer is a different being (lines 366–67).

368   *The snarys that I shal set wher nevyr set at Troye.* The devil's allusion to the snares,
        or tricks, whereby the Greeks overcame the city of Troy bears witness to the deep
        knowledge of the Trojan story in late medieval England. Resources on this topic
        are vast; for a foundational study see Benson, *History of Troy.*

375   *skowte.* Possibly from *MED, scouten* (v.): "to search, scout."

377   *Wyth wrath or wyhyllys we shal hyrre wynne.* A potentially confusing shift of
        pronouns occurs suddenly here. In the preceding speech Satan has spoken of his
        desire to besiege the human soul; accordingly he uses specifically masculine or
        gender-neutral plural pronouns ("he" in lines 366, 370; "hym" in line 372;
        "hem" in lines 366, 369, 370). The use of feminine singular pronouns by Wrath
        and Envy ("hyrre" in line 377; "hur" in line 378) signals an abrupt shift of focus
        to Mary Magdalene. See also BMH (p. 202) on variant readings of this line.

383   *afyauns.* The rhyme scheme here may have prompted the playwright to conflate
        MED, affiaunce (n.), sense 2; and *MED, affinité* (n.), sense 1c.

384   *A woman of whorshep ower servant to make.* Satan employs the feudal language of
        service to signify the relationship of the World, the Flesh, and the Devil to their
        minions. For example, Satan commands "knythtys" (line 373) and is the head
        of a "howshold" (line 403). Lechery tempts Mary Magdalene by offering her

"servyse" and "atendauns" (line 424). See *MED*, *servaunt* (n.), sense 1a; *service* (n.), sense 3c; and *worship(e* (n.), sense 3b. The spelling of "whorshep" (worship) may involve a pun here, given Mary Magdalene's traditional reputation for sexual profligacy.

387   *asemlanus*. *MED*, *as(s)emble* (n.), sense 2: "a group of people gathered for a purpose."

407   *arere*. *MED*, *areren* (v.), sense 13a: "to arouse or stir up (somebody), stimulate or incite (to action)."

412   *comprehend*. *MED*, *comprehenden* (v.), sense 3a: "to put . . . into words, describe, explain."

413   *devyse*. *MED*, *devis* (n.), sense 3c: "a device, scheme, stratagem, intrigue."

414–17   *Serys . . . . beryt the pryse*. Mary Magdalene is also targeted by disguised allegorical tempters in Lewis Wager's *Life and Repentaunce of Mary Magdalene* (White, *Reformation Biblical Drama*, pp. 11–28), where the evil crew includes Pride of Life, Cupiditie, and Carnall Concupiscence.

420   *She shal byn abyll to dystroye helle*. Mundus' extraordinary claim about the unfallen Magdalene seems to conflate her powers with those of the Virgin Mary; as such, his is the first of many allusions aligning the play's heroine with the mother of Jesus. In fearing that Mary Magdalene may be able to "destroy hell," Mundus invokes scriptural commentary that identified the Virgin Mary as the woman of Genesis 3:14–15 who will "crush" the serpent's head. Hence Mundus' statement seems to associate the defeat of the serpent (Genesis 3:14–15 reports God's warning to the successful tempter of Adam and Eve) with a more general destruction of hell, the serpent (Lucifer/Satan's) home. Spector (*NT*, 2:421n2/259–66; 434n7/51–2) cites allusions to this attribute of the Virgin Mary in the N-Town plays of the "Fall of Man" (1:32, lines 259–66) and "Jesse Root," or the Prophets' Play (1:67, lines 49–56), noting that this symbolic understanding of Marian power also appears in the Anglo-Norman *Jeu d'Adam* and Philippe de Mézières' play on the Presentation of Mary in the Temple. For the texts, see B, p. 101, lines 479–90; and *Philippe de Mézières' Campaign*, ed. Coleman, p. 102, lines 19–21.

425   *beral of bewte*. F (pp. 59–60) notes the frequent appearance of the beryl in medieval English lyric poetry. Medieval lapidaries describe the beryl as a gemstone "that fostered love between man and woman" (p. 59), alluding also to the gem's potentially erotic meanings. At the same time, lapidaries also speak to the beryl's healing properties.

428   *Spiritus malyngny*. The designation of the Bad Angel as a "spiritus malyngny" (or "malyng" as in line 434) anticipates the play's later interest in establishing the authenticity and moral probity of spiritual visitations. See notes to lines 601–02, 716, 1376, and 2010.

430   *all the six*. That is, the remaining six deadly sins, excluding Lechery, who is already engaged in the effort to bring Mary Magdalene to sin.

438   *I trotte hyr to tene.* MED, *tenen* (v.), sense 1: "to do somebody harm; harass, annoy, oppress."

439, s.d.   *Her shal alle . . . . Lechery shall entyr the castell.* Luxuria's easy access to Mary Magdalene's castle, which is also her namesake, suggests the architectural allegorization of the body as castle of the soul, capable of warding off malevolent moral intruders through the exercise of virtue but also vulnerable to succumbing to them. See note to line 81 above; Findon, "'Now is aloft,'" p. 249; and Whitehead, *Castles of the Mind*, pp. 87–116.

440–44   *Heyl, lady . . . . your aungelly delycyté.* Luxuria's address ("Heyl . . . Heyl") ironically echoes Gabriel's Annunciation to the Virgin Mary portrayed in other English biblical plays. In the Towneley Annunciation, Mary similarly inquires about her visitor's identity: "What is thi name?" (*Towneley*, lines 77–107). D. Williams (*French Fetish*, pp. 114–17) notes how quickly Mary Magdalene picks up Lechery's seductive language, an idiom, coded as French and feminine, that "removes Mary from the humdrum quotidian, and places her . . . within the rarified world of French romance" (p. 115). Williams suggests that Lechery, even though she is "Lady Lechery," is intent on seducing Mary Magdalene, thereby creating opportunities for homoerotic play that would only be compounded if both parts were played by boys or young men. Lechery's language becomes more obscure and convoluted as the scene unfolds, e.g., lines 456–59.

440   *alyauuns.* MED, *allia(u)nce* (n.), sense 3: "family connections established through marriage."

441   *oryent.* MED, *orient* (adj.), sense c: "brilliant, shining, fair."

447   *ravyssyt.* See MED, *ravishen* (v.), sense 4. The sense of ravishment carries a wide semantic range in ME, connoting both physical and spiritual senses of being emotionally and mentally moved or transported.

457   *obusyons may brede myche dysese.* MED, *abusioun* (n.), sense 1: "misuse, perversion, abuse"; *dysese.* MED, *disese* (n.), sense 1b: "that which inflicts hardship, misery, or misfortune; grievance, harm, injury, wrong." The naming of Mary Magdalene's "dysese" introduces here the notion of physical as well as spiritual illness that will eventually be healed by Christ, the "hartys leche" to which Magdalene's speech ironically alludes in line 461.

459   *Prynt.* MED, *emprenten* (v.), sense 8: "to stimulate, arouse, or move (a person) to a state of mind or a course of action."

462–69   *Brother Lazarus . . . . place from wreche.* Here Mary Magdalene entrusts the keeping of her castle to her brother Lazarus and sister Martha. The guardianship of property and household was a constant preoccupation of East Anglian landed families. See *PDD*, pp. 347–49.

463   *in substawns.* MED, *substaunce*, sense 6e. When used with "in," the phrase means "for all intents and purposes, in the main, generally."

469   *wreche.* MED, *wrech(e* (n.), sense 2: "destruction; misery; harm; also, calamity, misfortune."

470   *I am a taverner.* The scene of Mary Magdalene's seduction in the tavern is one of
       the playwright's major additions to her traditional vita. Taverns appear
       frequently in medieval comic and homiletic writing, where they figure as sites of
       both amusement and sin. Scherb (*Staging Faith*, pp. 175–76) highlights the
       pleasures and dangers of some medieval literary taverns. As Coletti observes, the
       Digby play's tavern is also implicated in, and evokes the values of, commercial
       exchange in the medieval mercantile economy. Mary Magdalene's tavern
       repartee, first with Luxuria and then Curiosity, is inflected by status-
       consciousness; see C, pp. 6–7, and sources cited therein. According to Strohm
       ("Three London Itineraries," p. 10), the medieval urban tavern was "a place
       where reconsideration . . . of social status might occur." In the Dutch play *Mary
       of Nemmegen*, another unruly girl meets trouble in a tavern similarly situated at
       the intersection of economics and morality. See Sponsler, *Drama and Resistance*,
       pp. 95–102. Streitman ("Face of Janus") discusses resemblances between the
       Digby saint play and the Dutch play.

474–80 *Of wynys . . . . ye can goo.* The international wine list of which the taverner boasts
       gives a worldly wise dimension to the site of Mary Magdalene's assignation,
       especially from a commercial perspective. BMH (p. 203) gloss the taverner's
       wine list primarily in terms of country of origin; however, "clary wynne,"
       "claret," and "vernage" signify types of wine or medicinal drinks. See *MED, clare*
       (n.1); *claret* (n.1); *vernage* (n.). The list is reminiscent of the list of countries
       where Aristorius' "merchaundyse renneth" in the *Croxton Play of the Sacrament*
       (lines 93–116).

481   *thee comfort and thee sokower. MED, comforten* (v.), sense 3a: "to refresh (somebody
       with food or drink); refresh oneself"; *MED, socouren* (v.), sense 1b: "to furnish
       sustenance; furnish (somebody) with the necessities of life." The two reflexive
       verbs here show the dramatist employing two words when one would have done.

486   *good restoratyff.* The taverner's recommendation of his wine as an effective cordial
       that provides relief from "stodyys and hevynes" (line 488) elides the wine's
       intoxicating functions with quasi-medicinal purposes.

490   *To me ye be courtes and kynde.* Mary's attention to the taverner's courtesy
       prefigures her interactions with the gallant.

491   *Hof, hof, hof! A frysch new galaunt.* By the mid-fifteenth century, the gallant was
       recognized as a satiric and socioeconomic type, especially by moralists and
       homilists who condemned the gallant's material excess, sartorial extravagance,
       and aspirations to high social status. The Digby play's gallant thus aligns Mary
       Magdalene's seduction with a well-developed discourse of social critique. See
       Davenport, "'Lusty Fresche Galaunts'" and C, pp. 7–12, and sources cited therein.
       According to Davenport (p. 114), "*hoff* (or *hof* or *huffa*)" is a signature of the
       gallant's speech. The gallant makes frequent appearances in medieval East
       Anglian drama. In Satan's prologue to N-Town's "Conspiracy" play and *Wisdom*,
       Lucifer dons the guise of the gallant. The eponymous protagonist of the Macro
       Mankind is lured into sin by a trio of gallants: Nought, New Guise, and
       Nowadays. Superbia, or Pride, in the *Castle of Perseverance* sports a gallant's
       attire. Cox (*The Devil and the Sacred*, pp. 64–65) claims that the Digby play's

Curiosity, like the gallants in the N-Town "Conspiracy" and the *Castle of Perseverance*, is aristocratic; in support, he cites Curiosity's affiliations with the "sevyn prynsys of hell" (line 324) and Satan's rousing of his "knythtys" (line 373). The social affiliations of the evil characters, according to Cox, mirror Mary Magdalene's identification as an aristocrat.

493–94   *Wene ye . . . . com to town.* The gallant's anxiety about a mercantile identity picks up on the taverner's commercial concerns. D. Smith ("'To Passe the See'") maintains that these issues point to the urban interests of the Digby play. See also C, pp. 8–9.

495   *rownd. MED, rounen* (v.), sense 1b: "to speak in private, speak in confidence, hold a private conversation."

496–502   *I have a shert . . . . evyr together abyde.* The Digby play gallant's inventory of his clothing is among the most detailed in medieval English drama. As C (pp. 9–10) observes, the gallant's investment in attire encodes anxieties about social status that late medieval sumptuary laws and didactic discourses about clothing sought to regulate. N. Smith's *Sartorial Strategies* analyzes the relationship between the gallant's exhibitionism, sartorial display, and the performance of sin, as well as the figurative possibilities of aristocratic attire. A rare illustration of Mary Magdalene's suitor appears in a late fourteenth-century Italian fresco cycle depicting the saint's life in ten scenes. See Anderson, "Her Dear Sister," pp. 49, 55–56.

500   *awye.* See *MED, avaien* (v.), sense a: "to inform, advise, or instruct (somebody)."

503   *I woll . . . to seme yyng.* On variable understandings of youth in the Middle Ages, see Dunlop (*Late Medieval Interlude*, pp. 9–21).

504   *With here agen the her I love mych pleyyng.* F (p. 64) notes the gallant's shift to coarser language here. BMH (p. 204) comment on his allusion to "an intimate encounter of hair against hair."

506   *I do it for no pryde.* The gallant's protestation is an ironic double-entendre; the Bad Angel who soon rejoices in Mary's seduction identifies her tempter as "Pryde, callyd Coriosté" (line 550).

511   *Coryossyté.* The gallant is given a name. The term *curiosity* bears a lot of semantic weight. See *MED, curiousité* (n.); all senses elaborated in the *MED*'s definitions seem to apply here. Zacher (*Curiosity and Pilgrimage*, p. 31) states that medieval *curiositas* was frequently associated with pride. The thirteenth-century play known as *Courtois d'Arras* bears interesting similarities to the dramatic scenario and characterization of the much later Digby *Magdalene*, though the late medieval English play splits between the gallant Curiosity and Mary Magdalene the attributes of the French dramatic protagonist. See Symes, *A Common Stage*, pp. 71–80.

515   *daysyys iee. MED, daies-ie* (n.). Curiosity invokes the European daisy or marguerite. A common native flower, the daisy also carries complex meanings. Citing works by Chaucer, Machaut, Usk, Froissart and others, F (pp. 67–70) notes the daisy's popularity as trope in medieval European courtly literature.

515–19   *A, dere dewchesse . . . . peynnes of perplexité.* Curiosity's come-on to the emotionally vulnerable Mary Magdalene and his contributions to their ensuing dialogue echo the convoluted, aureate idiom and rhetorical situation of the late ME poem known as "The Craft of Lovers," as do Lechery's wooing of Mary Magdalene (lines 440–59) and the dialogue that introduces the king and queen of Marseilles (lines 942–60). "The Craft of Lovers" stages a conversation between a lover and a lady initially identified as a "curyous" argument (ed. Kooper, line 2); wildly metaphoric, its evocation of courtship calls attention to the manner and terms of courtly language (e.g., lines 78–79). The three extant manuscript versions of the poem are associated with John Shirley; John Stow included "The Craft of Lovers" in his 1561 edition of Chaucer's *Works*. See Kooper, "Slack Water Poetry." F (p. 64) notes the poem's relevance to the play.

516–17   *Splendaunt of colour . . . . Your sofreyn colourrys. MED, colour* (n.), sense 3a: "color . . . of the face; complexion"; sense 5c: "manner." Curiosity seems to pun here on various meanings of ME *colour*, including sense 4 ("a stylistic device, figure, or embellishment"), thereby commenting on the florid rhetoric with which he first addresses Mary Magdalene.

520   *wene ye that I were a kelle.* Without citing a source, BMH (p. 251) define "kelle" as "a fishnet or a woman's cap," which they extrapolate to mean "prostitute" or "loose woman." *AND* variously defines *kalle* (n.) (also *kele* and *kelle*) as "net"; "hair-net"; "head-gear." To gloss this line Karras ("Holy Harlots," p. 23n69) cites *MED, kelis* (n. pl.): "ill-bred" or "low-class people." Mary Magdalene, then, seems to respond to Curiosity's sudden come-on, by asking "What do you think I am, a loose woman?"

526   *I can nat refreyn me. MED, refreinen* (v.2), sense 2c: "to restrain, contain, or control oneself."

           swete lelly. Like the daisy, the lily makes frequent appearances in courtly literature. F (p. 70) suggests Curiosity invokes the more elegant flower in response to Mary Magdalene's concern expressed in line 520. The lily is also a common symbol of the Virgin Mary chastity.

527   *Syr, curtesy doth it yow lere.* To Curiosity's declaration that he cannot restrain himself, Mary Magdalene retorts, "Courtesy should teach you how to do that"; or "You should know better." Her invocation of courtesy here, as C (pp. 12–16) argues, points to the larger drama of social identities that the playwright weaves into the saint's vita.

529   *ye conne. MED, connen* (v.), sense 3a: "to have mastery of (a skill), be versed or competent in (a craft, occupation, activity)."

530   *wol yow dawns.* F (p. 74) places Mary Magdalene's dance in a complex set of imaginative and epistolary intertexts. The gallant's invitation implicitly signals the presence of instrumental music in this scene. Brokaw (*Staging Harmony*, pp. 12–49) considers how the play uses music to express "temptation, sin, and the entrapments of fleshly pleasures" (p. 17); she stresses the importance of musical *sound* in the sensory reception of medieval drama. Brokaw also compares the Digby *Magdalene* to *Wisdom* as examples of East Anglian drama that stage

complex religious confessions through their musical appeals; as these notes indicate, the two plays bear other similarities to each other. On Mary Magdalene as a dancer, see Davidson, "Middle English Saint Play," p. 83. Loewen ("Conversion of Mary Magdalene") analyzes the German Passion Plays' extensive use of music to dramatize Mary Magdalene's conversion from sin to pious living. In these plays, musical performance integrates the homiletic rhetoric of Franciscan preachers and the spiritual possibilities expressed in musical notation. For a general discussion of musical performance in the play, see Rastall, *Heaven Singing*, pp. 173–74.

533 *beryt. MED, beren* (v.1), sense 7a: "to possess (a quality, capacity, power, virtue, etc.)."

534 *ye be with other ten.* I adapt this gloss from BMH, p. 204, based on *MED, tene* (n.2), sense 3a.

536 *Soppes in wynne.* Wine figures prominently in Mary Magdalene's seduction. Birney ("'Sop in Wyn'") explains that the sop, a small amount of food, in wine was thought to have medicinal properties.

543–46 *Evyn at your wyl . . . . for your sake.* C (pp. 1–4) notes the congruence of Mary Magdalene's moral demise with negative examples of medieval English conduct literature. Still, compared to English Reformation portrayals of Mary Magdalene's transgressions and those in continental medieval dramas, the Digby play's portrait of Mary Magdalene's sinful behaviors in this scene and at lines 564–71 is relatively tame. For continental examples, see Loewen, "Conversion of Mary Magdalene." Badir (*Maudlin Impression*, pp. 32–40) and Atkin (*Drama of Reform*, pp. 109–14) discuss the sexually explicit, salacious exchange between Mary and her tempters in Wager's *Life and Repentaunce of Mary Magdalene*; see White, *Reformation Biblical Drama* (pp. 16–28). Citing *The Old English Martyrology*, *The Northern Passion*, *The South English Legendary*, and Bokenham's *Legendys of Hooly Wummen*, Badir (p. 31) notes that medieval English accounts of the saint's life tend not to draw out Mary's profligate past, focusing instead on her roles as contemplative and preacher. See also *MDS*, pp. 100–50.

549 *grogly gromys.* D. Williams (*French Fetish*, p. 116) glosses this phrase as "unsavory chaps," but as BMH note (p. 204), the phrase "fallyn in owr" does not allow this meaning. (See *MED, grom* (n.), sense 3a.) BMH suggest the dramatist "may well have been employing a traditional alliterative phrase with no clear idea of its sense."

550 *Pryde, callyd Coriosté.* The gallant's lavish clothing and smooth rhetoric also enable his disguise in *Wisdom (MP*, p. 125), where Lucifer masquerades as a gallant.

555 *tremyl and trott.* BMH (p. 204) call the phrase "a common tag" that means to "shake and jump for joy," citing Mundus in the *Castle of Perseverance* (line 457).

559 *of hure al helle shall make rejoysseyng.* Allegorical tempters never explain why Mary Magdalene is considered such a welcome target by those who want to bring her down. Their approach to her, through courtliness and flattery of her social status, resonates in their celebration of her downfall: she is paradoxically a "soveryn," or mighty, elevated, "servant" (line 556) who "hath hure fet in synne."

560   *to nobyl kyngys*. Rex Diabolus here addresses the World and the King of Flesh.

564–71   *A God be . . . . halse and kysse*. This final image of Mary Magdalene before she
           responds to the Good Angel's imprecations depicts her as a romance heroine,
           longing and waiting for her lover. F (pp. 75–79) notes the scene's important
           intersection with the imagery and idiom of secular love poetry. Occurring in
           none of the sources for the play, this scene provides the play's "only glimpse .
           . . of Mary's sensual life" (F, p. 75). Within a few decades, English reformist
           drama would turn the fallen woman into a complicated icon of all that needed
           reform in traditional, medieval religious practice, especially the use and
           veneration of images and other material realizations of devotional expression.
           Badir *(Maudlin Impression*, p. 40) says that Wager turns Mary into a decorated
           idol; Atkin *(Drama of Reform*, p. 106) finds her standing in for all religious
           imagery that the reformed church would replace with the Word of God.

564   *my valentynys*. F (pp. 76–78) aligns Mary Magdalene's plea on behalf of her
           putative lovers with the medieval Valentine poetry of courtly writers such as
           Geoffrey Chaucer, John Clanvowe, John Gower, John Lydgate, Oton de
           Granson, and Charles d'Orléans.

565   *byrd*. *MED*, *birde* (n.1). The *MED* cites very contrary meanings: a "bird" (sense 1)
           is most often "a woman of noble birth, a damsel," a fair lady, etc. But the word
           (sense 3a) can also denote "a man of noble birth, scion, lord." The latter would
           seem to be what Mary Magdalene intends here; alternatively, she may be
           punning on ME *brid* (sense 1a), that is, the avian creatures whom Chaucer in *The
           Parliament of Foules* also associates with the "valentines" whose arrival Mary
           awaits in her arbor. F (pp. 76–77) discusses the connection between birds and
           lovers in medieval Valentine poetry.

566   *bote*. *MED*, *bote* (n.1), sense 1a: "advantage, help, profit, good, benefit."

568   *this erbyre*. *MED*, *herber* (n.1). Mary Magdalene's arbor taps the *MED*'s multiple
           meanings for this word; it is a "pleasure garden" (sense a); an "herb garden"
           (sense b); a "bower covered with flowers, vines, [and] shrubs" (sense e). F (pp.
           98–100) surveys these multiple possibilities. For example, Mary's arbor calls to
           mind both the medieval Garden of Love, frequently depicted in illustrated
           manuscripts of the *Roman de la Rose*, and the Garden of Eden. The sensuous
           language of the female speaker in the garden also evokes the *hortus conclusus*, or
           enclosed garden of the Song of Songs, unleashing potential for her
           identification with the Song's Bride. Scherb *(Staging Faith*, p. 177) finds religious
           valences in Mary's speech, including echoes of biblical imagery of the garden in
           Song of Songs 4:5–6; Ecclesiastes 24:42, and Isaias 58:11.

571, s.d. *Her shal Mary lye doun and slepe in the erbyre*. According to F (pp. 93–98), the arbor
           scene is part of a major romance "meme" in the play, the motif of "the sleeper
           in the garden." In this framework, the arbor or garden is a liminal space where
           "life-changing intervention from a realm beyond the everyday world" can occur
           (p. 94). F surveys appearances of and variations on this important motif in a
           wide range of Middle English romances.

572   *Symont Leprus* (speech heading). The playwright seems to have confused Simon the Pharisee of Luke 7:36–50, with Simon the Leper in Matthew 26:6–16 and Mark 14:3–11. In all three passages Jesus is anointed by an unnamed woman, but only in the home of Simon the Pharisee does Jesus relate the parable of the two debtors, as he also does in the Digby play. Jesus' parable of the two debtors does not appear in Jacobus' life of Mary Magdalene.

573   *solas. MED, solasen* (v.), sense 1a: "to entertain (somebody), amuse; please (one's heart or soul); cheer up (one's life)."

576–79   *Into the seté . . . . with this ordynowns.* Simon's concern for proper provisions for his dinner guests is consistent with other instances in the play that highlight the household and its management, perhaps addressing the values of the play's target audience and/or its producers. Simon's reference to officers performing "this ordynowns" situates his action squarely within the arena of rules and regulations, proper behavior and social custom. See *MED, ordinaunce* (n.).

577   *porvyawns. MED, purveiaunce* (n.), sense 3a: "the act of procuring or providing that which is necessary, especially food, equipment, etc.; provisioning."

581   *perfytnesse.* See *MED, parfitnes(se* (n.), sense 1. In characterizing Jesus as the "prophet" of perfection, Simon invokes the ideal that will become the goal of Mary Magdalene's spiritual life. Devotional works such as Walter Hilton's *Scale of Perfection* promoted these ideals for religious and sometimes lay contemplatives. As *MDS* (pp. 100–101) elaborates, Hilton singles out Mary Magdalene for her achievement of contemplative perfection.

587, s.d.   *Her entyr Symont into the place, the Good Angyll thus seyyng to Mary.* The simultaneity of these different actions, Simon entering the playing place to welcome Jesus in the next scene and Mary's imminent conversion, furnish a clear instance of dramatic possibilities afforded by the play's platea and loca staging. Like the evil allegorical beings who tempt Mary and the "spiritus malyngny" (line 428), the Good Angel is the playwright's invention. No other version of the saint's life makes her the subject of such spiritual visitations.

588   *Woman, woman, why art thou so onstabyll.* Compare Lady Lechery's very different salutation at lines 440–44, a difference that marks the spiritual and psychological distance Mary Magdalene has traveled in the interval between the two greetings.

590   *veryabyll. MED, variable* (adj.), sense 2a: "of a person: inconstant, unsteadfast; treacherous, untrustworthy."

594   *Salve for thi sowle. MED, salve* (n.1), sense 1c: "a spiritual or religious remedy."

598–99   *remembyr how sorowful . . . . angure and ir.* The Good Angel reminds Mary Magdalene of the torment that will await her in hell if she remains unrepentant.

601   *I am the gost of goodnesse.* The angel's self-identification as a "good" spirit (and Mary Magdalene's confirmation of that attribute in the next line) is the first of the play's several allusions to late medieval discourses on *discretio spirituum*, or the discernment of spirits: admonitions and guidelines intended to educate the

devout soul on the truth or falsehood, sacred or demonic origins of spiritual visitations that took the form of visions, sensations, and/or voices. A frequent topic of works of spiritual direction such as Hilton's *Scale of Perfection, The Chastising of God's Children*, and *The Cloud of Unknowing*, proper discernment of the sources of spiritual visitation was of major concern to late medieval women mystics such as Margery Kempe and Bridget of Sweden. See *MDS* (pp. 117–21) and Voaden, *God's Words*.

602–07   *how the speryt . . . . on every syde*. Mary Magdalene's self-assessment and self-reproach echo themes of medieval confessional literature, as does her occupation by and release from seven devils (line 691, s.d.; see also lines 631–40; 748–57). More specifically, her delineation of her spiritual condition as the interplay of exterior forces and interior inclinations resembles what Raskolnikov ("Confessional Literature") calls "vernacular psychology."

603   *temtyd me*. Noting an Augustinian parallel between the three goals of rhetoric — to teach, delight, and persuade — and the three steps of temptation — suggestion, pleasure, and consent — Scoville (*Saints and the Audience*, pp. 38–39) explains Mary Magdalene's unusual word choice here.

605   *wonddyd. MED, wounden* (v.), sense 5a: "to inflict emotional pain, distress."

612   *oyle of mercy*. Mary Magdalene's metaphor for the mercy she seeks from prophet Jesus is a fitting counterpoint to the "swete bawmys" (line 613) with which she will anoint him in Simon's house and also seek out his dead body in his tomb. The conflation of several anointing women in scripture, including the unnamed one who approaches Jesus in the home of Simon the Pharisee, and the Mary Magdalene who bears witness to the resurrection in all four gospels, enabled Gregory the Great's creation of the composite Magdalene, thereby joining the anointer to the sinner. The anointing scene of Luke 7 provides the core of Gregory's influential Homily 33; see Gregory the Great, *Forty Gospel Homilies*, pp. 268–79. Dugan (*Ephemeral History of Perfume*, p. 39) calls Mary Magdalene's exchange of her arbor's precious balms (line 569) for the sweet balms of anointing an instance of *contrapasso*, "a structure of penitence demanding that any absolution match the nature of the sin." Dugan also introduces the notion that the play's staging itself may have employed its various scents.

615   *mastyr most of magnyfycens*. Note the play's use of epithets for the deity.

639–40   *Thow knowyst . . . . hart reward me*. Mary makes an unusual claim about Jesus' knowledge of her spiritual intentions, her "hart and thowt"; see also line 696. The focus on interior piety, in contrast to outward religious expression, was an important strain of late medieval devotion. As C (p. 17) explains, such pieties were especially congenial to the habits and preferences of the prosperous late medieval laity, whose interests are otherwise so frequently addressed in the Digby *Magdalene*.

642–44   *For this grett repast . . . . seyn to thee*. In the verses from Luke 7 from which this scene draws, Jesus reprimands Simon because he identifies the anointing woman as a sinner. In the play, Jesus admonishes Simon even though he has not expressed displeasure about the woman. See BMH, p. 204, and the note to line 674 below.

643   *fectually. MED, effectualli* (adv.), sense 2: "diligently, earnestly, zealously."

660   *as my reson yef can.* In this difficult phrase, the scribe has written *ʒef*, perhaps by mistake.

649–77   *Symond, ther was a man . . . . be thou made therby.* Luke 7:41–49.

672   *aplye. MED, applien* (v.), sense 5a: "to strive or undertake (to do something)."

674   *Wherfor, in thi conscyens, thou owttyst nat to replye.* Jesus' statement here may explain his rebuke of Simon even though the man says nothing about the anointing woman in the Digby play. (See note to lines 642–44 above.) Jesus suggests knowledge of Simon's inward expression, "in . . . conscyens," that is, of his disapproval. See *MED, conscience* (n.), sense 1.

678–85   *blessyd be thou . . . . pacyens and charyté.* Mary Magdalene's words upon receiving Jesus' forgiveness constellate important themes and metaphors elaborately developed elsewhere in the play. After addressing Jesus as "lord of evyrlastyng lyfe," she immediately invokes his birth from his mother Mary, "that puer vergynne" who, though she makes no appearance in the play, nonetheless figures in it as an abiding reference point for Mary Magdalene. See *MDS*, pp. 151–54. As Coletti ("Design of the Digby Play") points out, the newly converted woman employs metaphors of nourishment ("repast contemplatyf") to describe Jesus' effect upon her and represents her own transformation through a trope of clothing, as she resolves to "enabyte" herself with humility. The trope of "enhabiting," as *MDS* (p. 263n28) notes, recalls the Pauline concept of 'putting on' the new man in Christ (Ephesians 4:23–24; Galatians 3:27–28; Romans 13:12–14; Colossians 3:9–10). It is tempting to speculate how these metaphoric changes of array might have been materially realized on stage. In Wager's *Life and Repentance* (White, *Reformation Biblical Drama*, p. 55, line 1765, s.d.), Mary Magdalene marks her conversion with a literal change of clothing.

681   *Agens my seknes, helth and medsyn.* The Digby play's saint also casts Mary's sinful condition as a "seknes" from which she is healed by *Christus medicus*, her "helth and medsyn." See also lines 594, 677, 693, 759, and 763, and Coletti, "Social Contexts," pp. 291–92. Keyser ("Examining the Body Poetic," pp. 145–58) discusses how the play's use of this figurative language conforms to the medieval medical paradigm.

683   *enabyte. MED, habiten* (v.), sense 2: "to attire oneself, dress."

687   *inward mythe.* See note to lines 639–40 above.

688   *desert. MED, desert* (n.2), sense 2. Negative connotations of the "desert" that Mary Magdalene's soul occupies before her conversion anticipate the positive associations of the wilderness (line 1971, s.d.) that later furnishes her contemplative retreat (sense 2a).

689   *And from therknesse hast porchasyd lyth.* Jesus employs a metaphoric commonplace of medieval discourses of redemption, which rendered the theology of salvation in economic terms. The foundation of these discourses is the idea that God redeemed the world by 'buying it back' (from the Latin *redimere*). See *PDD*, pp.

341–42; Rosenthal, *Purchase of Paradise*; Georgianna, "Love So Dearly Bought," p. 89.

691   *Vade in pace*. Luke 7:50.

691, s.d.   *Wyth this word . . . . hell with thondyr*. This remarkable stage direction points up the Digby play's fondness for vivid dramatic spectacle. The second part of the direction, complete with sound effects, demonstrates the playwright's inventive depiction of Mary Magdalene's life of sin, which the play develops in an elaborate allegory. The "dyllys" here are the Seven Deadly Sins. The first portion of the stage direction, though, draws upon the composite Magdalene's biblical identity, specifically the Gregorian construction that conflated the woman named Magdalene, from whom Jesus cast seven devils (Mark 16:9; Luke 8:2) with the sinful woman of Luke 7. Tamburr (*Harrowing of Hell*, p. 146) notes echoes here of the Harrowing of Hell, wherein Christ's conquering of the devil within the soul of the individual believer parallels that greater redemptive action. Christ was, according to Tamburr, channeling Justin Martyr, the great exorcist. The exorcism of Mary Magdalene's deadly sins or demons is one of three such scenes in East Anglian drama. In *Wisdom* (*MP*, pp. 143–46, lines 901–80), Anima emerges as a Magdalene figure by virtue of this and other similarities. As *MDS* notes (p. 98), *Wisdom* "reads and plays like an allegorical dress rehearsal for the more elaborate . . . treatment of related themes in the Digby *Magdalene*." Sixteenth-century marginalia in the Macro manuscript (*MP*, p. xxix) include a ballad that mentions Mary Magdalene, Mary of Egypt, and the Virgin Mary. N-Town's "Last Supper" conflates Mary Magdalene's scriptural exorcism in the gospels of Luke and Mark with the anointing episode from Luke 7, and relocates this conflation to the scene of the Last Supper. See *NT*, 1:269–71, lines 141–92; and for discussion of these episodes see *MDS*, pp. 84–94.

693   *Sowle helth attys tyme for to recure*. See *MED*, *soule-hele* (n.); *MED*, *recuren* (v.), sense 2a. Mary Magdalene's recovery of "soul health" and Jesus' promise to make her "hol in sowle" (line 677) invoke a specialized term from medieval devotional literature analyzed by Raskolnikov in *Body Against Soul*.

694   *whanhope*. See *MED*, *wanhope* (n.), sense 1a. Wanhope, or despair (Latin *tristitia*), was a subject of extensive commentary on the part of the Church fathers and later medieval exegetes. Discussions focused on whether despair was itself a "deadly" sin and, if not, what its relationship to sin must be. In the later Middle Ages despair was considered a subset of the sin of sloth (Latin *acedia*). Wenzel (*Sin of Sloth*, pp. 68–96) provides a basic account. For a recent overview and analysis, see Huber, "'Y am sorwe,'" pp. 1–22.

697   *the techeyng of Isaye in scryptur*. Revealing a precocious knowledge of the Old Testament, Mary Magdalene proclaims her trust in Isaiah's prophecies of the coming savior. Possible allusions here include Isaias 9:6–7, which announces the birth of the child who will sit on David's throne and whose "name shall be called Wonderful, Counsellor, God the Mighty, the Father of the world to come, the Prince of Peace." The mention of the names to be ascribed to the deity ("et vocabitur nomen eius") resonate with the play's sustained interest in the name

of Jesus. See the note to lines 93–94 above. Mary Magdalene may also have in mind here Isaias 11:1–2, which speaks of the flower and rod that will rise from the root of Jesse and upon whom the spirit of the Lord will rest.

699–700   *Blyssyd be they . . . . in credens*. John 20:29. BMH (p. 206) mistakenly cite John 10 but nonetheless correctly note the oddity of a comment that in John's gospel Jesus makes to Thomas, not Mary Magdalene. The remark directly follows Mary Magdalene's attestation of the scriptural, i.e. written, foundations of her renewed faith. Citing the unusual placement of this scriptural citation, *MDS* (pp. 192–93) suggests that its admonition regarding the relationship of sight to belief applies to both the Magdalene's outrageous corporeal testimony of faith and the material resources of theater.

705–21   *Holy God . . . . we desyern*. M (p. 264) declares this speech "theologically speaking . . . very odd" and states it "could hardly have been written for an angel." Citing the *Play of Mary Magdalene*, ed. Lewis, p. 132, BMH identify the speech as "a tripartite hymn to the Holy Trinity" that treats "each person of the Trinity in succession" (p. 206). Coming immediately after Jesus' exit from the stage, the Good Angel's metaphorically rich and conceptually challenging speech, or hymn, directs attention to the Digby play's representation of the deity, and more specifically, to its Christology. In sharp contrast to important strands of medieval piety that emphasized Christ's human nature, the Good Angel focuses on exceptional attributes that foreground his "devynyté" and "soverreyn sapyens." The Good Angel even implies that Jesus' humanity, his "blessyd mortalyté," has "obscuryd" his divine nature. As *MDS* explains (pp. 114–17), this characterization recalls the Christology that Walter Hilton, in the *Scale of Perfection*, propounds in relation to a program of contemplation.

716   *spryte of errour*. The Good Angel once more refers to the discernment of spirits in its "rejoysyng of Mawdleyn" (line 704, s.d.). See note to line 601 above.

719   *consyngne*. *MED*, *signen* (v.1), sense 2c: "to sign (a document, letter, an act, etc.) with one's name or signature; also, authenticate . . . with a signature or seal."

720   *malyngne*. *MED*, *maligne* (n.), sense b: "wickedness, treachery."

721   *gostely bred*. The Good Angel appears to allude to the eucharistic sacrament, but the various references to material and spiritual consumption in the play suggest that the term "gostely bred" involves more expansive forms of spiritual nourishment.

722–47   *A, owt, owt . . . . ower felaws blake*. Comedic antics of demons were a staple of medieval English dramatizations of the Harrowing of Hell and the Last Judgment. Cox (*The Devil and the Sacred*, p. 70) notes demonic infighting here.

722   *hampord wyth hate*. *MED*, *hamperen* (v.), sense c: "to attack; harass (the heart), vex, torment." As Tamburr notes, (*Harrowing of Hell*, pp. 159–61), the disturbance of the devils registered here anticipates Christ's Harrowing of Hell, reported later in lines 963–92.

724   *betyll-browyd bycheys*. The alliteration employed in the devils' repartee calls attention to the play — and the playwright's — awareness of distinct linguistic idioms.

725   *Belfagour and Belzabub*. BMH (p. 206) suggest that Belfagour is probably the Moabite deity mentioned in Numbers 25:3–5, to whom the Israelites are initiated. Belzabub, or Beelzebub, appears variously in the Old and New Testaments as a Philistine god, a demon, and as a synonym for Satan.

727–28   *The jugment . . . . judycyal-lyke astate*. The theme of judgment has recently surfaced in the scene of Mary Magdalene's repentance and Jesus' intuition of Simon's opinion about her. The mock trial to which the devils submit Spiritus Maligni, or the Bad Angel, is reminiscent of the mock court that occurs in *Mankind* (*MP*, pp. 175–77, lines 662–725).

730   *As flat as fox*. Whiting F601 cites the Digby play as the sole instance of this phrase.

731   *Primus Diabolus* (speech heading). Mostly likely the scribe, rather than the playwright, changes the name of the character identified as Rex Diabolus at line 722. Similarly, Spiritus Maligni at line 730 becomes Malinus Spiritus at line 733. Inconsistency in speech headings, both in actual names and the spelling of names, is a regular feature of the manuscript; see Introduction, p. 19.

735–36   *thys hard balys . . . . I wol be wreke*. The punishment inflicted by the devils upon the Bad Angel and the Seven Deadly Sins corresponds to the iconography of the Last Judgement window at St. Mary's Church in Fairford, Gloucestershire. See Ross' webpage: http://www.britainexpress.com/attractions.htm?attraction=1564, window 15.

737   *skore awey the yche*. MED, *scoren* (v.), sense a: "to cut (something)."

738   *wyth thys panne, ye do hym pycche*. MED, *pichen* (v.) In blackening their failed minions with pitch, the devils transfer to them their own iconographic associations with blackness; some reference to festive customs may also be at work here. See Vaughn, *Performing Blackness*, pp. 18–22.

739, s.d.   *Here shall they serve all the sevyn as they do the frest*. The stage direction indicates that "all the sevyn," the Seven Deadly Sins, accompany Spiritus Maligni when he delivers the message about their collective, failed attempt to secure Mary Magdalene's place in hell. Findon ("'Now is aloft,'" p. 251) comments that "the expulsion of Deadly Sins is a positive development for Mary, but a disaster for the sins themselves."

741   *lordeynnys*. MED, *lording(e* (n.). The term, which denotes persons occupying positions of mastery or lordship, may be used ironically here.

743, s.d.   *Here shall the tother deyllys sett the howse on afyere . . . and to Martha*. The "howse" situates this spectacle of demonic punishment in physical terms, probably identifying a specific *locus*, or place, in the playing space. The fire and smoke produced here indicate medieval dramatists' appreciation for pyrotechnic thrills, as well as the technical capacities of medieval drama's sponsors and players to create burning spectacles. Dramatic records from Coventry report payments for "kepyng of hell mowthe & the fyer" and document many uses of gunpowder. See Schreyer, *Shakespeare's Medieval Craft*, pp. 140–41, 228n33.

748–59   *O brother . . . . helyd myn infyrmyté*. This abrupt and unremarked shift of scene finds Mary Magdalene returned to her siblings in Castle Magdalene. Her speech of greeting to Martha and Lazarus rehearses metaphors and motifs appearing earlier in the play: a Christology that focuses on God as "kyng" and creator, and the representation of her sin as an "infyrmyté" to be healed.

751   *delectary*. This word seems to combine the idea of being "spiritually or intellectually delightful" and "a state or condition of happiness." See *MED*, *delectable* (adj.), sense b, and *MED*, *delectacioun* (n.), sense 3b. Compare lines 337 and 791.

757   *Revertere*. Jeffrey ("English Saints' Plays," p. 87) links Magdalene's account to the wordplay on *vertere/revertere/convertere* in Augustine's *Confessions*.

760–61   *Now worchepyd . . . . is callyd Savyower*. Martha's praise of the "hey name Jhesu" and its Latin rendering as *Savyower* signals the play's attention to the late medieval cult of the Holy Name of Jesus. See note to lines 93–94 above.

762   *evyn of dewe*. *MED*, *dever* (n.), sense 3b: "whatever is due or proper."

763   *To alle synfull and seke, he is sokour*. Martha too recognizes the motif of Jesus as physician, *Christus medicus*. See note to lines 678–85 above.

765   *obessyawnse*. *MED*, *obeisaunce* (n.), sense 3a: "respectful submission, homage; deference, reverence."

768–75   *Cryst, that is the lyth . . . . nyth and day*. M (pp. 265–66) notes that Mary's speech translates the opening lines of *Christe qui lux es et dies*, a Compline hymn from the Sarum rite used from the first Sunday of Lent to Passion Sunday. The hymn was frequently translated into ME. M (p. 279) cites *Breviarium ad Usum Insignis Ecclesiae Sarum*, 1:dlxxiii, 2:228–29.

773   *ded slep*. M (p. 266) notes that references to "grevos slepe" (line 852) or the *gravis somnus* of the hymn, throughout the play suggest that the playwright "worked from the Latin text rather than from the translation. Instances of dramatic *gravis somnus* apply not only to Mary Magdalene but to Lazarus (line 852) and the queen of Marseilles (line 1896).

777–80   *deth is sett . . . . wax alle swertt*. The play represents the death of Lazarus from John 11 in graphic detail. Apparently stumbling ("I faltyr and falle"), Lazarus first experiences distress as he becomes "onquarte"; see *MED*, *unquert(e* (adj.). He reports "a bome," or buzzing in his head (*MED*, *bomben* (v.)) and appears to lose consciousness, as he waxes "swertt" (*MED*, *swart* (adj.), sense b). Keyser ("Examining the Body Poetic," pp. 145–58) discusses the deaths of Lazarus and Cyrus in light of medieval medical knowledge. The Digby play's interest in physical illness, considered alongside its awareness of medicinal herbs and its use of metaphors of health and healing in spiritual as well as material contexts, may suggest that at some point its auspices were connected to the culture of the medieval hospital. See Coletti, "Social Contexts."

782   *no lengar now I reverte*. *MED*, *reverten* (v.), sense 3. See note for line 757 above.

783   *I yeld up the gost*. Like the death of Cyrus earlier in the play, the death of Lazarus depicts the late medieval awareness — and fear — of sudden death. In fact, Lazarus does not die when he here yields up the "gost," but forty lines later at line 823, s. d.

787   *shal gete yow leches*. The *Christus medicus* trope returns here and when Lazarus and Mary Magdalene affirm poetically, in rhyme, the congruence of his "bodely helth" (line 823) and his "gostys welth" (line 825). On the trope, see Rawcliffe, *Medicine for the Soul*, pp. 103–08.

        devyde. *MED*, *dividen* (v.), sense 1a(c): "to break (something) up; demolish, destroy."

794   *mellefflueus swettness*. See *MED*, *swetenes(se* (n.), sense 5, but overlapping with other senses. Carruthers ("Sweetness," p. 1001) states that medieval "'sweetness' — *dulcedo, suavitas* — is among the most mixed and trickiest of concepts"; but Mary and Martha's intended meaning here seems unambiguous. In light of the play's representation of Mary Magdalene as a mystic and contemplative (see *MDS*, pp. 100–50), Richard Rolle's account (in *Fire of Love*) of the contemplative's experience of spiritual love as *calor, dulcor, and canor* (heat, sweetness, and song) also resonates with the sisters' devout testimony.

796   *Lover to thee, Lord*. See *MED*, *lover(e* (n.2), sense 1b. The idea of the loving relationship between Jesus and Lazarus originates in the Gospel of John 11:3, where Mary and Martha seek Jesus' help for their brother, "whom [he] loves" ("quem amas"). But the playwright's term here (and at lines 798 and 800) to represent Lazarus' relationship to Jesus is also a familiar trope of medieval devotional and mystical writing, used to describe the devout individual's relationship to the deity in his humanity. Julian of Norwich's *A Vision Showed to a Devout Woman* famously begins: "Methought I wolde have bene that time with Mary Maudeleyne and with othere that were Cristes loverse"; *Writings of Julian*, ed. Watson and Jenkins, p. 63. The notion of the believer as Christ's beloved derives from allegorical interpretations of the Song of Songs.

802–10 *Of all infyrmyté . . . . in heven gloryfyed*. The opening of Jesus' speech is inspired by John 11:4. Jesus "said to them: 'This sickness is not unto death, but for the glory of God'" (*Infirmitas haec non est ad mortem, sed pro gloria Dei*). The Digby playwright, however, departs from the biblical prompt to have Jesus proclaim the inscrutability of both death and the eternal joys of heaven, which can be understood neither by reason nor academic knowledge ("counnyng of clerke"); or such at least is the point that the speech develops, despite the difficulties of line 802, which might also be the result of scribal confusion. *MDS* (pp. 121–24) discusses the play's critique of clerical learning and its portrayal of sacred cognition. Cockett ("Actor's Carnal Eye," p. 71) cites this passage as one of three addressing the limitation of words to express spiritual matters (the others occur at lines 1100–03 and 1364–65). The play's interest in affective and somatic forms of religious knowledge, he contends, not only comports with practices of late medieval affective pieties (as exemplified by East Anglian women mystics Julian of Norwich and Margery Kempe), but also anticipates the work of the actor who might "operate as a medium for sacred truth."

804   *werke*. Especially in opposition to "the joye . . . [of] Jherusallem hevenly" in the next line, the meaning of "werke" here is difficult to determine. For the many options, see *MED, werk* (n.1).

805   *Jherusallem hevenly*. To gloss this difficult passage, BMH (p. 207) cite 1 Corinthians 2:9, where Paul speaks of the inability of human knowledge to access God's sacred mysteries and wisdom.

817   *weyys*. *MED, wei* (n.4), sense a: "misery, trouble, woe."

822   *sharp showyr*. *MED, shour* (n.), sense 4a: "An attack of physical or emotional suffering."

831   *drewyn*. *MED, drauen* (v.), sense 1e(d): "to tear down, fell, . . . kill."

832–33   *We must nedys . . . . hym wythowt delay*. John's gospel does not mention the necessity for Lazarus' speedy burial.

834–37   *As the use . . . . wythowtyn lesyng*. The weepers gathered by Mary Magdalene are the late medieval stand-ins for the consoling Jews of John 11:19 and 31; Mary's consciousness of how the act of mourning "must be donne" links the burial of Lazarus not only to Jewish and Middle Eastern funeral customs but also to those of late medieval England. Mourners "clad in blake" frequently appeared in late medieval funerals, especially those of the well-to-do (see also the stage direction after line 841). The 1519 will of Anne Sulyard of Suffolk provided for 24 poor men and women "to be clad in Blak with hoodes of the same." Such mourners were often recipients of the deceased person's charity. See *PDD*, p. 350 and the sources cited therein.

846   *very*. *MED, verrei* (adj.), sense 6b(a) lists the word as "an emphatic."

849   *Jude*. John 11:7. The Digby play's representation of the death and raising of Lazarus follows John's gospel closely, but not slavishly; e.g., the play sharply differentiates Jesus' separate encounters with Mary and Martha by showing Lazarus die in between them.

850   *Lazar, my frynd*. Although she focuses on a twelfth-century Lazarus play from Fleury, Ashley's analysis ("Fleury *Raising of Lazarus*") of that play's complex Christology resonates here: she notes that the Fleury Jesus is both friend and intimate of Lazarus and a powerful victor. See the Digby Lazarus' praise of Christ's "werkys of wondyre" at lines 912–13.

852   *grevos slepe*. Jesus introduces the metaphor of death as sleep in John 11:11. See note to line 773 above.

854   *be skyll*. See *MED, skil* (n.), sense 7a. The disciple's remark may collapse John 11:12, "Lord, if he sleep, he shall be well" (*Domine, si dormit, salvus erit*), and John 11:37, "Could not he that opened the eyes of the man born blind have caused that this man not die?" (*Non poterat hic, qui aperuit oculos caeci nati, facere ut hic non moreretur?*). The mention of Jesus' "skyll" picks up on the latter, while

the disciple's anticipation that Lazarus might be "savyd" suggests a mistranslation of the Latin *salvus*.

855–64   *That is trew . . . . of my deité*. In another noteworthy addition to John's account of the Lazarus episode, Jesus here both gives notice of his virgin birth and briefly summarizes his imminent Passion.

857   *nemyows*. BMH (p. 258) note the derivation from Latin *nimium*, meaning "beyond measure" or "excessive."

865   *folow me now*. Fitzhenry ("Vernacularity and Theater," p. 227) notes the coincidence of the Digby Christ's "mobile, preaching" ministry and Wycliffite models of Christ.

866   *For Lazar is ded, verely to preve*. It is unclear why Jesus would want to openly "preve" Lazarus' death. In an alternative parsing of this line, that which Jesus seeks to demonstrate openly might be the "deité" of line 864.

868, s.d. *Here shal Jhesus . . . on Jew tellyt Martha*. John's gospel identifies the companions of Mary and Martha as Jews. See note to lines 834–37 above.

873–92   *A, Lord . . . . doth this dyscus*. See John 11:20–32.

886   *son of sapyens*. Scripture provides foundations for the association of Christ, as the second person of the Trinity, with Wisdom: Isaias 11:1–2; Luke 7:35; Luke 11:31 and 49; and 1 Corinthians 1:24. See Riggio, *Play of "Wisdom,"* p. 184. The Macro play known as *Wisdom* (*MP*, pp. 114–52) elaborates on late medieval understanding of Christ as Wisdom; a substantial fragment of that play is also preserved in the manuscript that contains the single extant version of the Digby *Magdalene*. Christ is addressed and appears as Wisdom in the N-Town "Assumption of Mary" play (*NT*, 1:390–91, lines 94–114).

889   *regent*. MED, *regent* (n.), sense b: "one who governs in place of a sovereign." Here "regent" is an apt designation for Jesus as the second person of the Trinity, albeit not yet recognized.

892   *dyscus*. MED, *discussen* (v.), sense 1a: "to investigate (a matter, an opinion); examine (one's conscience, a belief); weigh (deeds) for judgment."

895   *wys*. MED, *wisen* (v.), sense 3a: "to guide (somebody along a route or toward a goal), direct."

903–10   *Now, Father . . . . hethyr to me*. Jesus' words once more depart from their gospel source (John 11:41–43), this time in his appeal as the human son of his divine father.

911–20   *A, my makar . . . . here ded apere*. Because the risen Lazarus of John's gospel does not speak, medieval writers who wanted to represent this episode had enormous leeway in devising words for the man newly returned from death. The Digby play's Lazarus perhaps alludes to a comment that John gives to Martha (11:39) when he refers to the rot that should have consumed his flesh and bones. Lazarus figures in medieval English drama display a range of responses to the miraculous testimony to Jesus' divinity that they represent. Ashley ("Resurrection of Lazarus") discusses Lazarus figures in medieval English and French dramas.

920, s.d.   *Here all the pepull . . . Jhesus, Jhesus, Jhesus.* John's gospel mentions no such spirited endorsement of faith. Like the stage directions at lines 44 and 841, this provision for dramatic action calls attention to the 'extras' that populate the stage of the Digby *Magdalene* even as it recalls Martha's devotion to the "hey name Jhesu" called "Savyower" (lines 760–61).

921   *advertacyounys.* A noun form, "that which is made known," derives from ME *adverten* (v.), "to observe, perceive" (*MED*, sense 1); but see also *MED, advertisen* (v.), sense 2c: "to make (something) known, make clear or manifest, declare, show."

922   *Wherethorow.* See *MED, wher-thurgh.* (adv. & conj.), sense 3a(c).

924   *Vade in pace.* These are Jesus' words to the woman who anoints him in the home of Simon the Pharisee in Luke 7:50, the woman whom the Digby play, and a preceding millennium of scriptural and religious tradition, identified as Mary Magdalene.

924, s.d.   *Here devoydyt Jhesus.* This stage direction marks the play's turn to Mary Magdalene's legendary, post-biblical life, developed in many of her medieval vitae but based fundamentally on Jacobus de Voragine's *Legenda Aurea*; see *GL*. Furnivall (*Digby Plays*, p. 98) divided the play here, indicating all that follows as "part two." The king and queen of Marcylle, or Marseilles, introduced here, are central figures in the legendary life.

925   *Avantt! Avant thee. MED, avaunt* (interj.), sense c: "away, be off, avaunt."

927   *Ye brawlyng breellys and blabyr-lyppyd bycchys. MED, braulen* (v.1), sense 1; *MED, brali* (adj.); and *MED, brauler(e* (n.); all these words denote noisy and quarrelsome people. See also *MED, bicche* (n.), sense 2. The redundant reprimand serves the alliterative poetic line, as the king's ranting speech marks a notable shift in the tone and idiom of the play at this point, perhaps explaining why Furnivall perceived the need to divide it here.

929   *I am a sofereyn.* Velz ("Sovereignty in the Digby") discusses this important motif in the plays.

934   *bemmys. MED, beme* (n.1), sense a: "a trumpet, especially one used in warfare or hunting."

942   *I have a favorows fode and fresse as the fakown. MED, fode* (n.2), sense 3b. The king shifts abruptly from tyrannical to amorous, courtly speech. According to F (pp. 79–81), the imagery of flowers, animals, and gemstones that punctuates the king and queen's exchange is common to medieval love lyrics. Of special interest, as F notes (p. 80), is the king's identification of his wife with the "fakown," an aristocratic bird of prey. The king associates himself with the lion (line 944), another aristocratic animal "common in . . . romance and courtly society as well as heraldry" (F, p. 81).

947   *felecyows*. This word derives from *MED*, *felicité* (n.), sense 2a: "happiness; delight, joy, pleasure."

950–57   *Regina* (speech heading) . . . . *is my prosperyté*. The queen's speech is difficult linguistically and syntactically. She continues the king's courtly discourse but takes it to the next level of obscurity. F (p. 81) states that line 952's "boldest ondyr baner bryth" echoes Song of Songs 2:4: "his banner over me is love."

953   *coroscant*. The word derives from Latin *coruscus* (adj.), meaning "flashing, gleaming, glittering."

956   *I privyde*. *MED*, *providen* (v.), sense 4a: "to take care . . . protect (somebody [or] oneself)."

958   *berel brytest of bewté*. In praising his wife as a bright, beautiful beryl, the king recalls Flesh's address to Lady Lechery (see note to "beral of bewte" at line 425). F (p. 82) comments on this similarity, suggesting that the carry-over to the queen of romantic and erotic attributes is complicated by her aristocratic status.

961   *Now, comly knygthys*. The king's call for his knights to follow their assumed duties turns his legendary kingdom into a medieval aristocratic household, very much like the one overseen by Mary Magdalene's father Cyrus (see line 112 and its note).

962, s.d.   *spycys and wynne*. See notes to lines 46 and 112 above.

963   *Owt, owt, harrow*. The devil who delivers news of Christ's Crucifixion, Harrowing of Hell, and Resurrection is remarkably well-informed about basic Christian doctrine. With its notice of the "Kyng of Joy['s] . . . . wondyrfull worke" (lines 967–76), his report of these events even gestures toward the Christology present elsewhere in the play. This counter-intuitive instruction in Christian theology by a character coded as evil also occurs in the *Croxton Play of the Sacrament* (lines 393–441), when Jonathas and the other Jews explain the eucharistic sacrament and rehearse the "substaunce of . . . [Christian] lawe." The non-scriptural Harrowing of Hell is derived from the apocryphal *Gospel of Nicodemus*. The episode, which provided for Christ's release of righteous souls in hell during the interval between his crucifixion and resurrection, was very popular in medieval English literature, appearing in all of the biblical cycles. DiSalvo ("Unexpected Saints," p. 74) notes that the devils who disappear from the play at this point are "replaced by the pagan priest of Marseilles."

968   *fray*. *MED*, *frai* (n.), sense 2: "a fit of fright."

989   *deleverans*. *MED*, *deliverance* (n.), sense 2c notes the term can refer to "Judgment Day."

992, s.d.   *Here shall entyr . . . . thus seyyng Mawdlyn*. This stage direction invokes a social identity ("chast women") and a visual image ("sygnis of the passon") extremely important in late medieval religious culture. The introduction of the three Marys as chaste women aligns them with the social role of the vowess, a lay woman who formally professed before ecclesiastical authority her intention to pursue a chaste life in world. The stage direction's notice of the women's array further signals the vowess' symbolic apparel. See *MDS*, pp. 50–53. The symbols of the Passion "pryntyd" on this attire allude either to the *arma Christi*, a cluster of images representing the instruments of the Passion, or to a more focused image, sometimes called 'arms of the Passion,' that showed Christ's wounds depicted against the background of the cross. See Duffy, *Stripping of the Altars*, p. 246; Cooper and Denny-Brown, eds., *Arma Christi*; and *MDS*, p. 248n3. The latter image was associated particularly with the late medieval Bridgettine orders, whose sisters wore white linen crowns on which were sewn, in cruciform pattern, pieces of red cloth in the shape of drops of blood and whose lay brothers wore mantles decorated with white crosses and red patches "'for the reuerence of the fyve woundys of crist.'" See Jones and Walsham, "Syon Abbey," p. 13. BMH (p. 209) compare this passage to *Mankind*, line 322 (*MP*, p. 164).

995–98   *For here . . . . For here.* See Luke 23:27–28. Scoville (*Saints and the Audience*, p. 49) connects the Marys' rhetorical emphasis with the "memorial techniques of antiquity and of medieval rhetorical education," here replacing the imaginary landscapes of memory theory with "the actual landscape of the playing space."

998–99   *For here . . . . ther kyng ryall.* Mary Jacobe's recollection of the mocking of Christ on his way to Calvary is as laconic as scriptural reports of it; BMH (p. 209) cite Matthew 27:30, Mark 15:19. "The Announcement to the Three Marys" in the *N-Town Play* fills in this picture with imaginative details drawn from scriptural exegesis and devotional writings.

1003   *mervelows mell.* Merveillous (adj.) has a wide semantic range, embracing the "wonderful" (sense 1a), the "miraculous" (sense 2a), and the "horrifying" (sense 4a). *MED, mel* (n.2), sense 1 ("occasion") may gloss ME "mell" here. But the word also resonates with French *mêlée* or *mellé*, denoting "combat" and/or "struggle" (*AND, mellé*).

1005   *Heylle, gloryows crosse.* BMH (p. 209) note the resemblance of the three Marys' speech to a hymn to the cross, citing the example of *Salve crux sancta.*

1016   *anoytt. MED, enointen* (v.), sense 2a: "to apply an aromatic unguent, to perfume" and sense 2b: "to embalm."

1023–30   *Ye women presentt . . . . natt be delayyd.* All of the synoptic gospels report the angels' announcement of the Resurrection to the three Marys: Matthew 28:1–6; Mark 16:1–6; Luke 24:1–10.

1027   *wyre. MED, wer(e* (n.5), sense 1a: "a feeling or personal condition of doubt or uncertainty; also, hesitancy, indecision."

1037   *defend. MED, defenden* (v.), sense 3b: "to protect, save (somebody)."

1045–46   *And also . . . . techeyng and exortacyon.* Peter alludes here to his denial of knowing Jesus, attested in all the canonical gospels: Matthew 26:73–75; Mark 14:68–72; Luke 22:56–62; John 18:15–27.

1049   *sudare cloth. MED, sudari(e* (n.), sense 2: "the piece of linen used to wrap Christ's head before his burial."

1052   *Where he is becum. MED, bicumen* (v.), sense 5a: "to happen." My gloss here follows modern usage of the word. A literal ME version might be "What has happened to him?"

1060, s.d. *Hic aparuit Jhesus.* The stage direction does not specify how Jesus looks when he appears, but Mary Magdalene's notice at line 1079 that she supposes he "had byn Symoud the gardenyr" suggests that the figure playing Jesus wears the clothing or, more likely, bears the implements of a gardener.

1061–95   *Woman, woman . . . . me byn meke.* Occurring only in John's gospel (20:11–17), Mary Magdalene's meeting with Christ as a gardener, the most famous of her few appearances in scripture, provided the foundation for influential exegetical traditions, as well as inspiration for popular iconographic motifs.

1068   *And I hys lover and cause wyll phy.* The final part of the sentence beginning at line 1065 is difficult to parse. BMH (p. 209) note the derivation of "phy" from the French *fier,* to trust. See Godefroy, *Lexique de l'ancien Français, fier* (v.), p. 270. The word "cause" is more problematic, perhaps denoting *MED, cause* (n.) sense 5: "aim, intent; purpose, end." Accordingly, Mary Magdalene would be saying "I am his lover and [I] trust his intent or purpose." But given the scribe's many errors, it is possible that here "cause" mistakenly stands in for another word.

1074–75   *Towche me natt . . . . and onto yowers.* Jesus' scriptural admonition to Mary Magdalene (John 20:17) has a long and productive presence in medieval English drama. In addition to the Digby saint play, all of the English biblical cycles stage the risen Christ's conversation with Mary Magdalene in John 20, as do the meditative texts preserved in Bodleian Library MS e Museo 160 (BMH edit these as "Christ's Burial" and "Christ's Resurrection"). *MDS* (pp. 205–09) analyzes the various interpretations that ME dramatists conferred on this biblical scene. Beyond these dramatic witnesses to John 20:17, the most infamous late medieval English account of Christ's *noli me tangere* has to be that of Margery Kempe (*Book,* p. 197), who reports her determined resistance to Christ's prohibition of physical contact. See *MDS,* pp. 82–84. For recent scholarly encounters with *noli me tangere,* see Bieringer, Demasure, and Baert, *To Touch or Not.*

1079   *Symoud the gardenyr.* On the motif of Christ as gardener, see BMH, p. 210.

1081   *Mannys hartt is my gardyn here.* The metaphor of the heart or soul as garden also appears in *Wisdom* (*MP,* p. 117, lines 89–92). A large fragment of *Wisdom* (about two-thirds of the play) is preserved with the other plays in Bodleian Library MS Digby 133; like *Mary Magdalene,* it too bears the initials of its one-time owner, Miles Blomefyld.

1085   *smelle full sote. MED, swet(e* (adj.), conflating senses 2 ("sweet-smelling, fragrant, aromatic") and 4 ("agreeable, delightful, pleasing").

1086   *Emperowere.* As *MDS* argues (pp. 112–14, 116–17), Mary Magdalene's attribution of imperial glory to the risen Christ contributes to a dramatic Christology that consistently focuses on his divine power, rule, and authority. At the same time, her imperial epithet is an unusual response to Christ's *noli me tangere,* the scriptural episode par excellence that medieval exegetes — and dramatists — understood as focusing on her longing for a human, accessible savior.

1090   *obteyne*. MED, *obteinen* (v.), sense b: "to gain (something spiritual or intangible)."

1093   *vervens*. MED, *fervence* (n.), sense 2: "the ardor or excitement (of love)."

1097   *Jhesus, Jhesus, Jhesus*. Mary's exclamation here points once again to the play's interest in and promotion of the late medieval cult of the Holy Name. See note to lines 93–94 above.

1099   *moryd*. MED, *moren* (v.2), sense a: "to increase; improve; augment . . . enhance; intensify."

1100–03   *Itt is innumerabyll . . . . itt doth excelle*. MED, *innumerable* (adj.), sense a. Mary Magdalene employs the inexpressibility topos, which appears elsewhere in the play (see note to lines 802–10 above). BMH (p. 210) query the possible significance of her numerical figure.

1104   *Now less us go to the setté, to ower lady dere*. Mary Salome's exhortation that the three women report their news about Christ's Resurrection to his mother ("ower lady dere") is not supported in scripture. In the *N-Town Play* (*NT*, 1:352–54, lines 73–136), Christ appears to his mother to provide irrefutable evidence of his resurrection. In his commentary on the scene, *N-Town* editor Spector (2:519–20) notes sources in Pseudo-Bonaventure's *Meditationes vitae Christi* and its English translation, Nicholas Love's *Mirrour of the Blessed Lyf of Jesu Christ*.

1111   *Awete*. The playwright employs the Greek word from Matthew 28:9, "Hail."

1112   *nymyos*. See line 857 and its note.

1115–16   *for to sosteynne . . . . sore refreynne*. See MED, *refreinen* (v.2), sense 2d. Jesus' opening line echoes Mary Salome's petition, picking up on the "–eynne" rhyme that concludes it. The change of speakers here calls attention to the way the Digby playwright's verse aspires to stanzaic form, in this case splitting the stanza between the two speakers.

1121–22   *Goo ye . . . . go into Gallelye*. Matthew 28:10.

1124   *Bodyly, wyth here carnall yye*. Jesus' reference to the "carnall yye" transforms the simple announcement of Matthew's gospel into commentary on forms of spiritual knowledge. As *MDS* (pp. 126–27) explains, at various moments the Digby *Magdalene* suggests investments in late medieval discourses dedicated to forms of spiritual knowledge, particularly those with a personal, experiential dimension.

1133   *aprise*. MED, *pris(e* (adj.), sense a: "of men or women: worthy, noble, excellent; also, most noteworthy, outstanding."

1140   *Mahond*. Although the king at line 1136 mentions plural "goddys" to be honored by a "sacryfyce," his queen here identifies the principal object of their devotion as "Mahond." See note to line 143 above.

1143–50   *Now, my clerke Hawkyn . . . . servyse is sayd.* The first exchange between the pagan priest and his clerk, named Hawkyn, is potentially confusing. The priest commands the clerk to prepare his altar for the sacrifice that the king of Marseilles has just proposed; Hawkyn responds with a *non sequitur*, alluding to the priest's illicit sexual relationships with women. Despite the priest's denials, the clerk's allusions turn preparations for the pagan rite into a competitive, salacious moment. The scene anticipates a similar conflict between the shipmaster and his boy later in the play. Weimann (*Shakespeare and the Popular Tradition*, pp. 138–42) associates the priest's boy with the Garcio type, named for the unruly servant in the Towneley "Mactacio Abel" play, whose role it is to challenge the master, employing verbal inversion and word play to unsettle the master's rule. Weimann identifies other Garcio figures in the Towneley and Chester Shepherds' plays, and the Towneley "Coliphizacio," or Play of the Buffeting. The Digby priest and boy are also reminiscent of the master-servant rivalry between the quack doctor Brundyche and his boy Colle in the *Croxton Play of the Sacrament* (lines 525–96). In this and subsequent comedic episodes at lines 1395–1422 and 1716–44, F (p. 124) suggests a resemblance to fabliaux and ventures a comparison to the interludes of masters and servants in the plays of Terence.

1148   *brayd.* MED, *breid* (n.1), sense 4a notes that the phrase "in a breid" means "in a moment, presently, instantly, forthwith; suddenly."

1151   *Sentt Coppyn.* The priest swears by an imaginary saint. BMH (p. 210) suggest several possibilities for the name's significance; for example, St. James/Jacob, with Cobbin as a diminutive, and a Jew named Copin, hanged for the murder of St. Hugh of Lincoln. The name also appears in "The Buffeting of Christ" in *Towneley*, where "King Copyn" seems to mean "impostor" (1:258, line 241). Stevens and Cawley observe that "Copyn" may derive from ME *cop*, "a crest on the head of a bird . . . [or figuratively a] coxcomb" (2:558n241).

1153   *jorny.* See *MED, journei* (n.). Several senses of the word are relevant here: a day's sport (sense 2a) or an undertaking or service (sense 3). With obvious sexual connotations, the clerk seems to say that he will have the first go at the imaginary "lemman" (line 1149) over whom he and the priest suddenly are competing.

1154   *Wattys pakke.* BMH (pp. 210–11) cite Whiting W56 and state the term means "that one is fat, or that one is deceived in love." In light of the clerk's insulting remarks about how the priest's great size affects his comeliness to women, both meanings seem possible here.

1155   *grett Morell.* BMH (p. 211) observe that "Morell" is "a common name for a black horse, especially a draught horse."

1157   *grett as the dywll of hell.* In late medieval iconography, devils are often represented with huge bellies, like the one apparently possessed by the priest.

1159–63   *Whan women comme . . . . I dare sey.* In the late Middle Ages, women were frequently singled out as the largest and most likely audience for sermons.

1160   *houkkyn*. See *MED*, *hoken* (n.) and *hokinge* (ger.), with a figurative sense, "to fish with hooks," especially with the sense of allurement and temptation. The priest's clerk thus boasts of his sexual prowess.

1161   *Kyrchon and fayer Maryon*. BMH (p. 284) identify these as girls' names.

1163   *ryde*. The clerk's boy comments on how his master's large size would trouble any horse that carries him; but in light of their exchange, the sexual connotation seems inescapable. See *MED*, *riden* (v.), sense 9.

1168   *quell*. *MED*, *quellen* (v.1), sense 1a: "to kill, slay."

1169   *belle*. *MED*, *bellen* (v.1): "to swell up"; and *belen* (v.): "to inflame."

1171   *grenne*. *MED*, *grein* (n.), sense b: "a fork of the body, crotch."

1173–74   *Loo, mastyrs . . . . is asprongyn late*. MDS (pp. 158–59) discusses the sexual innuendo and homoerotic potential in this display of unruly masculine desire.

1179   *Yower servyse*. The king's remark signals that the action to follow both resembles and parodies services conducted by more familiar "prystys and clerkys" (line 1178). The preparation of the altar, the donning of vestments, and the recitation of a "lesson" or reading (lines 1182–84) are elements of late medieval Christian religious practice, as is the reference to "offyse" at line 1225. Weimann (*Shakespeare and the Popular Tradition*, pp. 5–6) locates this episode in a long tradition that parodied ecclesiastical and liturgical forms, rites, and teachings.

1186   *Leccyo mahowndys viri fortissimi sarasenorum*. That is, the *lectio* (lesson) of Mahound, mightiest of Saracens.

1187–97   *Glabriosum ad glumandum . . . . Castratum raty rybaldorum*. The clerk's garbled, incomprehensible lesson employs dog-Latin, identified by the adding of the genitive plural (*–orum*) to a series of nouns. Scherb ("Blasphemy and the Grotesque," p. 236) notes that the mock *lectio* "consists of a series of gnomic utterances rather than a linear argument or narrative"; its "phrases fail to form coherent sentences, but they do invoke motifs that . . . associate the pagan temple with blasphemy and grotesque." According to Scherb, these motifs focus on food and bodily consumption ("Gormoerdorum alocorum" and "fartum cardiculorum"); sex ("Castratum"); and the "perversion or inversion of ideal Christian religious values." BMH (p. 211) state that the mock reading's "Snyguer snagoer werwolfforum / Standgardum lamba beffettorum" is a "common figure for the careless priest." The playwright here seems also to be taking delight in the comic possibilities of sound: "Snyguer snagoer" and "Rygour dagour." Brokaw (*Staging Harmony*, p. 34) suggests a musical dimension, noting the "mock plainsong" of the boy's chant. Such play with ecclesiastical and liturgical Latin idioms occurs elsewhere in medieval English drama. See Rastall, "Sounds of Hell," pp. 106–08, 123; The Play of the Dice or "Processus Talorum" in *Towneley*, 1:309–10, lines 1–46. As Goldie ("Audiences for Language-Play," pp. 199–202) demonstrates, linguistic play with differences between Latin and English was a regular feature of medieval English drama. He notes its appearance in the Macro plays *Mankind* and *Wisdom* as well as biblical dramas.

Goldie locates this dramatic language play in larger contexts of audience reception, using evidence from medieval grammatical and preaching texts to suggest possible horizons of audience expectation and complex possibilities for the apprehension of linguistic play.

1198   *Howndys and hoggys, in heggys and hellys.* BMH (p. 211) usefully deem this a "roundabout way of saying hell-hounds and hedgehogs."

1200   *Ragnell and Roffyn.* BMH (p. 211) identify these as common names for demons, appearing in *Chester*'s "Fall of Lucifer" (line 260) and "Antichrist" (line 647).

        in the wavys. BMH (p. 211) note that the scribe here may have misconstrued the word as *wayys*, meaning "ways or paths."

1213   *Wyth thi wesdom and thi wytt.* Ashley ("'Wyt' and 'Wysdam'") discusses this theological commonplace in the *N-Town Plays*.

1218   *besawnt.* MED, *besaunt* (n.). In medieval usage, the word signifies various coins, some of them biblical; a *besaunt* was also a gold coin originating in Byzantium, an exotic locale that is consistent with the play's evocation of the geographical world.

1227   *the trebyll to syng.* MED, *treble* (n.), sense b. The priest's clerk indicates that their singing will be done in parts, with the clerk taking the "trebyll," or high part, suggesting the boy is truly a youth whose voice has yet to change. Whatever the two perform ("Syng both"), the priest reprimands the clerk's poor performance at line 1229. Rastall ("Sounds of Hell," p. 106) comments on the failure of this moment as musical performance.

1232–37 *For here may . . . . Mahowndys own yeelyd.* Like the Pardoner in Chaucer's *Canterbury Tales*, the priest invites (line 1236) his audience to "kisse the relikes" (*CT* VI[C] 944). The priest's appeal invokes the medieval cult of relics, which ascribed spiritual power to fragments of the physical remains of holy people, i.e. Christ and his saints, as well material objects associated with them. Extending the play's representation of a conflated Muslin/pagan religion in terms of the practices of late medieval Christianity, the priest touts the benefit of contact with Mahound's "nekke bon" and "yeelyd," just as the Pardoner impresses upon the Canterbury pilgrims the virtues of the Virgin Mary's veil and Saint Peter's sail (*CT* I[A] 694–97). But the Digby priest also undercuts his promise by inverting the usual benefit believed to follow from contact with holy relics; his relics will make their devotees "blynd forevyr more" (line 1240). Akbari (*Idols in the East*, pp. 217–20) aligns the Digby play with other late medieval representations of Islam that make relics central to Muslim worship, comparing the king of Marseilles to Muslim rulers in the *Sowdone of Babylone* and other ME romances. Unlike literary versions in which the disavowal of a caricatured Muslim worship results in the convert's destruction of the idols, the Digby play makes the demise of the "maments" (lines 1553, s.d.; 1561, s.d.) the direct result of Mary Magdalene's prayer (lines 1552–61). On the medieval cult of relics, see Geary, *Furta Sacra*.

1241   *bede.* MED, *bed(e* (n.), senses 1a and b: "prayer" or "a supplication." The priest's language is difficult here because the "ytt" of line 1240 seems to have several referents, "cause" in line 1239 and "bede" in line 1240.

1243   *Mahownd the holy.* See the textual note for this line.

        Dragon. BMH (p. 212) suggest that the scribe intends "Dagon," a Philistine deity. This reading comports with the priest's inclusion of "Golyas" (line 1244) in his prayer, probably signifying Goliath, the Philistine giant killed by David in 1 Samuel 17. Both names contribute to the exoticism of the pagan religion of Marseilles. The collocation of Mahownd, Dragon, and Golyas may reflect a tendency in medieval representations of Islam (Akbari, *Idols in the East*, p. 203) to make proponents of the religion worshipers of a three-fold pantheon of false gods, usually Muhammad, Apollo, and Tervagant.

1245   *Belyall.* See note to line 21 above.

1255–56   *He was put . . . . in my thowth.* Self-identifying earlier in the play as "juge of Jherusalem" (line 231), Pilate expresses misgivings about the legal proceedings that led to Jesus' death. Late medieval English drama variously characterizes Pilate as a morally complex figure, ranging from an actively evil person to someone who finds himself in difficult circumstances and tries to make the best of a bad deal, the latter with foundations in scripture. See A. Williams, *Characterization of Pilate.* Like ME biblical plays from Chester and York and in the Towneley and N-Town compilations, the Digby saint play fashions far more elaborate plotting amongst the Holy Land officials than is provided for by scriptural accounts.

1260   *Joseph of Baramathye.* All the canonical gospels identify Joseph of Arimathea as a follower of Jesus; he is best known for retrieving Jesus' body after his crucifixion and, with Nicodemus, burying it in a rocky tomb.

1262   *sotylté.* See *MED, sotilté* (n.), senses 1 and 2, especially "a clever device, an apt contrivance."

1267   *a pystyll of specyallté.* The Second Sergeant calls attention to the role of letters as a mode of political communication, adding to the play's interest in the power of writing. Lim ("'Take Writing,'" pp. 134–78) discusses this aspect of the play in relation to late medieval documentary culture.

1280, s.d.   *Her goth the masengyr to Herodys.* As in the play's early scenes, the platea and loca staging effectively represents the sharing of documentary communication across distances.

1302–03   *In every place . . . . be hys ofyce.* Pilate's acknowledged obedience to imperial authority as well as the hierarchy of secular power that the play illustrates may conjure more local images of political control and the service expected of particular appointments and political positions in the late medieval East Anglian environment from which the Digby *Magdalene* emerged. For illustrative examples, see Moreton, *Townshends and Their World* and Richmond, *The Paston Family.*

1308   *deversyté. MED, diversité* (n.), sense 4a: "an adverse circumstance; an unkind or hostile act." Compare line 955.

1322–24   *The therd nyght . . . . away they yode.* This notion — that Christ did not rise from the dead but rather was simply stolen away through a conspiracy of his disciples — resonates with skepticism about or attempts to suppress news of the resurrection in other ME biblical dramas. See, for example, the Towneley "Resurrection," 1:335–55.

1323   *dyleccyon. MED, dileccioun* (n.), sense a: "divine or spiritual love," and sense b: "mundane love."

1326   *froward fode.* See *MED, froward* (adj.), sense 1. BMH (p. 212) question whether this line refers to the Last Supper. But the playwright here puns on both senses of "fode" as nourishment and as person. See *MED, fode* (n.1 and n.2). The Provost's notice of the "froward fode" fed to those who stole Christ's dead body, with its "corupcyon" (line 1325), would then indicate the unfortunate circumstance of their having to make off with a smelly corpse. The Middle English eucharistic pun on Christ as creature and as food seems inescapable too.

1335, s.d.   *dysypyll.* The disciple who enters with Mary Magdalene here is otherwise unremarked in the play. With respect to the disposition of space in the play, Mary's location at this direction is unclear.

1336–48   *A . . . . brothyrn departyd asondyr.* The speech condenses a significant period of time, since Mary last spoke at the scene of Resurrection. Since then, Christ has ascended to heaven, and his disciples have begun their evangelical work in "dyvers contreys her and yondyr" (line 1346). See Acts 2:1–12.

1342   *mencyon. MED, mencioun* (n.), sense 2a: "recollection, remembrance."

1348, s.d.   *Her shall hevyn opyn, and Jhesus shall shew.* The appearance of Jesus in heaven, from which he praises his mother and commands Mary Magdalene to "converte the land of Marcyll" (line 1371), has no precedent in textual and iconographic traditions of the medieval Magdalene. The scene underscores the complexity of the play's staging, including its dependence on multi-level *loci* that provided for up and down movement. This disposition is essential for the activity of the angels from this moment to the end of the play, as well as for Mary Magdalene's own ascent into the heavens. Davis ("As Above, So Below") constructs a stage plan for the play based in part on its requirement for elevated playing stations. Davidson (*Technology*, pp. 81–100, 119–22) discusses the ingenuity and technological know-how that enabled such dramatic raising and lowerings, for example at line 1375, s.d.: *Tunc decendet angelus.* Meredith and Tailby (*Staging of Religious Drama*, pp. 94–96) cite uses of such stage machinery in French, Italian, and Spanish plays.

1349–71   *O . . . . land of Marcyll.* Containing some of the play's most densely metaphoric language, Jesus' encomium to the Virgin Mary is a compendium of familiar and unusual Marian tropes, drawing upon both scriptural exegesis and medical horticulture. The temple of Solomon (3 Kings 10:18–20) and fleece of Gideon (Judges 6:36–40) are common Marian figures, as are images of her illuminating capacities, represented here by the "paleys of Phebus bryghtnesse." Noting this passage's dependence on ME Marian lyrics and liturgy, F (p. 60) comments on Mary's association with heavenly bodies and light. The paratactic structure of this passage accumulates metaphoric attributes of the Virgin without providing an overarching narrative or statement. The speech extends the play's Christological interests by underscoring the Virgin Mary's crucial role in the production of Jesus' manhood, and therefore, his godhead, as *MDS* (pp. 163–68) explains. Bennett ("Meaning of the Digby") notes the Marian allusions in these and other scenes. Scherb (*Staging Faith*, p. 200) suggests that Jesus may be addressing an actual representation of the Virgin Mary located somewhere in the playing space.

1352–55   *She was my tapyrnakyll . . . . my manhod myth.* Jesus employs three different metaphors of architectural or other material enclosure — "tapyrnakyll," "paleys," "vessell" — to signify the incarnation of Christ in the Virgin Mary's womb. As Gibson observes ("*Porta Haec Clausa Erit*") scriptural exegesis frequently figured Mary's inviolate womb through images of enclosure, such as the tabernacle.

1356–59   *My blyssyd mother . . . . to make resystens.* The idea of the Virgin Mary as protector against the devil was common in medieval spiritual lore; her triumph over hell was established in scriptural exegesis. See note to line 420 above.

1359   *resystens. MED, resistence* (n.), sense 2a: "nonphysical opposition, e.g., moral, political, etc."

1360–63   *She is . . . . the cardyakyllys wrech.* Jesus shifts metaphoric registers in order to praise the Virgin Mary's identification with medicinal plans and herbs. Unable to describe Mary's virtue in language (lines 1364–65), Jesus "describes her instead through an epistemology of scent" that displaces, according to Dugan (*Ephemeral History of Perfume*, p. 40), the King of Flesh's "worldly amalgamation of ambergris, galingale, and clary with powerful musk, precious incense, cinnamon, and English gillyflower." As Keyser ("Examining the Body Poetic," pp. 161–218) shows, John Lydgate's *Life of Our Lady* similarly explores the Virgin as an agent of health and healing.

1361   *seche. MED, sechen* (v.), sense 10b: "to visit," or "of a medicinal herb, [to] make its way to . . . a wound."

1362   *vyolens. MED, violence* (n.), sense 1c: "drastic or excessive efficacy, potency."

1363   *cardyakyllys. MED, cardiacle* (n.), sense a: "a malady characterized by pain in the heart and palpitation; also, a disease characterized by feebleness and profuse sweating" or sense b: "a similar condition caused by excessive emotion."

1364–65   *The goodnesse . . . . joyys can wryth.* The playwright again invokes the inexpressibility topos, See note to lines 802–10 above.

1367   *cast. MED, casten* (v.), sense 19c: "to give or devote (oneself) to."

1368   *Raphaell.* The angel Raphael is named only in the Book of Tobias 12:15.

1370–71   *Byd here passe . . . . land of Marcyll.* In no other ME version of the life of Mary Magdalene does the saint's journey to Marseilles issue from Jesus' direct command. Most lives of the saint follow *LA*'s master narrative, which provided for Mary Magdalene to leave the Holy Land, with companions Lazarus, Martha, and Maximin, on a rudderless ship. According to F (pp. 104–11), this crucial departure from the traditional vita makes Mary Magdalene's dramatic story into an instance of another medieval romance meme, that of the "woman cast adrift." F surveys illustrations of this important motif in Chaucer, Gower, and ME romance. The Digby play's significant departures from the influential account in *LA* are worthy of detailed comparison with other versions of the saint's vita.

1372–75   *O gloryus Lord . . . . them to porchasse.* Unique to the play's life of the saint are the angelic messengers who fulfill such a crucial role here and elsewhere. See Scherb, "Worldly and Sacred Messengers."

1376   *Abasse.* See *MED, abaishen* (v.), sense 1a. The angel's reassurance echoes Gabriel's words to the Virgin Mary in Luke 1:30; see also the angelic reprise of the Annunciation in the N-Town "Assumption"; *NT*, 1:393, line 151. In Mary Magdalene's case, Voaden (*God's Words*, p. 62) notes that angel Gabriel's identical words to Zacharias (Luke 1:13) were invoked by a fifteenth-century preacher to emphasize the importance of correct discernment of spirits. See note to line 601 above. A different form of the word ("abaffe") occurs at line 1438.

1381   *holy apostylesse. MED, apostlesse* (n.): "female disciple." By designating Mary Magdalene's mission to Marseilles as that of a holy apostle, the play draws upon and affirms the long tradition of scriptural commentary that accorded spiritual authority to Mary Magdalene deriving from her role as witness to and messenger of Christ's resurrection. In the later Middle Ages, this tradition was invoked to authorize women's sacred speech and their role as teachers and preachers. See *MDS*, pp. 134–47; Jansen, "*Apostolorum Apostola*"; and Davis, "*Apostolesse*'s Social Network."

1386   *He that from my person seven dewllys mad to fle.* Mary Magdalene here confirms Gregory the Great's conflation of the witness to Christ's resurrection in John 20 with the woman from whom he exorcized seven devils in Luke 7.

1391–92   *Now to the see . . . . sheppyng to asspy.* When Mary acts on the angel's command to convert the land of Marseilles, she inaugurates a series of sea voyages that give geographical credibility to the many real-world locations — Jerusalem, Rome, Marseilles — that the play depicts. D. Smith ("'To Passe the See'") observes that the play demonstrates a new awareness of the physical and geographical world ushered in by extensive maritime travel, an awareness that departs from spiritualized spaces depicted in medieval *mappa mundi*. On the play's geographical awareness see also Scherb, "Worldly and Sacred Messengers."

1394, s.d. *Here shall entyre a shyp with a mery song.* Among the many demanding requirements of the Digby *Magdalene*'s staging, none is more ambitious than the ship that must cross the playing place for three different journeys. Godfrey ("Machinery of Spectacle," pp. 155–56n6) discusses practical requirements for the ship in performance, identifying visual analogues in late medieval manuscripts and paintings. Pierre Gringore's illustrations for pageants designed to welcome Mary Tudor to Paris in 1514, in BL MS Cotton Vespasian B.II, include one for a fully-rigged ship, complete with sailors in a festive mood. See Baskerville, *Pierre Gringore's Pageants*. The Digby play's association of the shipmen with merriment may pick up on the appearance of ship pageants in public entertainments (Baskerville, p. xxi). Meredith and Tailby (*Staging of Religious Drama*, pp. 98–99) cite dramatic records reporting the appearance of boats in European medieval drama.

1395   *Stryke! Stryke! Lett fall an ankyr to grownd.* From this dramatic moment until Mary Magdalene concludes her spiritual mission to Marseilles, the play represents the mariner and seafaring in general with notable historical accuracy and material specificity. Despite the comedic encounters that introduce the shipmaster, the play's portrait of the personnel and economics of seafaring provides a window on medieval maritime practices. See Ward, *World of the Medieval Shipmaster.*

1397   *sownd. MED, sounden* (v.1), sense b: "to measure the depth of (water), sound."

1400–01   *I may natt . . . . were my syere.* The exchange between the shipmaster and his boy that begins here is challenging to unpack, full of cryptic allusions to sexual themes and rivalry. Citing lack of evidence about indentured apprenticeships to train shipmasters, Ward (*World of the Medieval Shipmaster*, p. 103) notes the adolescent boys could be committed by their families to learn seafaring. As *MDS* (pp. 160–61, 183) notes, the shipmaster and his boy reprise the conflict between the pagan priest and Hawkyn.

1408   *poynt. MED, pointe* (n.1), sense 5b notes that the phrase to "ben a pointe" means "to be about (to do something)."

1411   *seyll. MED, seilen* (v.), sense 3a; and *seil(e* (n). The term "seyll" functions as a metonymy for the occasion of the journey itself.

1412   *fayer damsell.* The shipman's boy alludes to the feminine presence of a "damsell" whom the master reinterprets in violent terms, as the "damsell" is implicated in the master's whip.

1414   *rue. MED, reuen* (v.1), sense 1a: "to regret (something)."

1415   *sped. MED, speden* (v.), sense 4a: "to give assistance; assist; help (somebody) to attain success." To "ben sped" means to "be successful."

1418–19   *skorn. MED, scorn* (n.), sense 2a: "mockery." The phrase "on scorn" means "mockingly, derisively."

1421   *corage. MED, corage* (n.), sense 3a: "valor, courage"; sense 3b: "fortitude." Following so closely upon the boy's expressed desire for a "damsel," his diminished "corage" here cannot help but invoke the sexual connotations of the term as in sense 2b. Such is the situation of aged January in Chaucer's Merchant's Tale (*CT* IV[E] 1808).

1432   *avayle. MED, availle* (n.), sense 4a: "monetary gain, income, profit; reward, remuneration."

1446   *O Jhesu, thi mellyfluos name.* The idiom of the play shifts abruptly here, as Mary Magdalene assumes her role as apostle. On her address to the name of Jesus, see notes to lines 93–94, 697, 760–61, 1097, and 1554–61. Scoville (*Saints and the*

Audience, pp. 30–54, 113–16) discusses the saint's rhetorical profile as a preacher, for example, her successful *ethos* and her use of the high style.

1450   *resortt*. *MED*, *resorten* (v.), sense 2a: "to advance, go; come, proceed."

       be grett convenyens. *MED*, *convenientli* (adv.), sense 2a: "fittingly, properly, rightly." The text captures the adverbial sense with the use of the preposition "be."

1453   *of hys Godhed and of hys powere*. Mary Magdalene's claim on behalf of Jesus' Godhead and power points to a dramatic Christology that was invested in the divinity of the savior, which Mary Magdalene elaborates in the remainder of this speech; e.g., her reference at line 1454 to "kyng Crist." *MDS* (pp. 110–17) observes that the play's Christology parallels that of Walter Hilton's *Scale of Perfection*, a popular late medieval spiritual and theological text.

1459   *mannys sowle the reformacyon*. Reforming the soul was a central goal of the spiritual program set forth in Hilton's *Scale of Perfection*. Although Mary Magdalene here identifies that goal for the king of Marseilles, her own spiritual development in the play corresponds to the stages of spiritual progress that Hilton describes. See *MDS*, pp. 103–10.

1465   *rebon*. *MED*, *rebound* (n.). BMH (p. 264) cite Old French *rebondir*. Compare *MED*'s definition of "rejoinder, reply."

1467   *compassyd*. *MED*, *compassen* (v.), sense 5b: "to go or travel around in (an area)."

1469   *losyd*. *MED*, *losen* (v.2), sense 4a: "to bring (somebody or something) to destruction, destroy, ruin, mar, break."

1483   *In principio erat verbum*. The saint invokes the gospel of John 1:1 and responds to the king's question with an account of the creation that follows Genesis 1, which also begins *"in principio."* This specificity marks a major departure from the play's major source in Jacobus' *LA*, which thus describes Mary Magdalene's preaching in Marseilles (*GL*, p. 123): "And when the blessyd Marie Magdalene sawe the peple assembled at this temple for to doo sacrefyse to th[e] ydollis, she aroos up peasibly with a glad visage, a dyscrete tongue and wel spekyng, and began to preche the faythe & lawe of Ihesu Cryst." Among all the medieval English vitae of the saint, the Digby playwright uniquely identifies Mary Magdalene as a public preacher of vernacular scripture. In so doing, the play draws upon a long tradition of exegetical and homiletic traditions that examined, and often asserted, Mary Magdalene's spiritual authority and her right to preach. *MDS* (pp. 134–47) traces this conversation from the twelfth to the fifteenth centuries, arguing that it directly informs the play's portrait of the saint as preacher.

1493–94   *The sonne to . . . . labor wythowtyn werynesse*. The sun's difficult "labor" recalls the work of illuminating the earth in which Apollo attempted, and failed, to instruct Phaeton. See Ovid, *Metamorphoses*, trans. Miller, book 2, pp. 62–77.

1500   *holy wrytt*. Mary Magdalene understands sacred scripture as a form of writing. On the importance of writing in the play, see Lim, "'Take Writing,'" pp. 134–78; and "Pilate's Special Letter."

1506	*Fysche in flod and fowle in flyth.* The account of creation evokes a common medieval topos, represented in the famous ME lyric, "Foweles in the frith." See Moser, "'And I Mon Wax Wod.'"
1526	*resonnys. MED, resoun* (n.2), sense 8a: "speech, talk, discourse; *pl.* words, remarks."
1529	*And cut the tong owt of thi hed.* The king's threat departs from the punishments promised by tyrants to other female saints revered in the Middle Ages. Virgin martyrs suffered other kinds of torture; but one, Saint Christine, did have her tongue cut out. According to Christine de Pizan's *Book of the City of Ladies* (trans. Richards, pp. 234–40), Saint Christine made the best of a bad situation by spitting out that tongue, which struck her torturer in the eye, blinding him. The association of women with transgressive speech is ubiquitous in western misogyny, particularly in its prohibitions of women's teaching and preaching.
1530	*return. MED, returnen* (v.), sense 1c: "to reverse the direction of (something) . . . also, change (wrong to right)."
1534	*ware. MED, waren* (v.1), sense 1b: "to be mindful of . . . heed." The sense of this line is "Let us go to the temple, of which we should take note."
1536–39	*Come on all . . . . se thow how.* The play exhibits an important tendency of the medieval West to represent followers of Islam as idol worshipers. As Akbari (*Idols in the East*, p. 216) notes, these representations mirror medieval Christian religious practice even as they invert Islam's monotheism and Christianity's worship of a triune god. Ironically, Islamic rejection of the use of images in religious worship is similarly inverted to identify a common Christian practice — using sacred images to approach the divine — with a transgressive idolatry. Akbari (pp. 210–16, 219) notes similar dramatic strategies of representation in the *Jeu de Saint Nicolas.*
1537, s.d.	*all hys atendaunt.* The stage direction suggests the king moves with an entourage, even though none of its members, except for his queen, speak in the play.
1542–45	*Speke, god lord . . . . of all blysse.* The king's attempt to demonstrate the power of his false gods or idols and all the trappings of the vaguely pagan religion that the play associates with Mahound ironically anticipate English reformers' identification of Mary Magdalene with the very material and imaginative excess of religious expression that they sought to suppress. Badir (*Maudlin Impression,* pp. 36–41) states that Wager's *Life and Repentaunce* makes the fallen Magdalene into a decorated idol who in effect represents the unreformed church. The Digby play's treatment of the deluded religious practices of Marseilles has complex historical and confessional resonances.
1554–61	*Now Lord of lordys . . . . rythwysnesse here dyscus.* Mary Magdalene's prayer offers the most elaborate instance of devotion to the Name of Jesus expressed in the play. As Renevey ("Name above Names") points out, worship of the holy Name was an important theme in late medieval English mystical and spiritual writings and was widely promoted by Richard Rolle and Walter Hilton. Devotion to the Name of Jesus is attested elsewhere in late medieval East Anglia. John Lydgate

makes it a notable theme of "The Testament"; see *Minor Poems*, ed. MacCracken, 1:329–62. Gibson (*Theater of Devotion*, pp. 49, 187–88n91) notes that fifteenth-century Bury St. Edmunds, Suffolk, was home to a large and popular lay confraternity dedicated to "The Holy Name of Jesus." The *Croxton Play of the Sacrament*, widely associated with Bury, concludes with a blessing offered "in wyrshyppe of thys name gloryows" (lines 1004–07). See also the note to lines 93–94 above.

1556   *violatt*. MED, *violaten* (v.), sense 1a: "to defile something, render impure or unholy, desecrate." Here, the past participle is used.

1561   *dyscus*. MED, *discussen* (v.), sense 1c: "to make something known, reveal."

1561, s.d.   *Here shall come . . . . thus seyyng*. This stage direction signals one of the most elaborate and complex instances of stage business in medieval English drama. For shock value it is on a par with the *Croxton Play of the Sacrament*'s provision for a boiling, bursting cauldron from which the voice of Jesus speaks (lines 713–40). Records of medieval performances in continental Europe show the frequent use of fireworks and gunpowder as well as of the cloud and possible trapdoor required for this scene (Meredith and Tailby, *Staging of Religious Drama*, pp. 107, 94–97). On the theatrical production of fire and other burning effects, see Butterworth, "Hellfire." A similar instance of female prayer enlisting divine power to overcome pagan worship appears in John Capgrave's East Anglian *Life of Saint Katherine* (ed. Winstead, book 5, lines 1321–58).

1564   *concludytt*. MED, *concluden* (v.), sense 6a. After the conflagration of his gods and the literal fall of his priest, the king experiences a moment of illumination. He acknowledges the deception that has hitherto controlled his beliefs and resolves to revenge, or "bewreke," its source (line 1562), which has caused him suffering and adversity. He is ready to strike a deal with Mary Magdalene, if her god can provide a son and heir for him and his wife.

1574–77   *I wax all seke . . . . me dyth*. The king's sudden illness is difficult to interpret, as is his invocation of the "yen suek" that afflicts him. BMH (p. 214) note the conundrum but do not venture a gloss. F (pp. 153–55) argues the comedic potential of this episode, noting the king's sudden illness cannot help but recall the quick onslaught of sickness — and death — experienced by Cyrus and Lazarus earlier in the play. But the king does not die. See also L. King, "Sacred Eroticism," pp. 196–97.

1577, s.d.   *Here the kyng . . . thus seyyng*. The stage direction's mention of an old lodge "wythowt the gate" points to a specific and evocative arrangement of stations on the platea, one able to accommodate the distinction between those inside (the king of Marseilles) and those outside (Mary Magdalene).

1579   *reddure*. MED, *reddour* (n.1), sense b: "severe treatment"; and possibly *reddoure*: "fear, fright."

1581   *demene me wyth mesuer*. MED, *demeinen* (v.), sense 2c: "to treat (somebody in a certain way)"; see MED, *mesure* (n.), sense 8a. It is worth noting that the phrase "withouten mesure" means "mercilessly, ruthlessly" (sense e).

1582–83   *As thou savydyst . . . . Abacuk thi masengyre.* Mary Magdalene compares her plight
           to that of Daniel, who was miraculously fed by Habakkuk while expecting to be
           devoured in the lions' den (Daniel 14:30–42).

1587   *Mary my lover.* See note to line 796 above.

1590   *Now, awngelys, dyssend.* The Digby playwright invents the angels' role in this
           scene, making Jesus a kind of stage manager for the illuminated spectacle of
           Mary Magdalene's appearance to the king and queen of Marseilles.

1592   *weyys pacyfycal.* Jesus' instruction to the messenger angels — that they tell Mary
           Magdalene to speak to the king in a "peaceful" manner — seems a deliberate
           counter to, and rebuke of, the nature of her appeal to the king in *GL* (p. 124).
           There she appears to the king only after having made two visionary appearances
           to the queen, without result. Mary Magdalene approaches the king "with a
           frownyng & angri visage lyke fire, lyke as al the hous had brennyd, and sayd:
           'Thou tyraunt & membre of thy fader the deuyl, with that serpent thy wife.'"

1597   *aplye. MED, ap(p)lien* (v.), sense 6: "to comply (with an agreement or request),
           submit (to certain conditions); obey."

1600–01   *Hym to asay . . . . hem to asaye.* The playwright, or possibly the scribe, lapses here
           with this circular sentence.

1604   *mentyll of whyte.* The notice of the "araye" that Mary Magdalene appears to share
           with the angels contributes to the play's awareness of clothing as a sign of
           spiritual states. Compare Mary at lines 1606–07; see Coletti, "Design of the
           Digby Play." *MDS* (pp. 181–82) discusses Mary Magdalene's white clothes as a
           token of her spiritual virginity.

1608   *wond. MED, wonden* (v.), sense 1a: "To hold back because of doubt or indecision,
           hesitate" and/or sense b: "to hold back because of fear, be afraid; shrink back."

1610–17   *Thow froward kyng . . . . from thi good.* Mary Magdalene's appeal to the king for
           sustenance resonates with medieval discourses that addressed the necessity of
           charity toward the poor. Anticipating the saint's preaching about poverty at lines
           1923–30, her interaction with the king here calls attention to her own
           involuntary poverty (when she later retreats to the wilderness, she will exercise
           voluntary poverty). Both of these were recognized in the complex social practices
           and discourses that accompanied medieval understandings of poverty and
           charity. For example, Mary's mention of "hongor, threst, and cold" specifies the
           three basic 'needs' identified in those discourses, just as the king's promise of
           "mete and mony, and clothys for the nyth" (line 1652) offers charity to assuage
           them. As Coletti argues (*PDD*, pp. 358–68), the Digby play represents Mary
           Magdalene's entire life, and especially her encounters in Marseilles, as an
           elaborate staging of these discourses' central terms and principles.

1610   *trobelows. MED, troublous* (adj.), sense 3: "mentally or emotionally agitated,
           distressed."

1613   *cold.* See the textual note for this line.

1617, s.d. *Here Mari voydyt . . . seyyng the kyng.* The change of clothing for Mary Magdalene signaled by the stage direction suggests that she here removes the "mentyll of whyte" that she donned, unremarked, at the bidding of Secundus Angelus (line 1604). The king confirms that he received a "shewyng" from a woman clad "[a]ll in whyte" (line 1623).

1626   *good.* BMH capitalize: *Good.* Although the manuscript clearly reads "good" here, the sense of the queen's exclamation suggests that "God" would be a more appropriate word to designate the source of the visions she and the king have just experienced. BMH's capitalization make the word a metonymy.

1630–33   *To us she spake . . . . wythowtyn dowthe.* The play's queen expands upon the advice given by her counterpart in *GL* by asserting that she and her husband must act charitably to those in "nede." Her response models the behavior of well-to-do, late-medieval East Anglian matrons, who promoted and engaged in the performance of the "comfortable works," including the provision of "almesse" mentioned at line 1641. See Hill, *Women and Religion*, pp. 118–66.

1646–48   *The mythe . . . . wyth yow be.* Mary Magdalene's Trinitarian focus anticipates her Latin blessing at line 1715 and enables her provocative assertion (lines 1662–64) that the conversion of the king and queen results from "the Holy Gost into thi brest sentt down," almost as if they have been subject to an incarnational visitation as in Luke 1:35.

1649   *sythe.* MED, *sith* (n.), sense 4a: "a specified point in time."

1654   *Goddys cummaundement.* Assisting the poor is a major theme of the New Testament; see e.g., Matthew 25:34–36; Mark 10:21; Luke 3:11, 14:12–14.

1660   *pryme.* BMH (p. 215) suggest that "the canonical hour is probably a metaphor of a new beginning."

1670   *O blyssyd woman, rote of ower savacyon.* The queen's apostrophe initiates the play's association of Mary Magdalene with divine attributes and links the queen's profession of faith with her new-found fecundity. The conflation of the saint's intercessory power vis-à-vis conception and aristocratic pursuit of an heir occurs in the *Vie de la Magdalene* that Louise of Savoy commissioned from François Demoulins de Rochefort in 1516. See Johnston, "The Magdalene and 'Madame,'" pp. 281–83.

1680   *Petyr, my mastyr.* The sequence of dramatic events whereby the king and queen conceive a child and profess faith in Mary Magdalene's Christian God differs from those of the *GL*, where the king remains skeptical, resolving to seek out Peter "to wyte yf it were trewe that Marie Magdalene had prechyd of Ihesu Cryste" (p. 126).

1687   *I sese yow this day.* MED, *seisen* (v.), sense 2a. The king's terminology identifies his turning over his kingdom to Mary as an act of feudal enfeoffment, a more legalistic gesture than the notice in *GL* (p. 127) that the king and queen "left alle theyr thynges in the kepyng of Marie Magdalene."

1691   *neythyr lond nore rekynyng*. *MED*, *rekening(e* (ger.), senses 2a ("a record of use of money or property; a statement of accounts") and b ("money owed, a debt"). The king employs the official idiom of property and commerce as he delivers "powere pleyn" (line 1692) to Mary.

1693–1711 *Now, worshepfull lord . . . . Mary Maugleyn*. The idiom of the king and queen's interaction departs markedly from the aureate language with which they first addressed each other, as if Mary Magdalene's intervention has clarified their speech as well as converted their souls.

1697–99 *worshepfull sovereyn . . . . made to be*. The queen's address to her husband associates their relationship with the hierarchical structures of late medieval royal families. Her desire to accompany him on pilgrimage, as Morrison observes (*Women Pilgrims*, pp. 3, 18), comports with the experience of medieval women who themselves frequented or sent proxies to pilgrimage sites associated with fertility and childbirth.

1701   *the wyttys of wommen, how they byn wylld*. The king's assessment of his wife echoes familiar associations of femininity and irrationality in misogynist discourse. *MDS* (pp. 162–63) discusses the play's multifaceted critique of femininity. See also F, pp. 58–61.

1702   *fallytt many a chanse*. *MED*, *fallen* (v.), sense 34a: "to come by luck or chance (to a person) . . . to happen (to a person), befall (a person)"; *MED*, *chaunce* (n.), sense 1a: "something that happens or takes place; an occurrence or event, especially one that is unexpected, unforeseen, beyond human control, or attributed to providence or destiny."

1708–09 *Wyff, syn that . . . . no more seyn*. The king's consent to the queen's request to accompany him marks the beginning of their story's resemblance to that of Pericles, most notably in Shakespeare's version. These similarities depend upon romantic elements of both plays' depictions of travel and pilgrimage. See Rochester, "Space and Staging"; Womack, "Sea of Stories."

1715   *In nomine Patrys, et Filii, et Spiritus Sancti. Amen*. Mary Magdalene's blessing of the departing king and queen renders her almost clerical, by virtue of the Latin idiom and the authority that assumes the spiritual power to bless in the first place.

1734–35 *Thou hast stollyn . . . . owt of lond*. The shipmaster's allegations of impropriety, signaled by the king's haste to depart, add another dimension to the play's attention to illicit and transgressive sexualities. Offering Chaucer's Shipman's Tale as an example, F (p. 152) cites "the discourse about sex, money, and exchange that often circulates through tales of merchants and mercantile exchange."

1739   *Ten marke I wyll thee gyff*. The king's financial negotiation with the shipmaster recalls Mary Magdalene's similar awareness of the cost of the sea journey (lines 1431–32). The *MED* identifies the *marke* (n.2), sense 2a as a "monetary unit equivalent to 160 pennies or 2/3 of a pound sterling." Morrison (*Women Pilgrims*, p. 54) notes that medieval shipmasters could improve upon a voyage's profitability by transporting pilgrims. F (pp. 148–52) also discusses the play's portrayal of the mariner and his crew and its relation to late medieval seafaring practices.

1745–65   *A, lady, hellp . . . . Domine.* At some point in these lines the queen gives birth, her distress causing her to appeal to "Mary, Mary." She laments the "defawte of wommen" (line 1762), i.e. midwives, who might have assisted in the birth that now brings about her death. Guillaume le Clerc's Anglo-Norman life of the saint ("Romance of Mary Magdalene," p. 192) depicts the queen's plight, and that of childbearing women generally with heightened emotional detail. The misfortune of the woman who endures an ordinary human birth without "wommannys help" (line 1759) recalls the very different situation of the Virgin Mary, who effortlessly gives birth to the baby Jesus with no midwives in attendance and retains her radiant virginity in the process.

1747   *flower of wommanned.* The queen's apostrophe, presumably to Mary Magdalene, as the "flower of womanhood" introduces an epithet more commonly applied to the Virgin Mary and signals the confusion between and identification of the reformed saint and the mother of Jesus that, as *MDS* notes (pp. 169–79, 185–89) figures prominently in the latter portions of the play. T. Williams' discussion of evolving gendered terminology in late medieval English writing observes that "womanhood" here signals the exercise of feminine power (*Inventing Womanhood*, p. 151).

1765   *In manus tuas.* An abbreviated echo of Luke 23:46: *Pater, in manus tuas commendo spiritum meum* ("Father, into your hands I commend my spirit").

1776   *What wethyr may this be.* Apart from the queen's mention of the "flod" in which she hopes not to "drench" (line 1746), this is the play's main notice of the storm at sea, described in greater length in *GL* (p. 127) and with notable meteorological detail in Guillaume le Clerc's Anglo-Norman life of the saint; see "Romance of Mary Magdalene," pp. 191–93.

1783   *Gyntyll serys.* The king sweetens his request to the mariner and his men by applying to them an attribute — gentility — that would seem not to pertain to persons of their social class. On the play's attention to the idiom of social class, see C; and for its application to the shipmaster and crew particularly, see *PDD*, pp. 353–57). Ward (*World of the Medieval Shipmaster*, p. 103) notes that the medieval shipping trade provided opportunities for class mobility and social advancement through the overlapping roles of owner, shipmaster, and merchant.

1784   *Yender is a roch.* In light of the king's journey in search of baptism by Saint Peter, Scherb (*Staging Faith*, p. 178) notes the possibility of the biblical pun, *petrus*, or rock.

1798   *Zaf.* This word has confused the play's previous annotators because, spelled with the ME yogh (ʒ), *ʒaf* bears resemblance to other ME words. BMH (p. 215) confirm Jaffa, the port city adjacent to Tel Aviv in ancient Palestine, as the correct referent. Whereas Mary Magdalene in *GL* tells the king that Peter resides in Rome, the Digby saint gives no indication of his whereabouts when she tells the king to seek him. The Digby playwright may have had the mariner call out "the portt Jaf" because Jaffa is the site of important miracles enacted by Peter in Acts 9:36–42 and 10:5–23.

1802–07   *here is all . . . . for yower wage*. The king confirms that he has met the terms of the economic agreement he made at lines 1739–41, employing vocabulary that suggests a charter-party, the name given to such agreements involving transport by ship. See Ward, *World of the Medieval Shipmaster*, pp. 229–34.

1802   *connownt. MED, covenaunt* (n.) sense 1a: "an agreement between parties binding them to certain provisions" and sense 2a: "*Law*. A formal contract; a contract under seal; the indentured contract of a servant or apprentice."

1804   *graunt. MED, graunt* (n.), sense 1d: "promise, assurance, guarantee."

1806   *styntt. MED, stent(e* (n.), sense b: "an allotted portion of income; a share."

1824   *this pylgramage*. In calling his journey a pilgrimage, the king aligns his voyage with spiritual practices familiar to the play's late medieval audiences.

1835–42   *Syr, than what . . . . fynd to stond*. In *GL* (p. 133) the king and queen, upon returning to Marseilles, are baptized together by Maximin, a companion of Mary Magdalene who drops out of the Digby play's version of the saint's life.

1843–44   *my hart wyll be sor . . . . nat the sentens*. I have modified BMH's literal rendering: "If you don't declare the meaning of God's commandments" (p. 216). See *MED, sor(e* (adj. 2), sense 5a and/or c; *MED, commaundement* (n.), sense 1; *MED, sentence* (n.), sense 2a.

1845–50   *Syr, dayly ye . . . . feyth to edyfy*. Peter insists that the king seek true "experyens" through his own direct "inspeccyon" of holy places. In late medieval religious and epistemological discourses, the term "experience" connotes knowledge acquired through sense perceptions, attributes, and behaviors of the perceiving subject in contrast to knowledge obtained from official culture as codified in written texts and institutional discourses. When Peter directs the king to seek "very experyens," he invokes an emergent value in late medieval spirituality that emphasized private, affective experiences as legitimate modes of knowing apart from traditional conceptions of authority. Increasing attention to knowledge acquired in this manner coincides with developments in lay, vernacular religious culture. See Watson, *Richard Rolle*, pp. 22–23; "Conceptions of the Word," pp. 102–03; and "Middle English Mystics," pp. 551–54.

1847   *eloquens. MED* definitions for this word do not readily explain its usage here. Perhaps Peter is suggesting that the king's proximity to him ("Wyth me shall ye dwall") will result in the king's acquisition (after *MED, eloquence* (n.), sense 1a) of greater fluency or powers of persuasion related to his newly found faith. Or, perhaps "eloquens" serves mainly to complete the rhyme with "experyens" (line 1846) and "delygens" (line 1849).

1848   *stacyons. MED, stacioun* (n.), sense 2a. Peter is clearly directing the king to visit famous Christian landmarks in the Holy Land, but some medieval pilgrims would have understood "visiting the stations" to mean a journey to the many churches of Rome associated with the dispensing of pardon. Appearing in the Vernon (Bodleian Library MS Eng. poet. a. 1) and other important manuscripts,

"The Stacions of Rome," provided pilgrims with an itinerary for such a visit and a catalog of available pardons (*The Stacions of Rome*, ed. Furnivall, pp. 1–24).

1853   *Itt is gon full to yere.* The king confirms the passage of the two years that, according to the *GL*, he spends in the Holy Land. The text contains nothing to indicate how the passing of that time might have been represented on stage.

1864   *callyd aftyr cold.* Neither BMH, who suggest the phrase is a formula (p. 216), nor B, who suggests the Boy is deliberately confusing "hold" with "cold" (p. 744, line 1865n), is satisfying. Perhaps Boy refers here to the abrupt manner in which the king calls out the shipman in the previous line. *MED, colde* (adv.): "unfeelingly," "distressingly," "cruelly."

1873   *Wythowtyn ony connownt.* Compare lines 1802–07.

1875–78   *Grobbe, boy . . . . as thou can.* The playwright's attention to nautical practices (e.g., reading the direction of the winds and casting sails) particularizes sea voyaging in the play far more than does *GL* and other narrative versions of Mary Magdalene's legendary life.

1893   *indure. MED, enduren* (v.), sense 1a: "to strengthen (the body), fortify (the spirit)."

1895   *that puer vergyn.* The king's apostrophe to "that puer vergyn" appears to refer to the Virgin Mary, mother of Jesus, whom the queen elusively invokes at lines 1747–48. But the king's exclamation also initiates a series of encomia to the Virgin and Mary Magdalene (lines 1899–1902) that elide the two women. *MDS* (pp. 151–54; 169–75) discusses the play's emphasis on this identification. Morrison's notice (*Women Pilgrims*, p. 74) that the Virgin Mary was an important symbol "for childbearing women in their pilgrimage activities" applies to the queen's situation here.

1905   *be Maryus gyddauns.* In *GL* (p. 132), the queen reports her sojourn in the Holy Land under Mary Magdalene's guidance.

1910   *For I have gon the stacyonnys. MED, stacioun* (n.), sense 2a. The queen's claim to have "gon the stacyonnys," i.e. to have made a pilgrimage to the holy places, resonates with recorded experiences of medieval women pilgrims. Elizabeth of York, wife of Henry VII who died in childbirth in 1503, paid proxy pilgrims to visit Marian and other shrines associated with healing influences for pregnant women; see Morrison, *Women Pilgrims*, p. 74. In April 1502, Elizabeth paid William Crowmer, gentleman usher, for delivering money to her for "hire offring to the high aultier at Richmond upon Estre day after high masse in going hire stacions." See Nicolas, *Privy Purse Expenses*, p. 6. Richmond's high altar refers to the Carthusian monastery at Sheen, a royal foundation from the time of Henry V.

1920   *nobyllys. MED, noble* (n.2), sense a: "an English gold coin usually equivalent to 6 shillings and 8 pence."

1923–38   *O dere fryndys . . . . Amen.* The king and queen disembark from their voyage to find Mary Magdalene preaching a sermon loosely based on the Beatitudes of Matthew's gospel (5:1–12). Although ME versions of the saint's life frequently report that she preached, the Digby play once more presents Mary Magdalene as a preacher of vernacular scripture. See *PDD*, pp. 357–59.

1927–28   *Thow yow in poverté . . . . nyth and day.* Mary Magdalene's endorsement of poverty and charity is of a piece with the Digby play's framing of her entire vita in terms of material and economic transactions. See note to lines 1610–17 above.

1929   *sowth.* MED, *soth* (adj.), sense 3: "of a person, the heart, etc.: honest, sincere; faithful."

1930   *paupertas est donum dei.* See 2 Corinthians 8:2, 9; and Ecclesiastes 11:14. BMH (p. 217) cite the response of Patience to Haukyn in *Piers Plowman* (B text, 14.275). Poverty as a *donum dei* derives from the opening of Augustine's *De Patientia.* See Schmidt's notes on passus 14.275 (Langland, *Piers Plowman*, p. 343).

1939–47   *Heyll be thou . . . . and prynsses bothe.* The king and queen resume their apostrophes to a Mary who bears attributes of the virgin mother of Jesus ("tabernakyll of the blyssyd Trenité"); yet these "hail Marys" also address the woman who sustained the abandoned queen and her child, identified as Mary Magdalene at line 1902. See note to line 1895 above.

1950   *alle yower pepyll.* Mary Magdalene's "alle yower pepyll present" implies supernumeraries on stage.

1952   *sowle helth.* In the most basic sense, soul health or ME *sowlehele* (from the Latin *salus anima*) denotes "healing of the soul, salvation" (*MED, soule-hele* (n.), sense b). But, as Raskolnikov (*Body Against Soul*, p. 10) notes, the term was also associated with medieval modes of didactic writing, addressed to lay people and the clerics who ministered to them, that anatomized the soul/self.

1953   *the Holy Gost hath take resedens.* Mary Magdalene provocatively describes the king and queen as imbued by the Holy Spirit in a manner that resembles the divine act whereby the Son of God was incarnated in the Virgin Mary. See note to lines 1646–48 above.

1954   *desepcyon of wrech.* This phrase is difficult to parse, but it seems to suggest that the Holy Spirit has driven out the errors of the couple's prior religious experience (and its vengefulness). See *MED, wrech(e* (n.), sense 1c; and *decepcioun* (n.), sense b.

1957–58   *But now . . . . yower hertys ese.* Mitchell-Buck ("Tyrants, Tudors") discusses Mary Magdalene's role as "governor" in light of the Digby play's possible mid-sixteenth century performance, suggesting its resonance with Tudor audiences thinking of the rule of Henry VIII's daughters. The argument about the play's 1562 performance in Essex is Coldeway's ("Chelmsford Records").

1960   *More gostly strenkth me to purchase.* Economic metaphors of redemption recur as Mary Magdalene prepares for her eremetic life. See note to line 689 above.

1961   *comprehend.* MED, *comprehenden* (v.), sense 5d: "to attain to, achieve, accomplish (something)."

1966   *bede woman. MED, bede-woman* (n.), sense b. In declaring her intention to be "bede woman" for the king and queen, Mary Magdalene locates their relationship in the context of late medieval almsgiving, which sought redeeming prayers for benefactors in exchange for their gifts. *MDS* (pp. 66–67) describes how late medieval women's religious communities offered prayers for their benefactors.

1971, s.d.   *Her goth Mary into the wyldyrnesse.* Wilderness is a figure for the eremitic desert, of which Mary Magdalene speaks at line 1989.

1977   *swete sypresse.* F (pp. 84–88) elaborates the complex significance of "sypresse," the plant known as galingale and bearing culinary and medicinal properties. Citing imaginative literature, herbals, and encyclopedia lore, F notes the potential for confusion between the cypress plant and the tree known by the same name. This verbal confusion parallels other overlapping meanings that bear upon allusions to cypress in the Digby play. All of these meanings are operative at line 2046, when the hermit priest describes Mary Magdalene as "swetter than . . . cypresse."

1981–82   *But my londdys . . . . Peter me badde.* The king's post-conversion zeal to build churches and destroy false gods follows *GL*, but neither that work nor earlier scenes of the play make these actions the result of Saint Peter's mandate.

1985   *perplyxcyon.* The playwright works changes on ME *perplextif* (n.) or *perplexité* (n.), sense c, to express the "perilous situation" that the king intends to inflict upon those who challenge his new faith.

1989–2002   *In this deserte . . . . be contemplatyff.* Mary Magdalene's allusive speech invokes gestures and attributes that align her declared intentions with late medieval pursuit of the contemplative life. See *MDS*, pp. 105–08; 124–27. F (pp. 26–32) also discusses the saint as contemplative.

1989   *deserte.* Mary Magdalene's withdrawal to the desert signals her pursuit of the contemplative life, attraction to which she anticipates earlier in the play. From its formation in the eleventh century, the saint's legendary *vita eremetica* incorporated elements of the life of Mary of Egypt, another penitent female saint associated with sexual sins. See Karras, "Holy Harlots" and *GL*, pp. 227–29. The iconography of Mary Magdalene as desert hermit called for her to be dressed only in the cloak of her flowing hair; see Friesen, "Saints as Helpers in Dying."

1991   *abyte.* Compare line 683.

1995   *concyens. MED, conscience* (n.), sense 2: "the faculty of knowing what is right, especially with reference to Christian ethics; the moral sense, one's conscience; awareness of right and wrong."

2003   *swettnesse of prayors.* Mary's vow, notes Dugan (*Ephemeral History of Perfume*, p. 40), reaches Jesus in heaven as "a sweetly scented prayer."

2006   *into the clowdys ye do hyr hauns. MED, enhauncen* (v.), sense 1a: "to raise (something) physically, make higher." Jesus' appearance and his command to the angels who will elevate Mary Magdalene so that she can partake of "the fode that commyt from heven" (line 2001) initiate complicated stage business, as the saint and the angels who guide and protect her move back and forth between heavenly and earthly locales.

2007   *Ther fede wyth manna.* The "refection celestial and no bodily metes" that Mary Magdalene receives through her ecstatic elevation in *GL* (p. 134) here becomes *manna*, the miraculous food mentioned in the Hebrew bible. Mary Magdalene's manna is identified with the eucharistic at line 2018, s.d. where the angels feed Mary an oble, or Eucharistic wafer.

2009   *afyawns. MED, affiaunce* (n.): "assurance, confidence, trust."

2010   *fynddys frawd.* In another invocation of the *discretio spirituum,* Jesus assures Mary Magdalene that her ecstatic elevation and the visionary experience accompanying it will not be an instance of fiendish deception; she confirms as much at line 2034. See note to line 601 above.

2011–14 *O thou redulent rose . . . . of ower Lady.* Primus Angelus' praise of Jesus incorporates tropes — rose, palm, gem — appearing elsewhere in the play, tropes notably associated with the Virgin Mary and Mary Magdalene.

2018, s.d. *oble. MED, oblé* (n.). According to the *MED,* this ME term for the sacramental wafer derives from the participial form (*oblatum*) of Latin *offerre,* "to offer." The Last Supper scene of *N-Town* (*NT* 1:277, line 372, s.d.) states: "Here shal Jesus take an oblé in his hand."

2019   *influens. MED, influence* (n.), sense 3a: "an inherent power or quality" and sense b: "inspiration."

2022   *Inhansyd in heven above vergynnys.* See *MED, enhauncen* (v.), sense 5a and c. Although Mary Magdalene's elevation to a heavenly state outranking virgins may seem an unlikely outcome for a woman known for her sexual transgressions, medieval scriptural exegetes and homilists, as *MDS* (pp. 176–79) explains, did signify her spiritual condition in those terms.

2023   *byggyd. MED, biggen* (v.), sense 2a: "to dwell or live (in a place, among people), reside; inhabit (the Earth)."

2027   *Fiat voluntas tua.* The phrase appears in Matthew 6:10, but the usage here also echoes the Virgin Mary's words at the moment of the Incarnation in Luke 1:38: *fiat mihi secundum verbum tuum* ("be it done to me according to thy word").

2030   *as hys blyssyd wyll isse.* BMH (p. 234) gloss the oddly spelled "isse" as the third person singular form of *MED, ben* (v.): "to be."

2030, s.d. *Her shall she be halsyd. MED, halsen* (v.2), sense 1 and/or 3. Several overlapping meanings of the ME verb *halsen* — to embrace, physically and spiritually; to encircle — point to the visual possibilities of this spectacular dramatic scene. The indications for song here and in the next part of the stage direction remind us of the importance of music and singing in the Digby saint play's final moments. See Brokaw, *Staging Harmony,* pp. 43–49.

Asumpta est Maria in nubibus. As M (p. 273) notes, the stage direction signals the singing of the Lauds antiphon for the liturgical celebration of the Virgin Mary's

Assumption; the hymn further reinforces the identification of Mary Magdalene with the mother of Jesus that appears elsewhere in the play. Cox (*The Devil and the Sacred*, p. 50) notes connections between this scene and the "Assumption of Mary" in N-Town, where the antiphon is also sung. See *NT*, 1:409, line 522. These intriguing prompts underscore the heightened potential for spectacular stage action and imagery called up by Mary Magdalene's legendary life.

2031–32   *O, thou Lord . . . . be thi name.* Despite Mary Magdalene's customary association with the human Christ whose body she seeks at his resurrection, the Digby playwright also appeals to the saint's connection with Christ as a figure of power and dominion.

2038, s.d.   *an holy prest.* Provided by the saint's legendary life, the appearance of the curious priest, primed to perform his clerical role, furthers the association of Mary Magdalene with Mary of Egypt.

2043   *namys sevynne.* As BMH (p. 217) note, this term probably refers to traditions of biblical commentary that identified seven names for the Hebrew God. In the Towneley "Second Shepherds' Play," Mak makes his entrance calling upon "Lord, for thy naymes vii." See *Towneley*, 1:134, line 274; 2:500n274.

2045–52   *Heyl, creature . . . . of yower Lord.* Casting Mary Magdalene in the role of Christ's beloved, the priest's first address to her invokes the scriptural commonplace of the heavenly Jerusalem. Walter Hilton makes Jerusalem the goal of the contemplative's spiritual pilgrimage, the perfection or "perfythnesse" that the priest attributes to Mary: "Jerusalem . . . bitokeneth contemplacion in perfighte love of God" (*Scale of Perfection*, ed. Bestul, book 2, ch. 21, lines 1129–30).

2046   *cypresse.* Once again, the word probably refers not to the tree, but to a species of the *cyperus* genus, many of which possess aromatic properties. BMH provide "galingale" as a gloss (p. 237). See note to line 1977 above.

2049   *expresse.* MED, *expres(se* (adv.), sense a: "(to state or show) clearly, plainly, explicitly, specifically."

2054   *selle.* Mary Magdalene identifies her hermit's desert abode with a term that also signified an individual's dwelling place within institutional monasticism.

2065   *Prest* (speech heading). The unnamed priest stands in for Maximin, companion of Mary Magdalene who, in the saint's legendary life, travels with her to Marseilles, where he eventually becomes bishop of Aix. As *MDS* (pp. 131–33) notes, the Digby play's omission of Maximin, an important figure in the *GL*'s vita, enables the dramatic Magdalene to exhibit a different relationship to clerical authority and institutions.

2070   *But tyme is comme that I shall asende.* See *MED, ascenden* (v.), sense 1a. Mary Magdalene ambiguously speaks of her anticipated death in terms that call to mind the literal, bodily ascension to heaven of Christ and the bodily assumption of his mother. Although the saint's death finds her enduringly connected to the earth, which she kisses at the moment of her passing (line 2114), the play's final scenes repeatedly elide her fundamental differences from the Virgin Mary, echoing the relationship between Christ and his mother made familiar through the account of the Virgin Mary's Assumption in *GL*. The N-Town "Assumption of Mary," based largely on Jacobus' version of that event, provides a useful lens on these similarities. Like the Digby play, the "Assumption" adapts for the stage a narrative account of female bodily exaltation: the Virgin Mary takes up eternal, bodily residence in heaven beside her son, and Mary Magdalene is raised up by angels to receive daily feedings of manna. In addition to specific verbal resemblances between the two works identified in these explanatory notes, N-Town's "Assumption" play occasionally departs from *GL* in the same ways as does the Digby *Magdalene*. For example, both plays show Jesus explaining from on high the special privileges he grants to the Virgin and Mary Magdalene. See *NT*, 1:387–409.

2074   *a crown to bere*. Jesus' promise to Mary Magdalene of a crown as her rightful reward looks back to the moment when he called for her to be "inhansyd" above virgins (line 2022). The crown was a material, visible sign of the virgin's spiritual state. As Hotchin ("Nun's Crown") explains, in late medieval monastic practice, the wearing of the crown symbolized the professed virgin's privileged spiritual status. M (p. 273) suggests a parallel with the coronation of the Virgin Mary.

2090   *In a vestment I wyll me aray*. Compare the pagan priest at lines 1182–83.

2094   *palme of grett vytory*. The palm is an emblem of martyrdom and virginity; for Mary Magdalene it must signify the latter, though she is herself victorious over worldly temptation and material travails. This symbol appears frequently in medieval iconography of the saints. In *LA's* (2:78) account of the Virgin Mary's Assumption, an angel presents Mary with a "palm branch from paradise," to be carried before the bier upon her death. N-Town's "Assumption" play includes a similar line: "A braunce of a palme — owth of paradis com this" (*NT*, 1:392, line 134). The Magdalene's reception of the palm here probably draws upon all of these associations.

2097   *veryawns*. MED, *variaunce* (n.), sense 3b notes that the phrase "withouten variaunce" means "without wavering, steadfastly."

2101   *inure*. MED, *inure* (adj): "in accordance with established practice, customary."

2106   *to determyn*. MED, *determinen* (v.), sense 2a: "to decide upon something; resolve to do something."

2106–08   *This celestyall bred . . . . to illumyn*. Mary receives the sacrament *in herimo*; but, as Morris ("German Iconography," pp. 90–91) states, illustrations of this moment in various genres of continental art often depicted her last communion occurring in a church or before an altar.

2110   *opprese*. MED, *oppressen* (v.), sense 2a: "to overcome, put down, or subdue (somebody) in battle; *fig.* overcome (a vice, virtue, etc.)." Here, the term is used in a passive construction.

2115–18   *In manus tuas . . . . Dominus Deus veritatis*. Along side other motifs in this final scene (the saint's receipt of the eucharist properly cared for and presented by an appropriately garbed priest, complete with acolytes), Mary Magdalene's words echo the liturgical rite for the dying. See M, p. 274.

2116 *wysse*. *MED*, *wissen* (v.), sense 1: "to instruct (somebody, oneself, a person's thoughts), enlighten, advise, admonish; also, guide the actions of somebody, direct."

2129–30 *Thys body . . . . reverens and solemnyté*. Mary Magdalene is peacefully interred in the play, but the site of her burial — and claims to possess her relics — were contested subjects from the thirteenth century, as her established cult at Vézelay in Burgundy gave way to powerful claims advanced by political and religious forces in Provence. See Jansen, "Mary Magdalen."

2131–39 *Sufferens . . . . lett us syng*. The text shifts abruptly as it moves from representing the saint's life to addressing a dramatic audience. The designation of that audience as "sufferens," or sovereigns, comports with other instances of audience address in East Anglian drama and also suggests frameworks for thinking about the important — and lost — social and institutional contexts for medieval East Anglian dramatic performances. For an inventory of examples across dramatic genres, see *MDS*, pp. 244–45n56. The reference in line 2138 to "clerkys" is tantalizing, especially in view of the grand ambitions of the Digby *Magdalene* text and the virtually invisible footprint, on the ground, of possible circumstances for the performance of this play.

2131 *sentens*. *MED*, *sentence* (n.), sense 5, especially sense c: "a passage of prose or verse in a written work; the text of such a passage."

2139 *Te Deum laudamus*. The play provides for the singing of a popular hymn that was put to many different religious and social uses in the Middle Ages, suggesting that the "clerkys" to whom the command to sing is addressed (line 2138) would have no difficulty responding; see Brokaw, *Staging Harmony*, pp. 45–47. The *Croxton Play of the Sacrament* (line 1007) and the *Castle of Perseverance* (line 3649) also conclude with the singing of *Te Deum*.

2139, s.d. *Explicit oreginale de Sancta Maria Magdalena*. BMH (p. 218) determine the reference to an "oreginale" as evidence that the scribe was "working from an 'official' copy, the play-book," an object that is clearly not the play's single extant manuscript. In the copious records of the Chester Cycle, the term "Regenall," or "orygenall," suggests a master text, like the York register, to which individual guilds regularly had recourse for the copying of their plays. See Clopper, "History and Development," pp. 241–42.

2140–43 *Yff ony thyng . . . . that to amend*. These lines may communicate the interests of the playwright or the scribe; presumably these are not the same person. In light of the obviously dramatic nature of the text whose transcription has just concluded, the reference to "redars" suggests a complex relationship between the performative and readerly dimensions of the Digby *Magdalene* as a textual artifact.

TEXTUAL NOTES

ABBREVIATIONS: B: Bevington, *Medieval Drama*, pp. 687–753; **BMH**: Baker, Murphy, and Hall, *Late Medieval Religious Plays*, pp. 24–95; **MS**: Bodleian Library MS Digby 133.

1	*INPERATOR*. MS: the speaker's name is written at the top center of the page. Appearing directly to the right of it are the initials M. B., the signature by which Myles Blomefield registered his ownership of the manuscripts of medieval drama in his possession (see Introduction, p. 8).
2	*audyens*. So MS. BMH: *audyeans*.
4	*be*. MS: inserted above the line.
	world. MS: *word*. So also at lines 304, s.d., 305, 380, s.d., 381, 408, s.d., hereafter silently emended.
12	*regeons*. So MS. BMH: *regeouns*.
22	*porchase*. MS has indeterminate letter or blotted error between *c* and *h*.
23	*am*. MS: written above the line.
25	*pesabyl*. MS: *s* cancelled after this word.
	possessyon. So BMH. MS: *possesson*.
26	*disobedyent*. So BMH. MS: *obedyent*.
28	*shall*. MS: *xal*. The scribe commonly used *x* rather than the digraph *sh* for [ʃ]. I emend silently hereafter.
32	*nat*. MS: inserted above the line.
36	*weryons*. So MS. BMH: *weryouns*.
38	*or₂*. MS: altered from *on*.
	grocth. So MS, BMH. B: *grocch*.
40	*swyche*. MS: indeterminate letter cancelled before this word; BMH identify cancelled letter as *w*.
45	*am I plesyd*. So BMH. MS lacks the personal pronoun.
49	*kyngges*. So BMH. MS: *kyggys*.
52	*commaund*. So BMH. MS: *commaud*.
58	*knett*. MS: Superscript *n*. BMH mistakenly identify superscript *n* in *knottys* in this line.
	caytyfys. So BMH. MS: *cayftyys*.
63	*al*. MS: written above the line.
66	*to me ful trew*. So MS. BMH emend as *ful trew to me* for the sake of rhyme.
71	*is*. MS: written above the line.
72	*of beuté*. So BMH. MS lacks preposition.
78	*Save*. Written in margin where MS has cancelled *of*.
86	*kyndnes*. MS: *d* written above the line.

90	*plesowns*. So MS. BMH: *plesowans*.
93	*Thatt*. So MS. BMH: *Thou*.
96	*Owt*. MS: superscript *t* here and throughout, silently emended hereafter.
99	*dowttyr*. MS: scribe has written abbreviation *-ys* instead of *-yr*.
109	*Whan ye shal hens passe*. MS: line bracketed and written to the right of lines 107 and 108.
110	*all*. MS: *h* cancelled before this word.
113	*Onto thes ladys of jentylnes*. MS: line written to the right of line 112.
121	*owit*. MS: *ow* with superscript *t*; thus emended by B. BMH: *wythowt*. I have adopted Bevington's emendation because *owit wrech* (owed harm) makes grammatical sense in light of the series of "if" clauses that follow this line. Nonetheless, the line may involve some scribal error.
125	*in*. MS: written above the line.
133	*Herowdys*. MS: indeterminate letter cancelled between *w* and *d*.
145	*faytours*. MS: *s* written above the line.
148	*shal*. MS: written above *make*.
160	*governons*. So MS. BMH: *governouns*.
162	*me*. MS: inserted above the line.
166	*ondyrstond*. MS: written as two words, with indeterminate letter cancelled between.
175	*in lumine tuo*. So BMH. MS: *in lumine*.
176	*splendore*. So BMH. MS: *spelndore*.
179	*me*. MS: written above the line.
184	*sceptrum de Juda*. So BMH. MS: *septrum Juda*.
185	*qui mitendus*. So BMH. MS: *imitendus*.
186	*I*. So BMH. MS: omitted.
187	*dastardys*. MS: *dastardus*.
190	*that*. MS: written above the line.
192	*marryd*. So BMH. MS: *marry*.
194	*ar*. MS: written above the line.
200	*ondyr*. MS: indeterminate letter cancelled before this word.
203	*replycacyon*. So BMH. MS: *replycayon*.
205	*voys*. MS, BMH: *woys*. B emends as *woth*.
208, s.d.	*masengyr*. So BMH. MS: omitted.
213	*Tyberyus*. The scribe frequently writes the *-us* abbreviation after the letter *u*, thus rendering the word *Tyberyuus*. Hereafter I silently omit the redundant *u*.
218	*Forto*. So BMH. MS: *for*.
219	*them*. So BMH. MS: *the*.
220	*wythin*. MS: *in* inserted over caret.
222	*swych*. Repeated in MS.
224	*perce*. So MS. BMH: *perce them*.
225	*wyth*. The scribe probably intended *wyght* (quickly), a word that appears at line 227 and whose meaning is also apt here.
227	*wygth*. MS: ~~sond~~ *wygth*.
229	*rychesse*. So BMH. MS: *rychsse*.
232	*Tyberius*. MS: *i* added above.

234	*pregedyse*. MS: *predy* cancelled before.
235	*yow*. MS: written above the line.
236	*ye*. So BMH. MS: *he*.
	to. MS: written above the line.
237	*prommyssary*. So BMH. MS: *prmmyssary*.
	and. MS: *ss* cancelled after this word. B: *ser*.
	presedent. So BMH. MS: *presdent*.
238	*inperrowpent*. So BMH. MS: *inper rowpent*. This word exemplifies an obscurity that editors have struggled to explain. My gloss follows BMH, p. 200.
240	*what*. MS: *qwat*. I silently emend hereafter.
	seye. So BMH. MS: *sye*.
248, s.d.	*Her*. MS: *y* cancelled after. Stage directions are written in red from this point to the end of the play.
280	*this*. So BMH. MS: *is*.
282	*God*. MS: *me* cancelled after.
288	*bryng*. So BMH. MS: *bryg*.
292	*lyf I*. MS: *lyf y*. B omits personal pronoun.
298	*exprese*. MS: written in right margin; *fulfylle* cancelled before.
303	*systyr*. So BMH. MS: *systyrs*.
305	*evyr*. MS: *b* cancelled after this word.
315	*perteynyng*. So BMH. MS: altered from *perteynyt*.
316	*mone*. MS: *sonne* cancelled before.
327	*dwellyn*. So BMH, silently emended. MS: *dwellyng*. B: *be dwellyng*.
333, s.d.	*Kyng*. So MS. BMH: *Kynge*.
	Lechery. MS: written above the line at the right margin.
358	*pyrles, prykkyd*. So MS. B: *pirked, prikkyd*
359	*yower*. So BMH. MS: *ower*.
362	*and*. So BMH. MS: omitted.
365	*wyth*. So BMH, B. Omitted in MS.
	may. MS: *d* cancelled before this word.
387	*asemlanus*. So MS. BMH: *asemlaunvs*.
389	*Thys tyde*. MS: line bracketed and written to the right of line 387.
393	*Com as fast as he may ryde*. MS: line bracketed and written to the right of lines 390 and 391.
395	*masege*. MS: *ge* written above the line.
402	*yow*. MS: written above line.
404	*counseyl*. BMH observe that the scribe used the incorrect abbreviation *yr* for the elided nasal. Similar substitutions occur in the spelling of *counsell* at lines 412, 421, and 436.
	for. So BMH. MS: *fo*.
405	*where*. So BMH. MS: *whre*.
410	*ye*. MS: *send* cancelled after.
417	*Of that castel beryt the pryse*. MS: line bracketed and written to the right of lines 415 and 416.
421	*But yf your counseyll may othyrwyse devyse*. MS: line bracketed and written to the right of lines 418–20.
422	*ye*. MS: superscript *e*.

431	Speaker's rubric (*Satan*) repeated at the top of fol. 104v.
436	*Syrrys.* So BMH. MS: *Syrrus.* r_1 is a superscript.
439, s.d.	*Mary.* So BMH. MS: omitted.
447	*debonarius.* MS: *debonariuus.* Letters *iu* written above the line, not *ius* noted by BMH.
449	*receyve.* MS: *ve* written above the line.
459	*yow.* MS: *yow* ~~yow~~. Repeated *yow* cancelled after this word.
	sportys. MS: *d* cancelled before this word.
465	*betake.* So MS, B. BMH: *beteche.*
469, s.d.	*seyyng.* So BMH. MS: *seyyg.*
475	*is.* So BMH. MS: omitted.
478	*Grome.* So MS, B. BMH: *Groine.*
480	*bettyr.* So BMH. MS: *berttyr.*
490, s.d.	*galaunt.* MS: *of* cancelled after this word.
493	*What.* MS: written above cancelled *w.*
	Wene. MS: possibly *mene.* BMH: *mene.*
	marchant. MS: *galaunt* cancelled before.
495	*sum.* MS: written above the line.
501	*somyr.* MS: *wyn* cancelled before.
508	*in.* MS: *i.*
514	*drynk.* So BMH. MS: *dryng.*
515	*CORYOSTÉ.* MS: repeated at top of fol. 107v as *CORIOSTÉ.*
525	*womanly.* MS: *m* written over *l*, but cancellation noted by BMH may be the nasal abbreviation.
531	*MARY MAUDLEYN.* MS: *Coriosté* cancelled before speech marker.
535	*sen.* MS: *seyn* cancelled before.
536	*love ye.* So MS, B. BMH: *love ye thos.*
538	*am.* MS: written above the line.
539	*My love in yow gynnyt to close.* MS: line bracketed and written to the right of lines 537 and 538.
546	*To dye for your sake.* MS: line bracketed and written to the right of lines 544 and 545.
563	*semlyest.* So BMH. MS: *semyest.*
585	*nere.* MS: *nye* cancelled before.
589	*wol.* MS: inserted above the line.
590	*veryabyll.* MS: *a* added above.
593	*lust.* So BMH. MS: *lost.*
597	*in.* MS: inserted above the line.
600	*mercy.* MS: *ye* cancelled before.
614, s.d.	*Leprus.* MS: written below the line in the right margin.
622	*wythinne.* MS: *ne* inserted above the line.
630	*syt.* MS: altered from *set.*
637	*hope is perhenuall.* So BMH. MS: *hope perhenuall.*
640, s.d.	*Jhesus dicit.* MS: repeated at top of fol. 109v.
642	*repast.* So BMH. MS: *rpast.*
650	*well.* So BMH. MS: *woll.*
658	*man.* MS: written below the line at the right margin.

659	*Symond*. MS: *Jhesus* cancelled before.
662	*quesson*. So MS. BMH: *quessyon*.
665	*al*. So MS. BMH: *all*.
670	*entent*. MS: *in* before this word.
674	*conscyens*. MS: *e* added above.
676	*wrecchednesse*. So MS. BMH note alteration of *e* to *ss*.
684	*wyl*. So MS. BMH: *wyll*.
686	*contrysson*. So MS. BMH: *contryssyon*.
689	*porchasyd*. MS: *l* cancelled before this word.
693	*tyme*. MS: *my* cancelled before.
694	*dred*. MS: written below the line at the right margin.
695	*thi*. MS: *I was* cancelled before.
701	*contrysson*. So MS. BMH: *contryssyon*.
705	*omnipotency*. So BMH. MS: *omipotency*.
706	*governons*. So MS. BMH: *governouns*.
708	*devyn*. MS: *dey* cancelled before.
709	*And*. MS: *ad* cancelled before this word.
723	*to*. MS: inserted above line.
725, s.d.	*dyvllys*. MS: *v* written above.
727	*TERCIUS*. So MS. BMH silently emend: *Rex*.
728	*judycyal-lyke*. MS: *d* cancelled before this word.
731	*PRIMUS*. So MS. BMH silently emend: *Rex*. Also at lines 735, 740, and 744.
736	*wreke*. So BMH. MS: *wroke*.
738	*hym*. MS: *y* altered from *e*.
739, s.d.	*serve*. MS and BMH: *serva*.
741	*lordeynnys*. MS: *the* cancelled before.
744	*fals*. So BMH. MS: *ffals* written below the line.
754	*deversarye*. MS: *de* added above the line.
768	*MARY MAUDLEYN*. MS: *Mary M* ~~*Mary M*~~. Repeated *Mary M* cancelled. BMH emend silently as *Magdalen*; also at lines 784, 815, 824, 834, 889, 894.
787	*gete*. MS: written above the line.
791	*prophet*. So BMH. MS: *prophe*.
	hatt. MS: inserted above the line.
793	*yower*. So BMH. MS: *yow*.
803	*impossyble*. So BMH. MS: *inpossible*.
815	*Lord*. MS: *c* cancelled before this word.
817	*weyys*. MS: *e* inserted above.
823, s.d.	*Mortuus*. So BMH. MS: *mortuis*. This is one of a few stage directions written in the right margin.
831	*drewyn*. It is unclear if this *w* is orthographically the same as *v*, the option B chooses. In either case there is little difference between being *drewyn* (drawn) and *drevyn* (driven) down by death.
836	*be*. MS: inserted above the line.
845, s.d.	*Lay him in*. MS: written in right margin.
846	*cogynysson*. So MS. BMH: *cognyssyon*.
851	*chyldyurn*. So BMH. B: *childyrne*. MS: *chyldynre*.
853	*DISSIPULUS*. So MS. BMH: *Dissipulys*.

	volunté. MS: *w* cancelled before this word.
865	*I.* So MS, BMH. B: omits.
867	*Wherfor.* So BMH. MS: *whefor.*
868, s.d.	The scribe has squeezed the stage direction between lines 868 and 869.
876	*thysse.* MS: written below the line at right margin.
888	*from.* MS: *fro* cancelled before.
889	*rythewys.* MS: *thow* cancelled before.
	equité. MS: written below the line at right margin.
891	*be.* MS: written below the line at right margin.
892	*Good.* MS: *o* inserted above word.
894	*monument.* So BMH. MS: *moment.*
895	*that.* MS: *that* and another indeterminate letter cancelled before; BMH identify cancelled letter as *o.*
	ye. MS: *the* cancelled before.
900	*remeve.* MS: *remembyr* cancelled before.
902, s.d.	The scribe has again squeezed the stage direction between two lines of the spoken text.
904	*glory.* MS: written below the line.
909	*me.* MS: inserted over caret. Ink is badly smudged at the beginning of this line.
912	*wondyre.* MS: *b* cancelled between *n* and *d.*
913	*nothyng.* So BMH. MS: *nothyg.*
916	*away.* MS: *was* cancelled between *a* and *w.*
921	*yower.* MS: *ower* cancelled before.
928	*Obedyenly.* MS: *Why lowt ye natt lo* cancelled before.
937	*the.* MS: *y* cancelled before this word.
	so bold. MS: written below the line at the right margin.
944	*losty.* So MS. BMH indicate here possibility of *lofty.*
	lyon. MS: written below line at the right margin.
949	*O, my blysse, in beuteus bryght.* MS: line written to the right of lines 946–48.
957	*plesant.* MS: *pleõant.* Here and elsewhere for the *s* the scribe has written the *yogh* for intervocalic *s* (/z/). See also lines 1304, 1490, 1503, 1505, 1513, 1519, 1539, 1547, 1585, 1689.
959	*ruby.* So BMH. MS: *rubu.*
960	*plesaunt.* So BMH. MS: *pleaunt.*
	my. MS: *l* before, incorrectly cited by BMH as cancelled.
962, s.d.	*a dylle.* MS: inserted above the line.
963	*yelle.* MS: *e* cancelled before this word.
966	*brasse.* MS: written below the line at the right margin.
967	*blase.* MS: written below the line at the right margin.
968	*asondyr.* MS: letter *y* altered from *e* or vice versa.
972	*passon.* So MS. BMH silently emend: *passyon.*
973	*On.* So BMH. MS: *O.*
979	*wrowth.* MS: written above cancelled *wethe.*
983	*atrey.* MS: indeterminate letter cancelled between *a* and *t.*
985	*Yet.* So BMH. MS: *ye.*
	eye. MS: *ye* cancelled before.

986   *everychon*. MS: written below the line at the right margin.

992   *in fine*. So MS. BMH note that the abbreviation employed here could also
           mean *in sum*, the option they and B choose. But *in fine* better comports
           with the idiom and meaning of the devil's speech.

992, s.d. *passon*. So MS. BMH: *passyon*.

           upon. So MS. BMH: *ypon*.

           Mawdlyn. So MS. BMH: *Mawdleyn*. My examination of the manuscript
           concurs with BMH's observation that the "red line drawn through [the]
           first line of directions" was "apparently" not intended to cancel it. This
           line resembles other red lines drawn at the tops of pages to mark the
           upper margin (e.g., see folios 119r and 121v). The scribe appears,
           however, to have written the first line of the stage direction over the red
           line, not the reverse as suggested by BMH.

997   *MARY JACOBE*. So BMH, expanding silently here and elsewhere. MS: *M Jacobe*.

998   *Jewys*. MS, BMH: *jevys*. Inserted above the line.

1001   *MARY SALOME*. So BMH, expanding silently here and elsewhere. MS: *M
           Salome*.

           intollerabyll. So BMH. MS: *s* cancelled after this word.

1003   *haddyst*. MS: *hast* cancelled before.

1004   *is*. MS: inserted above the line.

1004, s.d. *folowyng*. MS: *yng* inserted above the line

           The speech marker *M Maudleyn* is cancelled in the right margin. I adopt at
           line 1005 the emended speech marker of BMH, which calls for all three
           Marys to speak.

1007   *Mannys sowle to bye from all thraldam*. So MS. BMH emend for consistency of
           rhyme: *Mannys sowle from all thraldam to bye*.

1008   *in*. MS: *shold a be* cancelled after. BMH: *in peyne shold a be boun*.

1011   *MARY MAUDLEYN*. MS: *M Magdleyn*. BMH expand silently here and at lines
           1031, 1055, 1059, 1063, 1070, 1078, s.d. 1095, etc.

1015   *MARY JACOBE*. MS: Speaker's rubric omitted here. I concur with the logic of
           BMH's emendation, which is based on the three Marys sequenced
           responses at this moment in the play. The red lines that precede and
           follow the speech at lines 1015–18 appear regularly in the manuscript to
           divide speeches by different speakers. B does not note a change of
           speaker here.

1017   *mynd*. So BMH. MS: *myd*.

1019   *boundys*. MS: *v* cancelled before this word.

1022, s.d. *angelys*. MS: *angelus*. BMH observe the scribe's erroneous abbreviation. The
           scribe has clearly employed the same *-us* abbreviation that we see in the
           speakers' rubrics at lines 1023 and 1027 and in *gracyus* at line 1016 and
           precyus at line 1018. A comparison with the final words in these lines
           (*wound[ys]* and *stoundd[ys]*, respectively) illustrates the scribe's distinction
           between *-us* and *-ys*. The correct form in the stage direction would
           produce the plural *angel[ys]*. Elsewhere the scribe confuses *angelus* and
           angelys; for example, see line 2066 and 2077.

1023   *ANGELUS*. So MS. BMH: *Primus Angelus*.

1026   *Go*. MS: written above cancelled *go*.

1039   *inward*. MS, BMH: *invard*.

1046, s.d.   *Here*. So BMH. MS: *how*.

1047   *[PETYR]*. The MS identifies no speaker here. BMH and B emend.

1053   *seyd*. MS: *d* written above word.

                resurrexon. So MS. BMH: *resurrexyon*.

1054   MS: speaker's rubric *Jhon* repeated here at top of fol. 119v.

1056   *and*. MS: inserted above the line.

1058   *Wom sekest*. MS: indeterminate letters inserted above the line, and cancelled,
                     between these words; BMH identify cancelled letters as *st*.

1060, s.d.   *Hic aparuit Jhesus*. MS: written in right margin.

1068   *I*. MS: inserted above the line.

1077   *hevnly*. So BMH. MS: *hevly*.

1078   *fyrst*. MS: *fr* cancelled before this word.

1079   *Symoud*. So MS. BMH: *Symound*.

                gardenyr. MS: first letter blotted; *g* added above.

1083   *fowle*. So BMH. MS: *flowle*. Scribe may have cancelled the superfluous letter *l*.

1086   *MARY MAUDLEYN*. MS: *J* cancelled before unnormalized manuscript speech
                     marker, *M Magdleyn*.

1091   *posybylyté*. So BMH. MS: *posybyle*.

1096   *systyrs*. So BMH. MS: *systyr*.

1100   *expresse*. MS: *a* cancelled before this word.

1111   *I*. MS: inserted over the line.

1120   *In nomine Patrys, ett Felii ett Spiritus Sancti, amen*. MS: line written in red.

1125   *O*. MS: added in margin.

1127   *thow*. MS: stroke of letter cancelled before.

1133   *aprise*. MS: *ri* added above.

1134   *meve*. MS: *ve* added above.

1139   *curteys*. MS: *r* added above.

1149   *syde*. MS: written below the line in the right margin.

1153   *ded*. MS: inserted above caret.

1158   *Onshapli thou art to see*. MS: line bracketed and written to the right of lines
                     1155 and 1156.

1159   *women*. So MS. BMH: *woman*.

1162   *They love me bettyr than thee*. MS: line bracketed and written to the right of
                     lines 1160 and 1161.

                me. So BMH. MS: partial letter cancelled after.

1170   *On thi ars com mych wondyre*. MS: line bracketed and written to the right of
                     lines 1168 and 1169.

1174   *This kenred is asprongyn late*. MS: line bracketed and written to the right of
                     lines 1171 and 1172.

1177, s.d.   *Bete hym. Rex diciit*. MS: written to the right of the line.

1178   *this*. MS: added above.

1181   *bryng*. So BMH. MS: *bryg*.

1186   *sarasenorum*. MS: *sarasensore*. BMH silently emend, probably for consistency
                     of final *orum* in all lines of this doggerel Latin. This line is written in red.

1188   *Gormoerdorum*. So MS. BMH: *Gormondorum*.

1193   *Snyguer*. MS: *Sy* cancelled before this word.

1194	*lamba.* So BMH. MS: *la* cancelled before this word.
1209, s.d.	*Rex dicitt.* MS: written in right margin.
1213	*Wyth thi wesdom and thi wytt.* MS: line bracketed and written to the right of lines 1210 and 1211.
1217	*Here in thi presens as I sett.* MS: line bracketed and written to the right of lines 1214–16.
1220	*be.* MS: *o* cancelled before this word.
1227, s.d.	*Syng both.* MS: written in right margin.
1228	*dyvll.* MS: indeterminate letter blotted before this word.
1230	*Butt now, syr, kyng, quene, and knyth.* MS: a red line separates lines 1229 and 1230, but there is no change of speaker.
1234	*er.* MS, BMH: *or.*
	ever. MS: A faint line through this word suggests its possible cancellation. In that case *er ye gon* (before you go) would make sense in the context of the speech.
1236	*this.* MS: five or six letters cancelled before; word(s) not discernable; BMH identify cancelled letters as *mewyer ye.*
1239	*And.* MS: ō cancelled before this word.
1241	*This same holy bede.* MS: line bracketed and written to the right of lines 1238 and 1239.
	bede. MS: final letter obscured by binding. BMH posit the letter *e*, hence their *bede*, which they gloss as "prayer." The scribe usually distinguishes the letters *e* and *o* and here clearly has written *be*; nonetheless, "this same holy *body*" offers a better fit with Presbiter's praise of the virtues of Mahownd's relics.
1243	*holy.* So BMH. MS, B: *body.* BMH reverse lines 1243 and 1244 based on the verse form. See BMH, pp. 211–12.
1246	*That.* MS: *t* altered from *e.*
1248	*That is ower god in fere.* MS: line bracketed and written to the right of lines 1245 and 1246.
1249	*serjauntys.* MS: *xall* cancelled before.
1260	*Baramathye.* MS: *m* cancelled before this word.
1261	*SERJANTT.* So MS. BMH add *Primus* before.
1277	*PYLATTI.* MS: final letter obscured by binding, but a second *t* can be discerned. BMH: *Pylatus.*
1278	*that.* So MS. BMH: *tho lordys.*
	ryall. MS: *l* cancelled before this word.
1283	*passon.* So MS. BMH: *passyon.*
1287	*am.* MS: inserted above.
1292	*nere.* MS: before this word the scribe appears to have cancelled a mistaken stroke of the pen.
1298	*aprise.* So BMH, emending silently. MS: *apise.*
1299	*Wych.* So MS. BMH emend silently: *Wyche.*
1303	*be.* MS: inserted above.
1309	*natt.* MS: *it* cancelled before.
1311	*sentens.* So BMH. MS: *sentellys.* BMH emend here and at line 1315.
1318	*to.* MS: inserted above.

1323	*desypyllys*. MS: *py* inserted above this word.
1329	*the$_2$*. MS: inserted above.
1333	*for*. So BMH. This line is bracketed and written in the margin to the right of lines 1331 and 1332; binding partly obscures the word after *Mery*.
	to. MS: *fo* cancelled before.
1334	*renown*. MS: *of* cancelled before.
1336	*ded*. MS: written below the line at the right.
1343	*alle*. So BMH. MS: *l* cancelled before this word.
1345	*dysyllpyllys*. So MS. BMH: *dysypyllys*.
1348	*ferr*. MS: inserted above.
1348, s.d.	*Jhesus*. This word is repeated at the end of the line. This stage direction is divided from the preceding line with a horizontal line drawn in red ink.
	shew. So MS. BMH emend: *shew [hymself]*.
1351	*the*. MS: *I* cancelled before this word. *In* added in margin.
1353	*Phebus*. MS: scribe has written character *yogh* instead of abbreviation for *us*.
1358	*hevnly*. So MS. BMH: *heuenly*.
1368	*myn*. MS: scribe has written *my* with superscript abbreviation for *er*.
1375, s.d.	*Tunc decendet angelus*. MS: written in right margin.
1376	*Abasse*. MS: indeterminate letter cancelled between *A* and *b*; BMH identify cancelled letter as *b*.
1385	*commaunddement*. So BMH. MS: *commauddement*.
1388	*thoys*. MS: *y* cancelled before this word.
1389	*be browth*. MS: written below the line.
1395	*Stryke! Stryke!* So BMH. MS: *stryke skryke*.
1404	*good*. MS: *o* inserted above.
1405	*forhongord*. So MS, BMH. B: *sor hongord*.
1409	*I$_1$*. So BMH. MS: *Cy* cancelled before this word.
1410	*forlorn*. MS: *lonr* cancelled between *for* and *lorn*.
1418, s.d.	*Bete hym*. MS: written in right margin.
1427	*same*. MS: *m* written over another letter.
1428	*to*. MS: inserted above.
1429	*I*. MS: inserted above.
1430	*Is of the lond of Marcyll*. MS: line bracketed and written to the right of lines 1428 and 1429.
1435	*Yondyr*. So MS. BMH: *Yond ther*.
	Torke. So MS. BMH: *Torkye*.
1437–38	*Yendyr is the lond of Satyllye / Of this cors we thar nat abaffe*. I follow the emendation of BMH, reversing lines 1437 and 1438. This order preserves the verse form employed by the playwright here and accords with the sequence of events. The stage direction at line 1438 is written to the right of lines 1436 and 1437. B retains the manuscript order of lines 1437 and 1438 and places the direction for singing between lines 1436 and 1437.
1439	BMH silently emend here, adding the speaker's rubric *Shepmen*.
1444	*Sett off! Sett off from lond*. So B. BMH give this line to the Boy. MS: The speech marker, *The Boy*, appears next to line 1445.
1448	*vyctoré*. MS: written above a cancelled *vytory*.
1452	*shew*. So BMH. MS: *she*.

1456	*yow.* MS: written twice.
	way. So BMH. MS: omitted.
1469	*mysbelef.* So BMH. MS: *mysbele.*
1476	*And.* MS: preceded by ampersand.
1480	*That wold I lerne; itt is my plesyng.* This is the last line on folio 129r. At the bottom right appears the speaker's rubric (*Mary*) for the speech beginning at the top of folio 129v. At the bottom of folio 129r the scribe has written *Jhesu mercy.* Furnivall believed these words to be part of Mary's speech. BMH (p. 213) suggest that they indicate the scribe's "pious outburst."
1492	*sterrys.* MS: *and* cancelled after; ampersand written above.
1503	*it.* MS: inserted above a cancelled *is.*
1526	*hast.* MS: *a* cancelled before this word.
1530	*return.* So BMH. MS: *retur.*
1541	*sestt.* MS: s_2 changed from *y.*
1542	*lord.* MS: added above the line.
1549	*Onto.* MS: *to* inserted above.
1551	*knees.* MS: indeterminate letter cancelled before this word.
1553	*mee.* MS: *q* cancelled after this word.
1560	*Good.* MS: one *o* added above.
1561, s.d.	*clerk.* So BMH. MS: *cler.*
1574	*I.* MS: *a* cancelled before this word.
1576	*suek.* So MS. BMH: *sueke.*
1577	*hath.* So MS. BMH: *heth.*
1588	*asstatt.* So BMH. MS: *assatt.*
1590	*awngelys.* So BMH. MS: *awngelus.*
1609, s.d.	*angelys.* So BMH. MS: *angelus.*
1613	*cold.* So MS. BMH emend as *chelle* for the sake of the rhyme scheme.
1617, s.d.	*chongg.* MS: *voyd* cancelled before. Final letter of *chongg* partially obscured by the margin.
1620	*shewyng.* MS: *is* cancelled before.
1622	*saw.* MS: *w* altered from *x* or *y.*
1626	*good.* So MS. BMH: *Good.* See the explanatory note for this line.
1627	*may.* MS: indeterminate letter cancelled before this word.
1633	*I tell yow, wythowtyn dowthe.* MS: line bracketed and written to the right of line 1632.
1638	*My.* MS: *I* cancelled before.
1639	*yower.* So BMH. MS: *ower.*
1641, s.d.	*transit.* So BMH. MS: *transiunt.*
1643	*the.* MS: *w* cancelled before this word.
1648	*wyth.* MS: inserted above.
1649	*yowre.* MS: inserted above cancelled *ow.*
1653	*wyth.* MS: *s* cancelled before this word.
1655	*myschef.* So BMH. MS: *mysch.*
1661	*malycyows.* So BMH. MS: *l* cancelled before this word.
1684	*God.* MS: inserted above.
1695	*onto.* MS: *to* added above.
1707	*me.* MS: inserted above.

1714   *save*. MS: *ſe* cancelled before.

1715, s.d.   *tunc*. MS: *tt* cancelled before this word.

1718   *And yf thou aspye ony lond*. MS: line written to the right of lines 1716 and 1717.

1721   *ondyrstond*. So BMH. MS: line is written to the right of lines 1719 and 1720; last three letters obscured by binding.

1724   *That stondyt upon a strond*. MS: line written to the right of lines 1722 and 1723.

1735   *Thou woldyst ledd hyr owt of lond*. MS: line bracketed and written to the right of lines 1733 and 1734.

1736   *God*. MS: a letter, probably *o*, has been cancelled before *d*.

1737   *shall*. MS: repeated and not cancelled.

1738   *Or ellys I woll nat wend*. MS: line written to the right of line 1737.

1740   *up*. MS: *I* cancelled before.

1741   *In the Holy Lond*. MS: line written to the right of line 1740.

1744   *Hens that we were*. MS: line written to the right of line 1743.

1749   *A*. MS: inserted above in red.

1766   *wyff*. MS: *ſ* cancelled before. BMH mistakenly note this change at line 1749.

1773   *me*. MS: inserted above.

1774   *Yf thi wyl it be*. MS: line bracketed and written to the right of lines 1771–73.

1777   *Ower mast woll all asondyr*. MS: line bracketed and written to the right of lines 1775–76.

1778   *ley*. MS: inserted above.

1780   *Cast hyr owt, or ellys we synke ondyr*. MS: line written to the right of lines 1778 and 1779; final two letters of *ondyr* not visible because of trimming. BMH emend.

1786   *And my chyld hyr by*. MS: line written to the right of lines 1784–85.

1790   *I sey yow, verely*. MS: line bracketed and written to the right of lines 1788 and 1789.

1790, s.d.   *Tunc remigant ad montem, et dicit rex*. MS: This stage direction appears as cancelled after line 1796, suggesting that the scribe realized he had written it in the wrong place but neglected to put the direction before the speech of the king that it clearly introduces. I follow the emendation of BMH. B omits.

              remigant. So BMH. MS: *remigat*.

1796   *To be ther gyde here*. MS: line bracketed and written to the right of lines 1794–95.

1796, s.d.   *remigant*. So BMH. MS: *remigat*.

              a monte. So BMH. MS: *a montem*.

1800   *And belyve go me fro*. MS: Line bracketed and written to the right of lines 1797–99.

1819   *shall*. MS: *thee seyn* cancelled after this word.

1822   *Mercyll*. So MS. BMH: *Marcyll*.

1825   *tell*. MS: inserted above.

1827   *the*. MS: inserted above.

1829   *Satyrnas*. So MS. BMH: *Saternas*.

1830   *commaundmenttys*. So BMH. MS: *commaundmettys*.

1838   *From the fyndys bond*. MS: line bracketed and written to the right of lines 1836–37.

1840   *baptysse*. MS: *bast* cancelled before. BMH do not note this cancellation.

1842	*Agens the fynd to stond.* MS: line bracketed and written to the right of lines 1839–41.
1844	*cummaunddementt.* So BMH. MS: *cummauddementt.*
1847	*dwall.* So B. MS: *wall.*
1848	*and₂.* MS: inserted above.
1850	*feyth.* MS: *e* inserted above.
1856	*lawe.* So B. MS, BMH: *lave.*
1859	*That feythfully I crave.* MS: line bracketed and written to the right of lines 1856 and 1857.
1862	*kepe.* MS: *ō* cancelled after this word. Line bracketed and written to the right of lines 1860–61.
1866	*Be₁.* MS: *b* cancelled after.
1870	*Help me over the se.* MS: line bracketed and written to the right of lines 1868–69.
1873	*ony.* MS: two letters, difficult to distinguish, cancelled before.
1874	*Comme in, in Goddys name.* MS: line bracketed and written to the right of lines 1871–73.
1878	*As well as thou can.* MS: line bracketed and written to the right of lines 1875–77.
1882	*I shall qwyt yower mede.* MS: line bracketed and written to the right of lines 1879–81.
1883	*In.* So BMH. MS: *I.*
1886	*Verely, indeed.* MS: line bracketed and written to the right of lines 1883–85.
1890	*thee.* MS: *ō* cancelled before this word.
1897	*shynne.* MS: *y* written over *e.*
1903	*wrappyd.* So BMH. MS: *wrppyd.*
	varyawns. MS: final two letters difficult to discern because of binding.
1904	*into.* So BMH. MS: *i to.*
1907	*precyus.* MS: inserted above.
1909	*Wherfor.* So BMH. MS: *Whefor.*
1914, s.d.	*nauta.* MS: partial letter cancelled before. BMH do not note this cancellation.
1916	*Mercylle.* So MS. BMH: *Marcylle.*
1918	*I prye yow for my sake.* MS: line bracketed and written to the right of lines 1915 and 1916.
1921	*thi.* So MS. BMH: *þe.*
1922	*Cryst save thee from wo and wrake.* MS: line bracketed and written to the right of lines 1919–21.
1924	*think.* So BMH, B. MS: omitted.
	yow. MS: *both* cancelled after.
1926	*he.* MS: inserted above.
1928	*Yitte.* So BMH. MS: *itte.*
1930	*donum.* So BMH. MS: *domum.*
1934	*men.* MS: written below the line at the right.
1935	*dysstroccyon.* MS: *ss* written over another letter.
1938	*Amen.* MS: written in red.
1938, s.d.	*qwuene.* So MS. BMH: *quvene.*
1939	*Lord.* MS: inserted above.

1944	*nobyllnesse*. MS: *l* cancelled between second *l* and *nesse*. So BMH.
1946	*thi*. MS: inserted above.
1949	*wythowt*. MS: *b* cancelled before this word.
1955	*knowlege*. So BMH. MS: *knowle*.
1958	*have*. MS: inserted above.
1966	*yower*. So BMH. MS: *ower*.
1971, s.d.	*thus*. MS: *x* cancelled before this word. BMH do not note this cancellation.
1985	*swych*. So BMH. MS: *wych*.
1992	*me*. MS: inserted above.
1996	*stryffe*. So BMH. MS: *styffe*.
2011	*sprong*. So BMH. MS: *sporng*.
2014	*born*. MS: written above cancelled *bornd*.
2015	*commaunddement*. So BMH. MS: *commauddement*.
2021	*Thou shall byn onoryd wyth joye and reverens*. This is the last line on fol. 141r. The scribe skipped fol. 141v and 142r, writing *turne on the othyr syde* in red at the top of 141v.
2030, s.d.	*Her shall she . . . . Et dicit Mari*. Only the first part of the stage direction is written is red, as is the scribe's practice for much of the manuscript. The use of black ink for the Latin verses of the hymn thus mark them as spoken text rather than stage direction.
2034	no_1. MS: inserted above, not no_2 as cited by BMH.
2038, s.d.	$prest_2$. MS: final word obscured by binding.
2044	*graunt*. MS: *gruant*. BMH: *gravnt*.
2051	*perfytnesse*. So BMH. MS: *perfynesse*.
2052	*shew*. So BMH. MS: *she*.
2066	*angelys*. So BMH. MS: *angelus*.
2073	*possesson*. So MS. BMH: *possessyon*.
2074	*enirytawns*. So BMH. MS: Probable letter *i* inserted above.
2075	*savacyon*. MS: In an interesting slip, the scribe has cancelled *damnacyon* and written the more appropriate *savacyon* above.
2076	*fere*. MS: *e* cancelled before this word.
2077	*angelys*. So BMH. MS: *angelus*.
2085	*cummaundytt*. So BMH. MS: *cummaudytt*.
2092	*Straytt*. MS: *a* written above.
2097	*thee*. MS: inserted above.
2101	*inure*. I follow the reading of BMH. MS: indeterminate word.
2107	*tyme*. MS: *tym* cancelled before.
	reseyve. MS: *ve* added above.
2108, s.d.	*Her she reseyvyt it*. MS: written directly to right of line 2108.
2112	*recummend*. So BMH. MS: *recumdmend*.
2118	*veritatis*. MS: final letters obscured by binding. Line written to the right of lines 2115–17.
2119	*reseyve*. MS: *s* altered from *r*.
2122, s.d.	*Gaudent in celis*. MS: written to the right of lines 2120 and 2121.
2126	*game*. So BMH. MS: *name*.
2131	*sentens*. MS: final letter missing with corner of this page.

BIBLIOGRAPHY

Akbari, Suzanne Conklin. *Idols in the East: European Representations of Islam and the Orient, 1100–1450*. Ithaca, NY: Cornell University Press, 2009.

Alfonso of Jaén. "The Middle English *Epistola solitarii ad reges* of Alfonso of Jaén: An Edition of the Text in London, British Library, MS Cotton Julius Fii." In Voaden, *Prophets Abroad*. Pp. 159–81.

Amos, Mark Addison. "'Somme lords & somme other of lower astates': London's Urban Elite and the Symbolic Battle for Status." In Biggs et al. Pp. 159–75.

Ancient Mysteries from the Digby Manuscripts. Ed. Thomas Sharpe. Edinburgh: Edinburgh Printing Co. for the Abbotsford Club, 1835.

Anderson, Joanne W. "Mary Magdalene and Her Dear Sister: Innovation in the Late Medieval Mural Cycle of Santa Maddalena in Rencio (Bolzano)." In Erhardt and Morris. Pp. 45–73.

Angela of Foligno. *Angela of Foligno: Complete Works*. Trans. Paul Lachance. Mahwah, NJ: Paulist Press, 1993.

Anglo-Norman Dictionary. Online at http://anglo-norman.net.

Anselm. *Prayers and Meditations of St. Anselm*. Trans. Sister Benedicta Ward. Harmondsworth: Penguin, 1973.

Antichrist and Judgement Day: The Middle French "Jour de Judgement." Trans. Richard K. Emmerson and David F. Hult. Asheville, NC: Pegasus Press, 1998.

Appleford, Amy. "Shakespeare's Katherine of Aragon: Last Medieval Queen, First Recusant Martyr." *Journal of Medieval and Early Modern Studies* 40 (2010), 149–72.

———. *Learning to Die in London, 1380–1540*. Philadelphia: University of Pennsylvania Press, 2015.

Ashley, Kathleen M. "'Wyt' and 'Wysdam' in N-Town Cycle." *Philological Quarterly* 58.2 (Spring 1979), 121–35.

———. "The Fleury *Raising of Lazarus* and Twelfth-Century Currents of Thought." *Comparative Drama* 15.2 (1981), 139–58.

———. "The Resurrection of Lazarus in the Late Medieval English and French Cycle Drama." *Papers on Language and Literature* 22.3 (Summer 1986), 227–44.

———. "Image and Ideology: Saint Anne in Late Medieval Drama." In *Interpreting Cultural Symbols*. Ed. Kathleen Ashley and Pamela Sheingorn. Athens: University of Georgia Press, 1990. Pp. 111–30.

Atkin, Tamara. *The Drama of Reform: Theology and Theatricality, 1461–1553*. Turnhout: Brepols, 2013.

Badham, Sally. "Mercantile Involvement in Religious Guilds." In Barron and Sutton. Pp. 221–41.

Badir, Patricia. "'To allure vnto their loue': Iconoclasm and Striptease in Lewis Wager's *The Life and Repentance of Marie Magdalene*." *Theatre Journal* 51 (1999), 1–20.

———. "Medieval Poetics and Protestant Magdalenes." In *Reading the Medieval in Early Modern England*. Ed. Gordon McMullan and David Matthews. Cambridge: Cambridge University Press, 2007. Pp. 205–19.

———. *The Maudlin Impression: English Literary Images of Mary Magdalene, 1550–1700*. Notre Dame, IN: University of Notre Dame Press, 2009.

Baigent, Michael, Richard Leigh, and Henry Lincoln. *Holy Blood, Holy Grail*. New York: Delacorte Press, 1982.

Baker, Donald C., and James L. Murphy. "The Late Medieval Plays of MS Digby 133: Scribes, Dates, and Early History." *Research Opportunities in Renaissance Drama* 10 (1967), 153–66.

Bale, John. *The Complete Plays of John Bale*. 2 vols. Ed. Peter Happé. Cambridge: D. S. Brewer, 1985–86.

Barratt, Alexandra, ed. *Womens' Writing in Middle English*. London: Longman, 1992.

Barron, Caroline M., and Anne F. Sutton, eds. *The Medieval Merchant. Proceedings of the 2012 Harlaxton Symposium*. Donington: Shaun Tyas, 2014.

Baskerville, Charles Read. *Pierre Gringore's Pageants for the Entry of Mary Tudor into Paris*. Chicago: University of Chicago Press, 1934.

Bates, David, and Robert Liddiard, eds. *East Anglia and Its North Sea World in the Middle Ages*. Woodbridge: Boydell Press, 2013.

Bateson, Mary, ed. "The Register of Crabhouse Nunnery." *Norfolk Archaeology* 11 (1892), 1–71.

Beadle, Richard. "The Medieval Drama of East Anglia: Studies in Dialect, Documentary Records and Stagecraft." 2 vols. Ph.D. dissertation. University of York, Centre for Medieval Studies, 1977.

———. "Plays and Playing at Thetford and Nearby 1498–1540." *Theatre Notebook* 32.1 (1978), 4–11.

———. "Prolegomena to a Literary Geography of Later Medieval Norfolk." In *Regionalism in Late Medieval Manuscripts and Texts*. Ed. Felicity Riddy. Cambridge: D. S. Brewer, 1991. Pp. 89–108.

———, ed. *The Cambridge Companion to Medieval English Theatre*. Cambridge: Cambridge University Press, 2006.

———. "Macro MS 5: A Historical Reconstruction." *Transactions of the Cambridge Bibliographical Society* 16 (2016), 35–77.

Beckwith, Sarah. "*Sacrum Signum*: Sacramentality and Dissent in York's Theater of Corpus Christi." In *Criticism and Dissent in the Middle Ages*. Ed. Rita Copeland. Cambridge: Cambridge University Press, 1996. Pp. 264–88.

Ben-Tsur, Dalia. "Early Ramifications of Theatrical Iconoclasm: The Conversion of Catholic Biblical Plays into Protestant Drama." *Partial Answers* 3.1 (2005), 43–56.

Bennett, Jacob. "The *Mary Magdalene* of Bishop's Lynn." *Studies in Philology* 75 (1978), 1–9.

———. "The Meaning of the Digby *Mary Magdalen*." *Studies in Philology* 101.1 (2004), 38–47.

Benskin, Michael. "The letters <þ> and <y> in Later Middle English, and Some Related Matters." *Journal of the Society of Archivists* 7 (1982), 13–30.

Benson, C. David. *The History of Troy in Middle English Literature: Guido delle Colonne's* Historia Destructionis Troiae *in Medieval England*. Woodbridge: D. S. Brewer, 1980.

Bériou, Nicole. "La Madeleine dans les sermons parisiens du XIIIe siècle." *Mélange de l'École français de Rome – Moyen Âge* 104.1 (1992), 269–340.

Bernard of Clairvaux. *On the Song of Songs I*. Trans. Kilian Walsh. Cistercian Fathers Series 4. Kalamazoo, MI: Cistercian Publications, 1976.

Bestul, Thomas H. "The Meditation on Mary Magdalene of Alexander Nequam." *The Journal of Medieval Latin* 9 (1999), 1–40.

Bevington, David, ed. *Medieval Drama*. Boston: Houghton Mifflin, 1975.

Biggs, Douglas, Sharon D. Michalove, and A. Compton Reeves, eds. *Traditions and Transformations in Late Medieval England*. Leiden: Brill, 2002.

Birney, Earle. "The Franklin's 'Sop in Wyn.'" *Notes and Queries* n.s. 6.9 (October 1959), 345–47.

Blamires, Alcuin, ed. with Karen Pratt and C. W. Marx. *Woman Defamed and Woman Defended*. Oxford: Clarendon Press, 1992.

Blamires, Alcuin. "Women and Preaching in Medieval Orthodoxy, Heresy, and Saints' Lives." *Viator* 26 (1995), 135–52.

Bloomfield, Morton W. *The Seven Deadly Sins: An Introduction to the History of a Religious Concept*. East Lansing: Michigan State University Press, 1952.

Boehnen, Scott. "The Aesthetics of 'Sprawling' Drama: The Digby *Mary Magdelene* as Pilgrims' Play." *Journal of English and Germanic Philology* 98 (1999), 325–52.

Bokenham, Osbern. *Legendys of Hooly Wummen*. Ed. Mary S. Sarjeantson. EETS o.s. 206. London: Humphrey Milford, Oxford University Press, 1938.

Bourgeault, Cynthia. *The Meaning of Mary Magdalene: Discovering the Woman at the Heart of Christianity*. Boston: Shambhala, 2010.

Brock, Ann Graham. *Mary Magdalene, The First Apostle: The Struggle for Authority*. Cambridge, MA: Harvard University Press, 2003.

Brokaw, Katherine Steele. *Staging Harmony: Music and Religious Change in Late Medieval and Early Modern English Drama*. Ithaca, NY: Cornell University Press, 2016.

Brown, Dan. *The Da Vinci Code*. New York: Doubleday, 2003.

Burgess, Clive. "Making Mammon Serve God: Merchant Piety in Later Medieval England." In Barron and Sutton. Pp. 183–207.

Burstein, Dan, and Arne J. De Keijzer, eds. *Secrets of Mary Magdalene: The Untold Story of History's Most Misunderstood Woman*. New York: CDS Books, 2006.

Bush, Jerome. "Resources of *Locus* and *Platea* Staging: The Digby *Mary Magdalene*." *Studies in Philology* 86.2 (1989), 139–65.

Butterworth, Philip. "Hellfire: Flame as Special Effect." In Davidson and Seiler. Pp. 67–101.

Capgrave, John. *The Life of Saint Katherine*. Ed. Karen A. Winstead. Kalamazoo, MI: Medieval Institute Publications, 1999.

Carruthers, Mary. "Sweetness." *Speculum* 81.4 (October 2006), 999–1013.

Carter, Susan. "The Digby *Mary Magdalen*: Constructing the *Apostola Apostolorum*." *Studies in Philology* 106.4 (2009), 402–19.

The Castle of Perseverance. Ed. David N. Klausner. Kalamazoo, MI: Medieval Institute Publications, 2010.

Cavalca, Domenico. *The Life of Mary Magdalen. Translated from the Italian of an Unknown Fourteenth-Century Writer*. Trans. Valentina Hawtrey. London: John Lane, 1904.

Chaganti, Seeta. "The *Platea*: Pre- and Postmodern: A Landscape of Medieval Performance Studies." *Exemplaria* 25.3 (2013), 252–64.

The Chastising of God's Children and the Treatise of Perfection of the Sons of God. Ed. Joyce Bazire and Eric Colledge. Oxford: Basil Blackwell, 1957.

Chaucer, Geoffrey. *The Riverside Chaucer*. Third edition. Ed. Larry D. Benson et al. Boston: Houghton Mifflin, 1987.

Chemers, Michael Mark. "Anti-Semitism, Surrogacy, and the Invocation of Mohammed in the *Play of the Sacrament*." *Comparative Drama* 41.1 (2007), 25–55.

The Chester Mystery Cycle. Ed. David Mills. East Lansing, MI: Colleagues Press, 1992.

The Chester Mystery Cycle. Ed. R. M. Lumiansky and David Mills. 2 vols. EETS s.s. 3 and 9. Oxford: Oxford University Press, 1974 and 1986.

Christine de Pizan. *The Book of the City of Ladies*. Trans. Earl Jeffrey Richards. New York: Persea Books, 1982.

Clichtove, Josse. "Epistle 124: Josse Clichtove to François du Moulin de Rochefort [Paris. Before July 22, 1518]." In Lefèvre, d'Etaples, Jacques. *The Prefatory Epistles of Jacques Lefèvre d'Etaples and Related Texts*. Ed. Eugene F. Rice, Jr. New York: Columbia University Press, 1972. Pp. 399–406.

Clopper, Lawrence M. "The History and Development of the Chester Cycle." *Modern Philology* 75.3 (February 1978), 219–46.

———. "*Communitas*: The Play of Saints in Late Medieval and Tudor England." *Mediaevalia* 18 (1995 [for 1992]), 81–109.

———. *Drama, Play, and Game: English Festive Culture in the Medieval and Early Modern Period*. Chicago: University of Chicago Press, 2001.

The Cloud of Unknowing and the Book of Privy Counselling. Ed. Phyllis Hodgson. EETS o.s. 218. 1944; rpt., London: Oxford University Press, 1981.

The Cloud of Unknowing and Related Treatises. Ed. Phyllis Hodgson. Analecta Cartusiana 3. Salzburg: Institut für Anglistik und Amerikanistik, Universität Salzberg, 1982.

Cockett, Peter. "The Actor's Carnal Eye: A Contemporary Staging of the Digby *Mary Magdalene*." *Baylor Journal of Theatre and Performance* 3.2 (2006), 67–83.

Coldewey, John. "The Digby Plays and the Chelmsford Records." *Research Opportunities in Renaissance Drama* 18 (1975), 103–21.

———. "The Non-Cycle Plays and the East Anglian Tradition." In Beadle, *Cambridge Companion*. 189–210.

Coletti, Theresa. "The Design of the Digby Play of *Mary Magdalene*." *Studies in Philology* 76.4 (1979), 313–33.

———. "Re-reading the Story of Herod in the Middle English Innocents Plays." In *Retelling Tales: Essays in Honor of Russell Peck*. Ed. Thomas Hahn and Alan Lupack. Woodbridge: D. S. Brewer, 1997. Pp. 35–59.

———. "Genealogy, Sexuality, and Sacred Power: The Saint Anne Dedication of the Digby *Candlemas Day* and the *Killing of the Children of Israel*." *Journal of Medieval and Early Modern Studies* 29.1 (Winter 1999), 25–59.

———. "'*Paupertas est donum Dei*': Hagiography, Lay Religion, and the Economics of Salvation in the Digby *Mary Magdalene*." *Speculum* 76.2 (2001), 337–78.

———. "'Curtesy doth it yow lere': The Sociology of Transgression in the Digby *Mary Magdalene*." *ELH* 71.1 (2004), 1–28.

———. *Mary Magdalene and the Drama of Saints: Theater, Gender, and Religion in Late Medieval England*. Philadelphia: University of Pennsylvania Press, 2004.

———. "Social Contexts of the East Anglian Saint Play: The Digby Mary Magdalene and the Late Medieval Hospital?" In *Medieval East Anglia*. Ed. Christopher Harper-Bill. Woodbridge: Boydell Press, 2005. Pp. 287–301.

———. "The Digby *Mary Magdalene*." In Kastan. Pp. 170–73.

———. "The Digby Plays." In Kastan. Pp. 174–77.

———. Review of *Lady, Hero, Saint: The Digby Play's Mary Magdalene*, by Joanne Findon. *The Medieval Review*. Indiana University. December 2012. Web. Online at https://scholarworks.iu.edu/journals/index.php/tmr/article/view/17638/23756.

———. "Afterward." In Loewen and Waugh. Pp. 276–90.

The Commonplace Book of Robert Reynes of Acle: An Edition of Tanner MS. 407. Ed. Cameron Louis. New York: Garland, 1980.

Cooper, Lisa H., and Andrea Denny-Brown, eds. *The* Arma Christi *in Medieval and Early Modern Material Culture, with a Critical Edition of 'O Vernicle.'* Farnham; Burlington, VT: Ashgate, 2014.

Cornelius, Roberta. "The Figurative Castle: A Study of the Mediaeval Allegory of the Edifice with Especial Reference to Religious Writings." Ph.D. dissertation. Bryn Mawr, 1930.

Cowling, Jane. "A Fifteenth-Century Saint Play in Winchester: Some Problems of Interpretation." *Medieval and Renaissance Drama in England* 13 (2001), 19–33.

Cox, John D. *The Devil and the Sacred in English Drama, 1350–1642*. Cambridge: Cambridge University Press, 2000.

Craymer, Suzanne. "Margery Kempe's Imitation of Mary Magdalene and the Digby Plays." *Mystics Quarterly* 19.4 (1993), 173–81.

The Croxton Play of the Sacrament. Ed. John T. Sebastian. Kalamazoo, MI: Medieval Institute Publications, 2012.

D'Ancona, Alessandro, ed. *Sacre Rappresentazione dei secoli XIV, XV, e XVI*. 3 vols. Florence: Successori Le Monnier, 1872.

Davenport, Tony. "'Lusty fresche galaunts.'" In *Aspects of Early English Drama*. Ed. Paula Neuss. Cambridge: D. S. Brewer, 1983. Pp. 110–28.

Davidson, Clifford. "The Digby *Mary Magdalene* and the Magdalene Cult of the Middle Ages." *Annuale Mediævale* 13 (1972), 70–87.

———, ed. *The Saint Play in Medieval Europe*. Kalamazoo, MI: Medieval Institute Publications, 1986.

———. "The Middle English Saint Play and Its Iconography." In Davidson, *The Saint Play*. Pp. 31–122.

———. *Technology, Guilds, and Early English Drama*. Kalamazoo, MI: Medieval Institute Publications, 1997.

———. "British Saint Play Records: Coping with Ambiguity." *Early Theatre* 2 (1999), 97–106.

———. "Saint Plays and Pageants of Medieval Britain." *Early Drama, Art, and Music Review* 22 (1999), 11–37.

———. "Violence and the Saint Play." *Studies in Philology* 98.3 (2001), 292–314.

Davidson, Clifford, and Thomas H. Seiler, eds. *The Iconography of Hell*. Kalamazoo, MI: Medieval Institute Publications, 1992.

Davis, Matthew Evan. "The *Apostolesse*'s Social Network: The Meaning of Mary Magdalene in Fifteenth-Century East Anglia." Ph.D. dissertation. Texas A&M University, 2013.

———. "As Above, So Below: Staging the Digby *Mary Magdalene*." *Theatre Notebook* 70.2 (2017), 74–108.

Delaney, Sheila. *Impolitic Bodies: Poetry, Saints, and Society in Fifteenth-Century England*. New York: Oxford University Press, 1998.

Delasanta, Rodney K., and Constance M. Rousseau. "Chaucer's *Orygenes upon the Maudeleyne*: A Translation." *Chaucer Review* 30.4 (1996), 319–42.

Deonise Hid Divinite and Other Treatises on Contemplative Prayer Related to "The Cloud of Unknowing." Ed. Phyllis Hodgson. EETS o.s. 231. 1955; rpt. with corrections, London: Oxford University Press, 1958.

D'Evelyn, Charlotte, and Frances A. Foster. "Saints' Legends." In *A Manual of the Writings in Middle English, 1050–1500*. Vol. 2. Ed. J. Burke Severs. Hamden, CT: Archon Books, 1970. Pp. 413–39, 556–635.

The Digby Plays. Ed. F. J. Furnivall. EETS e.s. 70. London: Oxford University Press, 1896; rpt. 1967.

The Digby Plays: Facsimiles of the Plays in Bodley MSS Digby 133 and e Museo 160. Introduction by Donald C. Baker and John L. Murphy. Leeds: University of Leeds, 1976.

DiSalvo, Gina Marie. "The Unexpected Saints: Hagiography and Early Modern Theater." Ph.D. dissertation. Northwestern University, 2014.

Dixon, Mimi Still. "'Thys Body of Mary': 'Femynyte' and 'Inward Mythe' in the Digby *Mary Magdalene*." *Mediaevalia* 18 (1995 [for 1992]), 221–44.

Dubruck, Edelgard E., and Barbara I. Gusick, eds. *Death and Dying in the Middle Ages*. New York: Peter Lang, 1999.

Duffy, Eamon. "Holy Maydens, Holy Wyfes: The Cult of Women Saints in Fifteenth- and Sixteenth-Century England." In *Women in the Church*. Ed. W. J. Sheils and Diana Wood. Oxford: Basil Blackwell, 1990. Pp. 175–96.

———. *The Stripping of the Altars: Traditional Religion in England 1400–1580*. New Haven: Yale University Press, 1992.

Dugan, Holly. "Scent of a Woman: Performing the Politics of Smell in Later Medieval England." *Journal of Medieval and Early Modern Studies* 38.2 (Spring 2008), 229–52.

———. *The Ephemeral History of Perfume: Scent and Sense in Early Modern England*. Baltimore, MD: Johns Hopkins University Press, 2011.

Dunlop, Fiona S. *The Late Medieval Interlude: The Drama of Youth and Aristocratic Masculinity*. Woodbridge: York Medieval Press, 2007.

Early English Drama. Ed. John C. Coldewey. New York: Garland Publishing, 1993.

English Wycliffite Sermons. Ed. Anne Hudson and Pamela Gradon. 5 vols. Oxford: Clarendon Press, 1983–96.

Ehrstine, Glenn. "Framing the Passion: Mansion Staging as Visual Mnemonic." In *Visualizing Medieval Performance*. Ed. Elina Gertsman. Aldershot: Ashgate, 2008. Pp. 263–77.

Erhardt, Michelle A. "Introduction." In Erhardt and Morris. Pp. 1–18.

———. "The Magdalene as Mirror: Trecento Franciscan Imagery in the Guidalotti-Rinuccini Chapel, Florence." In Erhardt and Morris. Pp. 21–44.

Erhardt, Michelle A., and Amy M. Morris, eds. *Mary Magdalene: Iconographic Studies from the Middle Ages to the Baroque*. Leiden: Brill, 2012.

Erler, Mary. "Spectacle and Sacrament: A London Parish Play in the 1530s." *Modern Philology* 91.4 (1994), 449–54.

———. "English Vowed Women at the End of the Middle Ages." *Mediaeval Studies* 57 (1995), 155–203.

Evans, Ruth. "Signs of the Body: Gender, Sexuality, and Space in York and the York Cycle." In *Women's Spaces: Patronage, Place, and Gender in the Medieval Church*. Ed. Virginia Raguin and Sarah Stanbury. Albany, NY: SUNY Press, 2005. Pp. 23–45.

Findon, Joanne. "Napping in the Arbour in the Digby *Mary Magdalene* Play." *Early Theatre* 9.2 (2006), 35–55.

———. *Lady, Hero, Saint: The Digby Play's Mary Magdalene*. Toronto: Pontifical Institute of Mediaeval Studies, 2011.

———. "'Now is aloft þat late was ondyr!': Enclosure, Liberation, and Spatial Semantics in the Digby *Mary Magdalene* Play." In Loewen and Waugh. Pp. 247–57.

Fitzhenry, William. "Vernacularity and Theater: Gender and Religious Identity in East Anglian Drama." Ph.D. dissertation. Duke University, 1997.

Freedman, Paul. *Out of the East: Spices and the Medieval Imagination*. New Haven: Yale University Press, 2008.

Friesen, Ilsa E. "Saints as Helpers in Dying: The Hairy Holy Women Mary Magdalene, Mary of Egypt, and Wilgefortis in the Iconography of the Late Middle Ages." In Dubruck and Gusick. Pp. 239–56.

Furnivall, Frederick J., ed. *The Fifty Earliest English Wills in the Court of Probate*. EETS o.s. 78. London: Trübner and Co., 1882.

Gardner, Edmund G., ed. *The Cell of Self-Knowledge: Seven Early English Mystical Works Printed by Henry Pepwell in 1521*. New York: Cooper Square Publishers, Inc., 1966.

Garth, Helen Meredith. *Saint Mary Magdalene in Medieval Literature*. Baltimore, MD: Johns Hopkins University Press, 1950.

Geary, Patrick J. *Furta Sacra: Thefts of Relics in the Central Middle Ages*. Princeton: Princeton University Press, 1978.

Georgianna, Linda. "Love So Dearly Bought: The Terms of Redemption in *The Canterbury Tales*." *Studies in the Age of Chaucer* 12 (1990), 85–116.

Gertsman, Elina. "The Loci of Performance: Art, Theater, and Memory." *Mediaevalia* 28 (2007), 119–35.

Gibson, Gail McMurray. "'*Porta Haec Clausa Erit*': Comedy, Conception, and Ezekiel's Closed Door in the *Ludus Coventriae* Play of 'Joseph's Return.'" *Journal of Medieval and Renaissance Studies* 8.1 (1978), 137–56.

———. "Bury St. Edmunds, John Lydgate, and the *N-Town Cycle*." *Speculum* 56 (1981), 56–90.

———. *The Theater of Devotion: East Anglian Drama and Society in the Late Middle Ages*. Chicago: University of Chicago Press, 1989.

———. "Saint Anne and the Religion of Childbed: Some East Anglian Texts and Talismans." In *Interpreting Cultural Symbols: Saint Anne and Late Medieval Society*. Ed. Kathleen Ashley and Pamela Sheingorn. Athens: University of Georgia Press, 1990. Pp. 95–110.

———. "Manuscript as Sacred Object: Robert Hegge's N-Town Plays." *Journal of Medieval and Early Modern Studies* 44.3 (2014), 503–29.

Gibson, Gail McMurray, and Theresa Coletti. "Lynn, Walsingham, Norwich." In *Europe: A Literary History, 1348–1418*. Ed. David Wallace. 2 vols. Oxford: Oxford University Press, 2016. 1:298–321.

Gilchrist, Roberta, and Marilyn Oliva. *Religious Women in Medieval East Anglia: History and Archaeology c. 1100–1540*. Norwich: Centre of East Anglian Studies, University of East Anglia, 1993.

Godefroy, Frédéric. *Lexique de L'Ancien Français*. Paris: Honoré Champion, 2003.

Godfrey, Bob. "The Machinery of Spectacle: The Performance Dynamic of the Play of *Mary Magdalen* and Related Matters." *European Medieval Drama* 3 (1999), 145–59.

———. "The Digby *Mary Magdalen* in Performance: A Merry Peripeteia." In *The best pairt of our play: Essays Presented to John J. McGavin*. Ed. Sarah Carpenter, Pamela M. King, Meg Twycross, and Greg Walker. Part 1. Special Issue, *Medieval English Theatre* 37 (2015), 105–18.

Goldie, Matthew Boyd. "Audiences for Language-Play in Middle English Drama." In Biggs et al. Pp. 177–216.

Goodall, John A. A. *God's House at Ewelme: Life, Devotion, and Architecture in a Fifteenth-Century Almshouse*. Aldershot: Ashgate, 2001.

Granger, Penny. *The N-Town Play: Drama and Liturgy in Medieval East Anglia*. Woodbridge: D. S. Brewer, 2009.

Grantley, Darryll. "The Source of the Digby *Mary Magdalen*." *Notes and Queries* 229 (1984), 457–59.

———. "Saints' Plays." In Beadle, *Cambridge Companion*. Pp. 265–89.

Greene, Richard Leighton. "Fortune." *Dictionary of the Middle Ages*. Vol. 5. Ed. Joseph Strayer. New York: Scribner's, 1985. Pp. 145–47.

Gregory the Great. *Homilia 33*. In *XL Homiliarum in Evangelia, Liber Secundus*. In Migne 76:1238–46.

———. "Homily 33." In *Forty Gospel Homilies*. Trans. Dom David Hurst. Kalamazoo, MI: Cistercian Publications, 1990. Pp. 268–79.

Guillaume le Clerc. "La vie de Madeleine." Ed. Robert Reinsch. *Archiv* 64 (1880), 85–94.

———. *Saint Mary Magdalene*. In Russell. Pp. 61–73, 187–98.

Harper-Bill, Christopher, ed. *Charters of the Medieval Hospitals of Bury St. Edmunds*. Woodbridge: Boydell and Brewer, for the Suffolk Record Society, 1994.

———, ed. *Medieval East Anlglia*. Woodbridge and Rochester, NY: Boydell Press, 2005.

Harrod, Henry. "Extracts from Early Norfolk Wills." *Norfolk Archaeology* 1 (1847), 111–28.

———. "Extracts from Early Wills in the Norwich Registries." *Norfolk Archaeology* 4 (1855), 317–39.

Haskins, Susan. *Mary Magdalen: Myth and Metaphor*. New York: Harcourt, Brace and Co., 1993.

Hill, Carole. *Women and Religion in Late Medieval Norwich*. Woodbridge and Rochester, NY: Boydell Press, 2010.

———. "The *Liber Celestis* of Bridget of Sweden (1302/3–1373) and Its Influence on the Household Culture of Some Late Medieval Norfolk Women." In Bates and Liddiard. Pp. 301–14.

Hill-Vàsquez, Heather. *Sacred Players: The Politics of Response in the Middle English Religious Drama*. Washington, DC: Catholic University of America Press, 2007.

Hilton, Walter. *Scala perfectionis*. Westminster: Wynkyn de Worde, 1494. STC 14045.

———. *The Scale of Perfection*. Trans. and intro. John P. H. Clark and Rosemary Dorward. Mahwah, NJ: Paulist Press, 1991.

———. *The Scale of Perfection*. Ed. Thomas H. Bestul. Kalamazoo, MI: Medieval Institute Publications, 2000.

Holsinger, Bruce. "Analytical Survey 6: Medieval Literature and Cultures of Performance." *New Medieval Literatures* 6 (2003), 271–311.

The Holy Bible: Douay-Rheims Version. Rockford, IL: Tan Books and Publishers, 1899.

Horstmann, Carl, ed. *Altenglische Legenden: Neue Folge*. Heilbronn: Henniger, 1881.

———. "Prosalegenden. Die Legenden der MS. Douce 114." *Anglia* 8 (1885), 102–96.

———. *Sammlung altenglischer Legenden*. 1878. Rpt. Hildesheim: Georg Olms Verlag, 1969.

Hotchin, Julie. "The Nun's Crown." *Early Modern Women* 4 (2009), 187–94.

Huber, Emily Rebekah. "'For Y am sorwe, and sorwe ys Y': Melancholy, Despair, and Pathology in Middle English Literature." Ph.D. dissertation. University of Rochester, 2008.

Hubert, Ann. "Performing Piety: Preachers and Players in East Anglia, 1400–1520." Ph.D. dissertation. University of Illinois at Urbana-Champaign, 2015.

Hudson, Anne, ed. *Selections from English Wycliffite Writings*. Cambridge: Cambridge University Press, 1978.

Hugh of Floreffe. *The Life of Yvette of Huy*. Trans. Jo Ann McNamara. Toronto: Peregrina Publishing, 1999.

Jacques Lefèvre D'Étaples and The Three Maries Debates. Introduction, text, and annotation by Sheila M. Porrer. Geneva: Droz, 2009.

Jacobus de Voragine. *The Golden Legend*. Trans. William Granger Ryan. 2 vols. Princeton: Princeton University Press, 1993.

Jansen, Katherine Ludwig. "Maria Magdalena: *Apostolorum Apostola*." In Kienzle and Walker. Pp. 57–96.

———. *The Making of the Magdalen*. Princeton: Princeton University Press, 2000.

————. "Mary Magdalen." In *Encyclopedia of Medieval Pilgrimage*. Leiden: Brill, 2009. Pp. 386–90.

Jeffrey, David L. "English Saints' Plays." In *Medieval Drama*. Ed. Neville Denny. London: Edward Arnold, 1973. Pp. 69–89.

Jennings, Margaret. "The Art of the Pseudo-Origen Homily *De Maria Magdalena*." *Medievalia et Humanistica* 5 (1974), 139–52.

Johnson, Ian. "*Auctricitas*? Holy Women and their Middle English Texts." In Voaden, *Prophets Abroad*. Pp. 177–97.

Johnston, Alexandra F. "*Wisdom* and the Records: Is there a Moral?" In *The* Wisdom *Symposium: Papers from the Trinity College Festival*. Ed. Milla Cozart Riggio. New York: AMS Press, 1986. Pp. 87–102.

Johnston, Barbara J. "The Magdalene and 'Madame': Piety, Politics, and Personal Agenda in Louise of Savoy's *Vie de la Magdalene*." In Erhardt and Morris. Pp. 269–93.

Jones, E. A., and Alexandra Walsham. "Introduction: Syon Abbey and Its Books: Origins, Influences and Transitions." In *Syon Abbey and Its Books: Reading, Writing and Religion: c. 1400–1700*. Ed. E. A. Jones and Alexandra Walsham. Woodbridge: Boydell, 2010. Pp. 1–38.

Jones, Mary Loubris. "How the Seven Deadly Sins 'Dewoyde from þe Woman' in the Digby *Mary Magdalene*." *American Notes and Queries* 16.8 (1978), 118–19.

Julian of Norwich. *A Book of Showings to the Anchoress Julian of Norwich*. Ed. Edmund Colledge and James Walsh. 2 parts. Toronto: Pontifical Institute of Mediaeval Studies, 1978.

————. *The Writings of Julian of Norwich: A Vision Showed to a Devout Woman* and *A Revelation of Love*. Ed. Nicholas Watson and Jacqueline Jenkins. University Park: Pennsylvania State University Press, 2006.

Kane, John. "Mary Magdala: The Evolution of her Role in Medieval Drama." *Studii medievali*, 3rd series 26 (1985), 677–84.

Karras, Ruth. "Holy Harlots: Prostitute Saints in Medieval Legend." *Journal of the History of Sexuality* 1 (1990), 3–32.

Kastan, David Scott, et al. *The Oxford Encyclopedia of British Literature*. Vol. 2. New York: Oxford University Press, 2006.

Kazik, Joanna. "Worshipping *Corpus Christi*: Mary Magdalene in the English Mystery Cycles." *Studia Anglica Posnaniensia* 38 (2002), 295–309.

————. "Public Body, Private Soul: Mary Magdalene in the Chosen Pageants in the English Mystery Cycles." In *Representing Gender in Cultures*. Ed. Elzbieta Oleksy and Joanna Rydzewska. Frankfurt: Peter Lang, 2004. Pp. 47–56.

Kempe, Margery. *The Book of Margery Kempe*. Ed. Sanford Meech and Hope Emily Allen. EETS o.s. 212. 1940. Rpt., London: Oxford University Press, 1982.

————. *The Book of Margery Kempe*. Ed. Barry Windeatt. Harlow: Longman, 2000.

Kerby-Fulton, Kathryn. *Books Under Suspicion: Censorship and Tolerance of Revelatory Writing in Late Medieval England*. Notre Dame, IN: University of Notre Dame Press, 2006.

Keyser, Linda Migl. "Examining the Body Poetic: Representations of Illness and Healing in Late Medieval English Literature." Ph.D. dissertation. University of Maryland, 1999.

Kienzle, Beverly Maryne, and Pamela J. Walker, eds. *Women Preachers and Prophets through Two Millennia of Christianity*. Berkeley: University of California Press, 1998.

King, Karen L. "The Gospel of Mary Magdalene." In *Searching the Scriptures*. Vol. 2, *A Feminist Commentary*. Ed. Elisabeth Schüssler Fiorenza. New York: Crossroad, 1994. Pp. 601–34.

————. "The Gospel of Mary." In *The Complete Gospels: Annotated Scholars Version*. Ed. Robert J. Miller. Sonoma, CA: Polebridge Press, 1994.

————. "Prophetic Power and Women's Authority: The Case of the *Gospel of Mary* (Magdalen)." In Kienzle and Walker. Pp. 21–41.

————. *The Gospel of Mary of Magdala: Jesus and the First Woman Apostle*. Santa Rosa, CA: Polebridge Press, 2003.

King, Laura Severt. "Sacred Eroticism, Rapturous Anguish: Christianity's Penitent Prostitutes and the Vexation of Allegory, 1370–1608." Ph.D. dissertation. University of California at Berkeley, 1993.

Kooper, Erik, ed. "Slack Water Poetry: An Edition of the *Craft of Lovers*." *English Studies* 68 (1987), 473–89.

Kuchar, Gary. "Gender and Recusant Melancholia in Robert Southwell's *Mary Magdalene's Funeral Tears*." In *Catholic Culture in Early Modern England*. Ed. Ronald Corthell, Frances E. Dolan, Christopher Higley, and Arthur F. Marotti. Notre Dame, IN: University of Notre Dame Press, 2007. Pp. 135–57.

"*La Règle des Fins Amans*: Eine Beginenregel aus dem Ende des XIII Jahrhunderts." Ed. Karl Christ. In *Philologische Studien aus dem romanische-germanischen Kulturkreise: Festsgabe Karl Voretzsch*. Ed. B. Schädel and W. Mulertt. Halle: Max Niemeyer, 1927. Pp. 173–213.

La vie de Marie Magdaleine. Ed. Jacques Chocheyras and Graham Runnalls. Geneva: Droz, 1986.

Lamentatyon of Mary Magdaleyne. Ed. Bertha Skeat. Cambridge: Fabb and Tyler, 1897.

Langland, William. *A Vision of Piers Plowman: A Complete Edition of the B-Text*. Ed. A. V. C. Schmidt. London: J. M. Dent and Sons, 1978.

The Late Medieval Religious Plays of Bodleian MSS Digby 133 and e Mus. 160. Ed. Donald C. Baker, John L. Murphy, and Louis B. Hall, Jr. EETS o.s. 283. Oxford: Oxford University Press, 1982.

Leshock, David. "The Representation of Islam in the Wakefield Corpus Christi Plays." *Medieval Perspectives* 11 (1996), 195–208.

The Life of Christina of Markyate: A Twelfth-Century Recluse. Ed. and trans. C. H. Talbot. 1959; rpt., Toronto: University of Toronto Press in association with the Medieval Academy of America, 1998.

The Life of Saint Mary Magdalene and of her Sister Martha. Ed. and trans. David Mycoff. Kalamazoo, MI: Cistercian Publications, 1989.

Lim, Hyunyang Kim. "'Take Writing': News, Information, and Documentary Culture in Late Medieval England." Ph.D. dissertation. University of Maryland, College Park, 2006.

———. "Pilate's Special Letter: Writing, Theater, and Spiritual Knowledge in the Digby *Mary Magdalene*." *Medieval and Early Modern English Studies* 22 (2014), 1–20.

Loewen, Peter V. "The Conversion of Mary Magdalene and the Musical Legacy of Franciscan Piety in the Early German Passion Plays." In *Speculum Sermonis: Interdisciplinary Reflections on the Medieval Sermon*. Ed. Georgiana Donavin, Cary J. Nederman, and Richard Utz. Turnhout: Brepols, 2004. Pp. 235–58.

———. "Mary Magdalene Preaches through Song: Feminine Expression in the Shrewsbury *Officium Resurrectionis* and in Easter Dramas from the German Lands and Bohemia." *Speculum* 82.3 (2007), 595–641.

———. "Mary Magdalene Converts Her Vanities through Song: Signs of Franciscan Spirituality and Preaching in Late-Medieval German Drama." In Loewen and Waugh. Pp. 181–207.

Loewen, Peter V., and Robin Waugh, eds. *Mary Magdalene in Medieval Culture: Conflicted Roles*. New York: Routledge, 2014.

Love, Nicholas. *Nicholas Love's Mirror of the Blessed Life of Jesus Christ*. Ed. Michael Sargent. New York: Garland, 1992.

Ludus Coventriae; or, the Plaie Called Corpus Christi. Ed. K. S. Block. EETS e.s. 120. 1922; rpt., London: Oxford University Press, 1960.

Lydgate, John. *The Minor Poems of John Lydgate*. Vol. 1. Ed. Henry Noble MacCracken. EETS e.s. 107. 1911; rpt., Oxford: Oxford University Press, 1961.

———. *Mummings and Entertainments*. Ed. Claire Sponsler. Kalamazoo, MI: Medieval Institute Publications, 2010.

Maci, Stefania Maria. "The Language of *Mary Magdalene* of the Bodleian MS Digby 133." *Linguistica e Filologia* 10 (1999), 105–39.

Maclean, Sally-Beth. "Saints on Stage: An Analytical Survey of Dramatic Records in the West of England." *Early Theatre* 2 (1999), 45–62.

The Macro Plays. Ed. Mark Eccles. EETS o.s. 262. London: Oxford University Press, 1969.

Maltman, Sister Nicholas. "Light In and On the Digby *Mary Magdalene*." In *Saints, Scholars, and Heroes: Studies in Medieval Culture in Honour of Charles W. Jones*. Vol. 1. Ed. Margot H. King and

Wesley M. Stevens. Collegeville, MN: Hill Monastic Manuscript Library, St. John's Abbey and University, 1979. Pp. 257–80.

Malvern, Marjorie. *Venus in Sackcloth: The Magdalen's Origins and Metamorphoses*. Carbondale: Southern Illinois University Press, 1975.

Marjanen, Antti. *The Woman Jesus Loved: Mary Magdalene in the Nag Hammadi Library and Related Documents*. Leiden: Brill, 1996.

The Mary Play from the N.Town Manuscript. Ed. Peter Meredith. London: Longman, 1987.

McCall, John. "Chaucer and the Pseudo-Origen *De Maria Magdalena*: A Preliminary Study." *Speculum* 46 (1971), 491–509.

McClain, Lisa. "'They have taken away my Lord': Mary Magdalene, Christ's Missing Body, and the Mass in Reformation England." *Sixteenth Century Journal* 38.1 (2007), 77–96.

McKinell, John. "Staging the Digby *Mary Magdalene*." *Medieval English Theatre* 6 (1984), 127–53.

Mead, Stephen X. "Four-fold Allegory in the Digby *Mary Magdalene*." *Renascence* 43.4 (1991), 269–82.

Mechtild of Hackeborn. *The Booke of Gostlye Grace of Mechtild of Hackeborn*. Ed. Theresa A. Halligan. Toronto: Pontifical Institute of Mediaeval Studies, 1979.

Meditations on the Life of Christ: An Illustrated Manuscript of the Fourteenth Century. Trans. Isa Ragusa. Ed. Isa Ragusa and Rosalie B. Green. Princeton: Princeton University Press, 1977.

Meredith, Peter, and John Tailby, eds. *The Staging of Religious Drama in Europe in the Later Middle Ages: Texts and Documents in English Translation*. Kalamazoo, MI: Medieval Institute Publications, 1983.

Middle English Legends of Women Saints. Ed. Sherry L. Reames. Kalamazoo, MI: Medieval Institute Publications, 2003.

Migne, J.-P. *Patrologiae Cursus Completus, Series Latina*. 221 vols. Paris: Garnier Press, 1844–64.

Milner, Susannah. "Flesh and Food: The Function of Female Asceticism in the Digby *Mary Magdalene*." *Philological Quarterly* 73.4 (1994), 385–401.

Minnis, Alastair, and Rosalynn Voaden, eds. *Medieval Holy Women in the Christian Tradition, c. 1100–c. 1500*. Turnhout: Brepols, 2010.

Mirk, John. *Mirk's Festial*. Ed. Theodor Erbe. EETS e.s. 96. London: Kegan Paul, Trench, Trübner & Co., 1905; rpt., Millwood, NY: Kraus, 1973.

Mitchell-Buck, Heather S. "Tyrants, Tudors, and the Digby *Mary Magdalen*." *Comparative Drama* 48.3 (2014), 241–59.

Moore, Samuel. "Patrons of Letters in Norfolk and Suffolk, c. 1450." *PMLA* 27.2 (1912), 188–207; and 28.1 (1913), 79–105.

Moreton, C. E. *The Townshends and Their World: Gentry, Law, and Land in Norfolk c. 1450–1551*. Oxford: Clarendon Press, 1992.

Mormando, Franco. "'Virtual Death' in the Middle Ages: The Apotheosis of Mary Magdalene in Popular Preaching." In Dubruck and Gusick. Pp. 257–74.

Morris, Amy M. "The German Iconography of the *Saint Magdalene Altarpiece*: Documenting Its Context." In Erhardt and Morris. Pp. 75–104.

Morrison, Susan Signe. *Women Pilgrims in Late Medieval England: Private Piety as Public Performance*. London and New York: Routledge, 2000.

Moser, Thomas C. Jr. "'And I Mon Wax Wod': The Middle English 'Foweles in the Frith.'" *PMLA* 102.3 (May 1987), 326–37.

"MS Digby 133." *Digital Bodleian*. Bodleian Libraries, University of Oxford. Web. Online at http://image.ox.ac.uk/show?collection=bodleian&manuscript=msdigby133.

Mycoff, David A., ed. *A Critical Edition of the Legend of Mary Magdalena from Caxton's Golden Legende of 1483*. Salzburg: Institut für Anglistik und Amerikanistik, Universität Salzburg, 1985.

The Myroure of Oure Ladye. Ed. John Henry Blunt. EETS e.s. 19. 1873; rpt., Millwood, NY: Kraus, 1981.

The N-Town Play, Cotton MS Vespasian D.8. Ed. Stephen Spector. 2 vols. EETS s.s. 11 and 12. Oxford: Oxford University Press, 1991.

The N-Town Plays. Ed. Douglas Sugano. Kalamazoo, MI: Medieval Institute Publications, 2007.

Nequam, Alexander. See Bestul, "The Meditation on Mary Magdalen."

The New Testament: Douay Version. Introduction by Laurence Bright. London: Sheed and Ward, 1977.

Nicolas, Nicholas Harris. *Privy Purse Expenses of Elizabeth of York: Wardrobe Accounts of Edward the Fourth. With a Memoir of Elizabeth of York, and Notes*. London: William Pickering, 1830.

Non-Cycle Plays and Fragments. Ed. Norman Davis. EETS s.s. 1. London: Oxford University Press, 1970.

Normington, Katie. *Gender and Medieval Drama*. Cambridge: D. S. Brewer, 2004.

Northway, Kara. "It's All in the Delivery: An Archival Study of Players' Off-Stage Letter-Carrying." *ROMARD: Research on Medieval and Renaissance Drama* 50 (2012), 73–92.

Odo of Cluny. *In veneratione sanctæ Mariæ Magdalenæ*. In Migne 133:713–21.

Oldland, John. "The Expansion of London's Overseas Trade from 1475 to 1520." In Barron and Sutton. Pp. 55–92.

Oliva, Marilyn. *The Convent and the Community in Late Medieval England: Female Monasteries in the Diocese of Norwich, 1350–1540*. Woodbridge and Rochester, NY: Boydell Press, 1998.

Ortenberg, Veronica. "Le Culte de Sainte Marie Madeleine dans L'Angleterre Anglo-Saxonne." *Mélanges de l'École Française de Rome – Moyen Âge* 104.1 (1992), 13–35.

Ovid. *Metamorphoses: Books I–VIII*. Trans. Frank Justus Miller; revised by G. P. Goold. Third edition. Vol. 1. Cambridge, MA: Harvard University Press, 1977.

Owen, Dorothy M., ed. *The Making of King's Lynn: A Documentary Survey*. London: Oxford University Press for the British Academy, 1984.

Palmer, Barbara D. "Gestures of Greeting: Annunciations, Sacred and Secular." In *Gesture in Medieval Drama and Art*. Ed. Clifford Davidson. Kalamazoo, MI: Medieval Institute Publications, 2001. Pp. 128–57.

The Passion Play from the N.Town Manuscript. Ed. Peter Meredith. London: Longman, 1990.

Paston Letters and Papers of the Fifteenth Century. Ed. Norman Davis. 2 vols. Oxford: Oxford University Press, 1971 and 1976.

Pearson, Andrea G. "Gendered Subject, Gendered Spectator: Mary Magdalen in the Gaze of Margaret of York." *Gesta* 44.1 (2005), 47–66.

Peter Chrysologus. *Sermo 74, De resurrectione Christi*. In Migne 52:408–11.

———. *Sermo 75, De resurrectione Christi*. In Migne 52: 411–14.

Peter Comestor (attributed to Hildebert de Lavardin). *In festo sanctæ Magdalenæ Sermo unicus*. In Migne 171:671–78.

Peter of Celle. *Sermo 60. In festivitate sanctæ Mariæ Magdalenæ I*. In Migne 202:822–25.

Pfaff, R. W. *New Liturgical Feasts in the Middle Ages*. Oxford: Clarendon Press, 1970.

Philippe de Mézières' Campaign for the Feast of Mary's Presentation. Ed. William E. Coleman. Toronto: Pontifical Institute of Mediaeval Studies, 1981.

Phillips, Kristina Rutledge. "Civil and Spiritual Disobedience in the Early Drama of East Anglia." Ph.D. dissertation. Catholic University of America, 2006.

The Play of Mary Magdalene. Ed. L. E. Lewis. Ph. D. dissertation. University of Wisconsin–Madison, 1963.

Preston, Michael J. *A Concordance to the Digby Plays and the e Mus[eo] 160 Christ's Burial and Resurrection*. Ann Arbor, MI: Xerox University Microfilms, 1977.

Proctor, Francis and Christopher Wordsworth, eds. *Breviarium ad Usum Insignis Ecclesiae Sarum*. Cambridge: Cambridge University Press, 1879–86.

Radulph Ardentis. *Homilia 25. In festo beatæ Mariæ Magdalenæ*. In Migne 155:1397–402.

Raskolnikov, Masha. "Confessional Literature, Vernacular Psychology, and the History of the Self in Middle English." *Literature Compass* 2.1 (2005), 1–20.

———. *Body Against Soul: Gender and Sowlehele in Middle English Allegory*. Columbus: Ohio State University Press, 2009.

Rastall, Richard. "Female Roles in All-Male Casts." *Medieval English Theatre* 7 (1985), 25–50.

———. "The Sounds of Hell." In Davidson and Seiler. Pp. 102–31.

———. *The Heaven Singing: Music in Early Religious Drama*. Vol. 1. Cambridge: D. S. Brewer, 1996.

Rawcliffe, Carole. *The Hospitals of Medieval Norwich*. Norwich: Centre of East Anglian Studies, University of East Anglia, 1995.

———. *Medicine for the Soul: The Life, Death, and Resurrection of an English Medieval Hospital*. Stroud: Sutton, 1998.

Records of Early English Drama: Chester. Ed. Lawrence M. Clopper. Toronto: University of Toronto Press, 1979.

Records of Early English Drama: Norwich, 1540–1642. Ed. David Galloway. Toronto: University of Toronto Press, 1984.

Records of Plays and Players in Norfolk and Suffolk, 1330–1642. Ed. David Galloway and John Wasson. Oxford: Oxford University Press, 1981.

Renevey, Denis. "Name above Names: Devotion to the Name of Jesus from Richard Rolle to Walter Hilton's *Scale of Perfection 1*." In *The Medieval Mystical Tradition: England, Ireland and Wales: Papers Read at Charney Manor, July 1999*. Ed. Marion Glasscoe. Cambridge: D. S. Brewer, 1999. Pp. 102–21.

Revelations of Saint Birgitta. Ed. William Patterson Cumming. EETS o.s. 178. 1929; rpt., Millwood, NY: Kraus, 1971.

Ricci, Carla. *Mary Magdalene and Many Others: Women who Followed Jesus.* Minneapolis, MN: Fortress Press, 1994.

Richmond, Colin. *The Paston Family in the Fifteenth Century: The First Phase.* Cambridge: Cambridge University Press, 1990.

Riggio, Milla Cozart. "The Allegory of Feudal Acquisition in *The Castle of Perseverance*." In *Allegory, Myth, and Symbol*. Ed. Morton W. Bloomfield. Cambridge, MA: Harvard University Press, 1981. Pp. 187–208.

———, ed. *The Play of "Wisdom": Its Texts and Contexts.* New York: AMS Press, 1998.

Ritchie, Harry M. "A Suggested Location for the Digby *Mary Magdalene*." *Theatre Survey* 4 (1963), 51–58.

Rochester, Joanne M. "Space and Staging in the Digby *Mary Magdalen* and *Pericles, Prince of Tyre*." *Early Theatre* 13.2 (2010), 43–62.

Rogers, Alan. "Contrasting Careers: William Browne of Stamford and Social Mobility in the Later Fifteenth Century." In Barron and Sutton. Pp. 93–110.

Rolle, Richard. *The Fire of Love* and *the Mending of Life* or *The Rule of Living*. Ed. R. Harvey. EETS o.s. 106. London: K. Paul, Trench, Trübner and Co., 1896.

———. *The Song of Angels.* In Gardner. Pp. 63–73.

———. *Richard Rolle: Prose and Verse from MS Longleat 29 and Related Manuscripts.* Ed. S. J. Ogilvie-Thomson. EETS o.s. 293. Oxford: Oxford University Press, 1988.

———. *Richard Rolle: The English Writings.* Ed. and trans. Rosamund Allen. Mahwah, NJ: Paulist Press, 1988.

Rosenthal, Joel. *The Purchase of Paradise: Gift Giving and the Aristocracy, 1307–1485.* London: Routledge and Kegan Paul, 1972.

———. "Local Girls Do It Better: Women and Religion in Late Medieval East Anglia." In Biggs et al. Pp. 1–20.

Ross, David, ed. "Fairford, St Mary's Church." *Britain Express*. Britain Express Limited, 1996. Web. Online at http://www.britainexpress.com/attractions.htm?attraction=1564.

Russell, Delbert W., trans. *Verse Saints' Lives Written in the French of England*. Medieval and Renaissance Texts and Studies 431. Tempe, AZ: ACMRS, 2012.

Sadlack, Erin A. *The French Queen's Letters: Mary Tudor Brandon and the Politics of Marriage in Sixteenth-Century Europe*. New York: Palgrave Macmillan, 2011.

Salih, Sarah. "Staging Conversion: The Digby Saint Plays and *The Book of Margery Kempe*." In *Gender and Holiness: Men, Women, and Saints in Late Medieval England*. Ed. Samantha J. E. Riches and Sarah Salih. London and New York: Routledge, 2002. Pp. 121–34.

Sanok, Catherine. "Performing Feminine Sanctity in Late Medieval England: Parish Guilds, Saints' Plays, and the *Second Nun's Tale*." *Journal of Medieval and Early Modern Studies* 32.2 (2002), 269–303.

———. *Her Life Historical: Exemplarity and Female Saints' Lives in Late Medieval England*. Philadelphia: University of Pennsylvania Press, 2007.

Scherb, Victor I. "Worldly and Sacred Messengers in the Digby *Mary Magdalene*." *English Studies* 73.1 (1992), 1–9.

———. "Blasphemy and the Grotesque in the Digby *Mary Magdalene*." *Studies in Philology* 96.3 (1999), 225–40.

———. *Staging Faith: East Anglian Drama in the Later Middle Ages*. Madison, NJ: Fairleigh Dickinson University Press, 2001.

Schmidt, Victor M. "Mary Magdalen and the Risen Christ: Changing Perspectives." In *To Touch or Not to Touch? Interdisciplinary Perspectives on the Noli me tangere*. Ed. Reimund Bieringer, Karlijn Demasure, and Barbara Baert. Leuven: Peeters, 2013. Pp. 179–225.

Schreyer, Kurt A. *Shakespeare's Medieval Craft: Remnants of the Mysteries on the London Stage*. Ithaca, NY: Cornell University Press, 2014.

Scoville, Chester N. *Saints and the Audience in Middle English Biblical Drama*. Toronto: University of Toronto Press, 2004.

Sebastian, John Thomas. "Lewd Imaginings: Pedagogy, Piety, and Performance in Late Medieval East Anglia." Ph.D. dissertation. Cornell University, 2004.

Shklar, Ruth. "Cobham's Daughter: *The Book of Margery Kempe* and the Power of Heterodox Thinking." *Modern Language Quarterly* 56.3 (1995), 277–304.

Shugar, Debora Kuller. "Saints and Lovers: Mary Magdalene and the Ovidian Evangel." *Bucknell Review* 35 (1992), 150–71.

Sister Catherine (*Schwester Katrei*). Trans. Elvira Borgstädt. In *Meister Eckhart: Teacher and Preacher*. Ed. Bernard McGinn, with Frank Tobin and Elvira Borgstädt. Mahwah, NJ: Paulist Press, 1986. Pp. 347–87.

Smith, D. K. "'To passe the see in shortt space': Mapping the World in the Digby *Mary Magdalene*." *Medieval and Renaissance Drama in England* 18 (2005), 193–214.

Smith, Nicole D. *Sartorial Strategies: Outfitting Aristocrats and Fashioning Conduct in Late Medieval Literature*. Notre Dame, IN: University of Notre Dame Press, 2012.

Speculum Sacerdotale. Ed. Edward H. Weatherly. EETS o.s. 200. Oxford: Oxford University Press, 1936.

Sponsler, Claire. *Drama and Resistance: Bodies, Goods, and Theatricality in Late Medieval England*. Minneapolis: University of Minnesota Press, 1997

———. *The Queen's Dumbshows: John Lydgate and the Making of Early Theater*. Philadelphia: University of Pennsylvania Press, 2014.

The Stacions of Rome, . . . and The Pilgrims Sea-Voyage, . . . with Clene Maydenhod. Ed. F. J. Furnivall and William Michael Rossetti. EETS o.s. 25. London: N. Trübner and Co., 1867.

Stokes, James. "Women and Performance in Medieval and Early Modern Suffolk." *Early Theatre* 15.1 (2012), 27–43.

Streitman, Elsa. "The Face of Janus: Debatable Issues in *Mariken van Nieumeghen*." *Comparative Drama* 27.1 (Spring 1993), 64–82.

Strohm, Paul. "Three London Itineraries: Aesthetic Purity and the Composing Process." In *Theory and the Premodern Text*. Minneapolis: University of Minnesota Press, 2000. Pp. 3–19.

Sugano, Douglas. "'This game wel pleyd in good a-ray': The N-Town Playbooks and East Anglian Games." *Comparative Drama* 28.2 (1994), 221–34.

———. "Apologies for the Magdalene: Devotion, Iconoclasm, and the *N-Town Plays*." *Research Opportunities in Renaissance Drama* 33 (1994), 165–76.

Symes, Carol. *A Common Stage: Theater and Public Life in Medieval Arras*. Ithaca, NY: Cornell University Press, 2007.

———. "The Medieval Archive and the History of Theatre: Assessing the Written and Unwritten Evidence for Premodern Performance." *Theatre Survey* 52.1 (2011), 29–58.

Tamburr, Karl. *The Harrowing of Hell in Medieval England*. Cambridge: D. S. Brewer, 2007.

Tanner, Norman P., ed. *Heresy Trials in the Diocese of Norwich, 1428–31*. London: Royal Historical Society, 1977.

Taylor, Larissa Juliet. "Apostle to the Apostles: The Complexity of Medieval Preaching about Mary Magdalene." In Loewen and Waugh. Pp. 33–50.

Testamenta Eboracensia: A Selection of Wills from the Registry at York. Ed. James Raine. Vol. 4. Surtees Society 53. Durham: Andrews & Co., 1869.

Thimmes, Pamela. "Memory and Re-Vision: Mary Magdalene Research since 1975." *Currents in Research: Biblical Studies* 6 (1998), 193–226.

Thomas à Kempis. *Imitatio Christi. The following of Christ, translated out of Latin into English*. London: 1556. STC 23967.

The Towneley Plays. Ed. Martin Stevens and A. C. Cawley. 2 vols. EETS s.s. 13 and 14. Oxford: Oxford University Press, 1994.

A Tretise of Miraclis Pleyinge. Ed. Clifford Davidson. Kalamazoo, MI: Medieval Institute Publications, 1993.

Two Coventry Corpus Christi Plays. Ed. Pamela M. King and Clifford Davidson. Kalamazoo, MI: Medieval Institute Publications, 2000.

Twycross, Meg, and Elisabeth Dutton. "Lydgate's *Mumming for the Mercers of London*." In Barron and Sutton. Pp. 310–49.

Tymms, Samuel, ed. *Wills and Inventories from the Registers of the Commissary of Bury St. Edmunds and the Archdeacon of Sudbury*. London: J. B. Nichols and Son, 1850.

Vaughn, Virginia Mason. *Performing Blackness on English Stages, 1500–1800*. Cambridge: Cambridge University Press, 2005.

Velz, John W. "Sovereignty in the Digby *Mary Magdalene*." *Comparative Drama* 2.1 (1968), 32–43.

Voaden, Rosalynn, ed. *Prophets Abroad: The Reception of Continental Holy Women in Late-Medieval England*. Woodbridge: D. S. Brewer, 1996.

———. *God's Words, Women's Voices: The Discernment of Spirits in the Writing of Late-Medieval Woman Visionaries*. Woodbridge: York Medieval Press, 1999.

Ward, Robin. *The World of the Medieval Shipmaster: Law, Business and the Sea, c.1350–c.1450*. Woodbridge and Rochester, NY: Boydell Press, 2009.

Warren, Nancy Bradley. *Spiritual Economies: Female Monasticism in Later Medieval England*. Philadelphia: University of Pennsylvania Press, 2001.

Waters, Claire M. *Angels and Earthly Creatures: Preaching, Performance, and Gender in the Later Middle Ages*. Philadelphia: University of Pennsylvania Press, 2004.

Watson, Nicholas. *Richard Rolle and the Invention of Authority*. Cambridge: Cambridge University Press, 1991.

———. "Censorship and Cultural Change in Late-Medieval England: Vernacular Theology, the Oxford Translation Debate, and Arundel's Constitutions of 1409." *Speculum* 70.4 (1995), 822–64.

———. "Conceptions of the Word: The Mother Tongue and the Incarnation of God." *New Medieval Literatures* 1 (1997), 85–124.

———. "The Middle English Mystics." In *The Cambridge History of Medieval English Literature*. Ed. David Wallace. Cambridge: Cambridge University Press, 1999. Pp. 539–65.

Weigert, Laura. *French Visual Culture and the Making of Medieval Theater*. Cambridge: Cambridge University Press, 2015.

Weimann, Robert. *Shakespeare and the Popular Tradition in the Theater: Studies in the Social Dimension of Dramatic Form and Function*. Ed. Robert Shwartz. Baltimore, MD: Johns Hopkins University Press, 1978.

Wenzel, Siegfried. *The Sin of Sloth: Acedia in Medieval Thought and Literature*. Chapel Hill: University of North Carolina Press, 1960.

White, Paul Whitfield, ed. *Reformation Biblical Drama in England, "The Life and Repentaunce of Mary Magdalene" and "The History of Iacob and Esau."* New York: Garland, 1992.

Whitehead, Christiania. *Castles of the Mind: A Study of Medieval Architectural Allegory*. Cardiff: University of Wales Press, 2003.

Whiting, Bartlett Jere, and Helen Wescott Whiting. *Proverbs, Sentences, and Proverbial Phrases from English Writings Mainly before 1500*. Cambridge, MA: Belknap Press of Harvard University Press, 1968.

Wickham, Glynne. "The Staging of Saint Plays in England." In *The Medieval Drama: Papers of the Third Annual Conference of the Center for Medieval and Early Renaissance Studies, State University of New York at Binghamton, 3–4 May 1969*. Ed. Sandro Sticca. Albany: SUNY Press, 1972. Pp. 99–119.

Williams, Arnold. *The Characterization of Pilate in the Towneley Plays*. East Lansing: Michigan State College Press, 1950.

Williams, Deanne. *The French Fetish from Chaucer to Shakespeare*. Cambridge: Cambridge University Press, 2004.

Williams, Tara. *Inventing Womanhood: Gender and Language in Later Middle English Writing*. Columbus: Ohio State University Press, 2011.

Winstead, Karen A. *John Capgrave's Fifteenth Century*. Philadelphia: University of Pennsylvania Press, 2007.

Wogan-Browne, Jocelyn. *Saints' Lives and Women's Literary Culture, c. 1150–1300: Virginity and Its Authorizations*. Oxford: Oxford University Press, 2001.

———. "Analytic Survey 5: 'Reading is Good Prayer': Recent Research on Female Reading Communities." *New Medieval Literatures* 5 (2002), 229–97.

Womack, Peter. "Shakespeare and the Sea of Stories." *Journal of Medieval and Early Modern Studies* 29.1 (1999), 169–87.

The Worlde and the Chylde. Ed. Clifford Davidson and Peter Happé. Kalamazoo, MI: Medieval Institute Publications, 1999.

Wright, Robert. "Community Theatre in Late Medieval East Anglia." *Theatre Notebook* 28 (1974), 24–39.

The York Plays. Ed. Richard Beadle. London: Edward Arnold, 1982.

Young, Karl, ed. *The Drama of the Medieval Church*. 2 vols. 1933; rpt. Oxford: Clarendon Press, 1962.

Zacher, Christian K. *Curiosity and Pilgrimage: The Literature of Discovery in Fourteenth-Century England*. Baltimore, MD: Johns Hopkins University Press, 1976.

Zieman, Katherine. "Monasticism and the Public Contemplative in Late Medieval England: Richard Methley and His Spiritual Formation." *Journal of Medieval and Early Modern Studies* 42.3 (2012), 699–724.

❦ GLOSSARY

abey *obey*
abyde, abydyn *await, endure*
agen(s), ageyn *against, with respect to*
and *if*
aplye *offer;* (refl.) *dedicate oneself*
arayyd *arrayed, dressed*
as *that, since, because, according to*
aspecyall *special*
audyens *audience, presence*
avansyd *advanced, put forward*
avayll *profit*

bale, balys *suffering*
bamys *balms, ointments*
be *is*
bed *bid*
bemys *beams*
bewte *beauty*
blysch *bless*
blysche *bliss*
bone *boon, request*
bote *remedy*
browth *brought, put*
bryth *bright*
but *unless*
byd *command, order*
byn (v. **to beyn**) *are, be,* (p. ppl.) *been*

cawt(h) *caught*
chance *circumstance*
chyr *cheer*
cler *clear*
closse *hidden*
cowd *could*

degré *social status*
departe *distribute, separate*

devodyt (v.) *exit*
devyde *disperse, oppose*
dew *due*
dissipulys, dyssyplys, dysyllpyllys
    disciples
don *do*
doth (v.) *does*
do(w)th (n.) *doubt*
dylf(e), dyllys *devil, devils*

ellys *else*
emperower, emprore, enperower
    emperor
erbyr(e) *arbor, bower*
especyal *especially*
exprese *expressly*
exprese (v.) *to say, speak of, fulfill*

fayn *gladly*
fe *payment*
femynyté *femininity*
fett *fetch*
for *as, for, because of*
fro *from*
ful *very*
fynd *fiend*

gef *gave*
g(e)yff *give*
governons *governance*
grawous *grievous*
gyde *guide*
gyn *begins*

hale *health*
halse *embrace*
harlottys *scoundrels*

hast *haste*
hawdyens *presence*
hem *them*
her (adv.) *here*
her *hair*
hey, hye *high*
heym *him*
ho *who, whoever*
holl *whole, healthy*
hungore, hongor, houngure *hunger*
hur(e), hyre, here *her*
hyre *their*

indu(e)re, induour *endure, remain*
insythe *quickly*

knyth, knytes, knythys *knight, knights*

lett *delay*
levyn *live*
lyst (n.) *choosing, pleasure*
lythly *quickly*

mede *reward*
mot(t), mown, myth (v.) *may*
mykyll *great*
mythe, mytys *might, power*
myty *mighty, powerful*

nesessyte *need*
nyth *night*

obbey *obey*
of *for*
ondyr *under*
ony *any, anyone*
onys *once*
ower (n.) *hour*
ower, owur *our*
owt *out*

perfytnes(se) *perfection*
pes *peace*
peynnes *pains*
plesauns, plesowns *pleasure*
porchase, porchasyd *purchase,*
    acquire, gained, attained

pryst *priest*
put *keep*
pystull, pystyll *letter*

quell *kill, silence*

recure *recover*
rede (n.) *counsel, advice*
rede (v.) *advise*
releff *reward, relieve*
r(e)yngne, regnyng *reign, reigning*
ryall *royal*
ryth, ryte (n.) *right*; (adv.) *directly*

save *except for*
sem(e)ly *attractive*
sentens *meaning*
serys, syrrys *sirs*
seté *city*
seyn *tell*
shew *show*
sokorer (v.) *to help*
soko(u)r, soko(w)re, socure (n.)
    succor, help, aid
sone *soon*
sore *sorrowful*; (adv.) *sorrowfully,*
    greatly
sote *sweet*
soth *truth*
soveryn, sovere(y)n, sofer(e)yn
    sovereign
soverreynte *sovereignty*
sowth *sought*
speceally *especially*
sprytys *spirits*
suere *surely*
swych(e) *such*
syn *since*
syn (p. ppl.) *seen*
syte, syth *sight*
syth *time*

tene *harm*
that (prep.) *who*
that *so that*
theyn, thine *yours*
tho *those*

thowt *thought*
tyde *time*

verely *truly*

werkytt *causes, works*
whech *who*
whyll *while*
wo, woo *who*
wold *would*

woll *will*
wom *whom*
wos *whose*
woso *whoso*
wrake *harm*
wrowth (p. ppl.) *wrought, made, done*
wy *why*
wyche *who*
wyth, wight *quick*
wythly, whytly *quickly, in haste*

William Dunbar, *The Complete Works*, edited by John Conlee (2004)

Chaucerian Dream Visions and Complaints, edited by Dana M. Symons (2004)

Stanzaic Guy of Warwick, edited by Alison Wiggins (2004)

Saints' Lives in Middle English Collections, edited by E. Gordon Whatley, with Anne B. Thompson and Robert K. Upchurch (2004)

Siege of Jerusalem, edited by Michael Livingston (2004)

The Kingis Quair and Other Prison Poems, edited by Linne R. Mooney and Mary-Jo Arn (2005)

The Chaucerian Apocrypha: A Selection, edited by Kathleen Forni (2005)

John Gower, *The Minor Latin Works*, edited and translated by R. F. Yeager, with *In Praise of Peace*, edited by Michael Livingston (2005)

Sentimental and Humorous Romances: Floris and Blancheflour, Sir Degrevant, The Squire of Low Degree, The Tournament of Tottenham, and The Feast of Tottenham, edited by Erik Kooper (2006)

The Dicts and Sayings of the Philosophers, edited by John William Sutton (2006)

Everyman and Its Dutch Original, Elckerlijc, edited by Clifford Davidson, Martin W. Walsh, and Ton J. Broos (2007)

The N-Town Plays, edited by Douglas Sugano, with assistance by Victor I. Scherb (2007)

The Book of John Mandeville, edited by Tamarah Kohanski and C. David Benson (2007)

John Lydgate, *The Temple of Glas*, edited by J. Allan Mitchell (2007)

The Northern Homily Cycle, edited by Anne B. Thompson (2008)

Codex Ashmole 61: A Compilation of Popular Middle English Verse, edited by George Shuffelton (2008)

Chaucer and the Poems of "Ch," edited by James I. Wimsatt (revised edition 2009)

William Caxton, *The Game and Playe of the Chesse*, edited by Jenny Adams (2009)

John the Blind Audelay, *Poems and Carols*, edited by Susanna Fein (2009)

Two Moral Interludes: The Pride of Life and Wisdom, edited by David Klausner (2009)

John Lydgate, *Mummings and Entertainments*, edited by Claire Sponsler (2010)

Mankind, edited by Kathleen M. Ashley and Gerard NeCastro (2010)

The Castle of Perseverance, edited by David N. Klausner (2010)

Robert Henryson, *The Complete Works*, edited by David J. Parkinson (2010)

John Gower, *The French Balades*, edited and translated by R. F. Yeager (2011)

The Middle English Metrical Paraphrase of the Old Testament, edited by Michael Livingston (2011)

The York Corpus Christi Plays, edited by Clifford Davidson (2011)

Prik of Conscience, edited by James H. Morey (2012)

The Dialogue of Solomon and Marcolf: A Dual-Language Edition from Latin and Middle English Printed Editions, edited by Nancy Mason Bradbury and Scott Bradbury (2012)

Croxton Play of the Sacrament, edited by John T. Sebastian (2012)

Ten Bourdes, edited by Melissa M. Furrow (2013)

Lybeaus Desconus, edited by Eve Salisbury and James Weldon (2013)

The Complete Harley 2253 Manuscript, Vol. 2, edited and translated by Susanna Fein with David Raybin and Jan Ziolkowski (2014); Vol. 3 (2015); Vol. 1 (2015)

Oton de Granson Poems, edited and translated by Peter Nicholson and Joan Grenier-Winther (2015)

The King of Tars, edited by John H. Chandler (2015)

John Hardyng Chronicle, edited by James Simpson and Sarah Peverley (2015)

Richard Coer de Lyon, edited by Peter Larkin (2015)

Guillaume de Machaut, The Complete Poetry and Music, Volume 1: The Debate Poems, edited and translated by R. Barton Palmer (2016)

Lydgate's Fabula Duorum Mercatorum and Guy of Warwyk, edited by Pamela Farvolden (2016)

The Katherine Group (MS Bodley 34), edited by Emily Rebekah Huber and Elizabeth Robertson (2016)

Sir Torrent of Portingale, edited by James Wade (2017)

The Towneley Plays, edited by Garrett P. J. Epp (2017)

❧ MEDIEVAL GERMAN TEXTS IN BILINGUAL EDITIONS SERIES

Sovereignty and Salvation in the Vernacular, 1050–1150, introduction, translations, and notes by James A. Schultz (2000)

Ava's New Testament Narratives: "When the Old Law Passed Away," introduction, translation, and notes by James A. Rushing, Jr. (2003)

History as Literature: German World Chronicles of the Thirteenth Century in Verse, introduction, translation, and notes by R. Graeme Dunphy (2003)

Thomasin von Zirclaria, *Der Welsche Gast (The Italian Guest)*, translated by Marion Gibbs and Winder McConnell (2009)

Ladies, Whores, and Holy Women: A Sourcebook in Courtly, Religious, and Urban Cultures of Late Medieval Germany, introductions, translations, and notes by Ann Marie Rasmussen and Sarah Westphal-Wihl (2010)

Neidhart: Selected Songs from the Riedegg Manuscript, introduction, translation, and commentary by Kathryn Starkey and Edith Wenzel (2016)

❧ VARIA

The Study of Chivalry: Resources and Approaches, edited by Howell Chickering and Thomas H. Seiler (1988)

Studies in the Harley Manuscript: The Scribes, Contents, and Social Contexts of British Library MS Harley 2253, edited by Susanna Fein (2000)

The Liturgy of the Medieval Church, edited by Thomas J. Heffernan and E. Ann Matter (2001; second edition 2005)

Johannes de Grocheio, *Ars musice*, edited and translated by Constant J. Mews, John N. Crossley, Catherine Jeffreys, Leigh McKinnon, and Carol J. Williams (2011)

Aribo, De musica *and* Sententiae, edited and translated by T.J.H. McCarthy (2015)

Guy of Saint-Denis, Tractatus de Tonis, edited and translated by Constant J. Mews, Carol J. Williams, John N. Crossley, and Catherine Jeffreys (2017)

Typeset in 10/13 New Baskerville
and Golden Cockerel Ornaments display

Medieval Institute Publications
College of Arts and Sciences
Western Michigan University
1903 W. Michigan Avenue
Kalamazoo, MI 49008-5432
http://www.wmich.edu/medievalpublications

 WESTERN MICHIGAN UNIVERSITY

PGIL2021USA